Edward Bond
Plays: Two

Lear, The Sea, Narrow Road to the Deep North, Black Mass, Passion

The three full-length plays printed here were written and first staged between 1968 and 1973 and they complete the cycle of works begun with *The Pope's Wedding* in 1962. They range from the reworking of Shakespearean tragedy in *Lear*, through its companion comedy *The Sea*, to the spare Japanese setting of the parable *Narrow Road to the Deep North*. The two short pieces, *Black Mass* and *Passion*, were specially written to be performed at demonstrations by the Anti-Apartheid Movement and the Campaign for Nuclear Disarmament respectively.

The Sea has been revised for this edition, and a change made to the ending of *Lear*. Also included is the original 'Author's Preface' to *Lear* and an Introduction by the author written specially for this volume.

Edward Bond was born and educated in London. His plays include *The Pope's Wedding* (Royal Court Theatre, 1962), *Saved* (Royal Court, 1965), *Early Morning* (Royal Court, 1968), *Narrow Road to the Deep North* (Belgrade Theatre, Coventry, 1968; Royal Court 1969), *Black Mass* (Sharpeville Commemoration Evening, Lyceum Theatre, 1970), *Passion* (CND Rally, Alexandra Palace, 1971), *Lear* (Royal Court, 1971), *The Sea* (Royal Court, 1973), *Bingo* (Northcott, Exeter, 1973; Royal Court, 1974), *The Fool* (Royal Court, 1975), *The Bundle* (RSC Warehouse, 1978), *The Woman* (National Theatre, 1978), *The Worlds* (New Half Moon Theatre, London, 1981), *Restoration* (Royal Court, 1981), *Summer* (National Theatre, 1982), *Derek* (RSC Youth Festival, The Other Place, Stratford-upon-Avon, 1982), *The Cat* (produced in Germany as *The English Cat* by the Stuttgart Opera, 1983), *Human Cannon* (Quantum Theatre, Manchester, 1986), *The War Plays* (*Red Black and Ignorant*, *The Tin Can People* and *Great Peace*), which were staged as a trilogy by the RSC at the Barbican Pit in 1985, *Jackets* (Leicester, Haymarket, 1989), *September* (Canterbury Cathedral, 1989); *In the Company of Men* (Paris, 1992); *Olly's Prison* (BBC 2 Television 1993); *Tuesday* (BBC Schools TV, 1993); His *Theatre Poems and Songs* were published in 1978 and *Poems 1978–1985* in 1987.

EDWARD BOND

Plays: Two

Lear
The Sea
Narrow Road to the Deep North
Black Mass
Passion

With an Introduction by the author

METHUEN DRAMA

METHUEN WORLD CLASSICS

This collection first published in 1978 by Eyre Methuen Ltd
Lear and 'Author's Preface' first published by Eyre Methuen Ltd in 1972,
revised for this edition, 1978. Copyright © 1972, 1978 by Edward Bond
Reprinted 1983, 1985 by Methuen London Ltd

Reprinted in 1989 by Methuen Drama
an imprint of Reed Consumer Books Ltd
Michelin House, 81 Fulham Road, London SW3 6RB
and Auckland, Melbourne, Singapore and Toronto
and distributed in the United States of America by Heinemann,
a division of Reed Publishing (USA) Inc.,
361 Hanover Street, Portsmouth, New Hampshire NH 03801 3959
Reprinted 1990, 1992
Reissued with a new cover design 1993
Reprinted 1994

The Sea first published by Eyre Methuen Ltd in 1973, revised for this
edition, 1978. Copyright © 1973, 1978 by Edward Bond
Narrow Road to the Deep North first published by Methuen & Co. in 1968,
revised for this edition, 1978. Copyright © 1968, 1978 by Edward Bond
Black Mass first published by Methuen & Co. in 1971 in a volume with
The Pope's Wedding. Corrected for this edition, 1978. Copyright © 1970 by
Edward Bond
Passion first published by Eyre Methuen Ltd in 1974 in a volume with
Bingo. Revised for this edition, 1978. Copyright © 1974, 1978 by Edward
Bond
Introduction first published in this collection. Copyright © 1978 by
Edward Bond
This collection copyright © 1978 by Edward Bond

The front cover shows a detail from Crowd Looking at Tied-up Object
*by Henry Moore (water colour, 1942). It is reproduced by kind permission of the
artist and of Lord Clark.*

Printed and bound in Great Britain by
Cox & Wyman Ltd, Reading, Berkshire

ISBN 0 413 39270 8

CONTENTS

Edward Bond
A Chronology

Introduction

The Rational Theatre

Recently I spoke to a man whose job it was to teach the meaning of Shakespeare's writings to students at a university. He told me Shakespeare had no opinions of his own, he could understand and retell everyone's opinion, he left it to others to judge. It is disturbing that students can still be taught this. Had Shakespeare not spent his creative life desperately struggling to reconcile problems that obsessed him he could not have written with such intellectual strength and passionate beauty. What were these problems ? The nature of right and wrong, in what way an individual should be part of his society, why some men are tyrants and others nearly saints, why some governments are despotic and why at other times reason appears briefly to rule a country or a city. He asked these questions as he passed from youth to age in a world that was both young and old.

Shakespeare's early literary work consists almost entirely of a long series of history plays. These plays were an attempt to show the need for good government and how that government was created. It would be strong enough to protect good and to punish or expel evil; and strong enough to protect itself against its own weaknesses and save itself from corruption. The last play in this series (*Henry V*) celebrates the establishment of such a government, under a king who had both wisdom and vitality. Shakespeare then wrote a series of plays about individuals and their psychologies. No one before Shakespeare had looked so closely at the human mind and the passions, fears and hopes raging in it. And not one of these individuals could have fitted into the society of the good government he had spent so long in describing and praising in the history plays. His honesty makes him reject his first explanations. The 'good' government of the history plays is not good. Historically it could not be good, and the question of its strength, and its internal freedom from corruption, is almost irrelevant to the sort of government it was. It was a class government administering class justice; and Shakespeare, like all other men, was too much a part of his own time to fully understand it.

He pursued his questions in many ages and countries, among many races and conditions of men. And although he could not answer his questions he learned to bear them with stoical dignity: this is at least an assurance that he was facing the right problems – otherwise his dramatic resolutions would have been sentimental and trite. Lear dies old, Hamlet dies young, Othello is deceived, Macbeth runs amok, goodness struggles, and there is no good government, no order to protect ordinary men. Shakespeare cannot answer his questions but he cannot stop asking them.

Next he writes a series of what are sometimes called romantic comedies. Really they are the first plays of the theatre of the absurd. Shakespeare's intellectual honesty and encompassing observation, which enabled him, forced him to create the supreme literature of the bourgeoisie, also forced him to anticipate the decadence of that literature. He did this from a position of strength, of someone who partly understood the future, the rational nature of political development and the rational structure of history. Writers of the theatre of the absurd in our time write only from weakness because they are trapped in the decadence of our time and have no rational view of the future or of anything else. In these late comedies Shakespeare asks the same questions but they are examined in a more grotesque way. He was older and the only solutions he understood could already be seen not to work; in future the questions would have to be understood in a new, revolutionary way. Shakespeare is not for all time, and even in his own time he was in many ways already out of date.

Cymbeline is an appalling slapstick (but not slapdash) rehash of *King Lear*. Sex is changed, the queen trapped in irredeemable, metaphysical evil, a headless body is embraced on stage, Posthumus seems as if he might have come back from the dead, a god descends from heaven to tell Shakespeare to stop asking his questions, and the play is closed by the ramblings of an idiotic old Lear, babbling of buffoons and giants who will one day bring the good government, the wise order, that will make men happy. Prospero is driven from his kingdom, he lives closely with good and evil and has magic to reconcile things mortals can't reconcile: but this magic could not save him from his political enemies. In the end he breaks his wand and goes home to die – or to reopen the finger-stained files in his office. There are no supernatural answers to natural problems. As Shakespeare himself knew, the peace, the reconciliation that he created on the stage would not last an hour on the street.

Finally there is the play usually treated as a historical pageant. It is Shakespeare's last struggle with his problems and recapitulates his earlier work. *Henry VIII* is derived from the world of the first history plays; but locked in the king's castle, in his administrative machine, are two tormented individuals from the middle plays – Katharine and Wolsey (an aristocrat and a butcher's son). Neither finds justice in Henry's world. Both are implausibly maligned for the sake of appearances; Wolsey, being of plebeian origin, has the less good excuses. All this could only be treated cynically in a modern production. And so the play passes deeper into the Absurd: Elizabeth, an infant Miranda, is cradled in the red hands of a monster and fussed over by a queen who will shortly have her head chopped off for sleeping with her brother. Shakespeare, in recording contemporary history, returns to the world of Titus Andronicus. After that, silence. His real will was not his houses and his second best bed, but his unanswered questions.

This isn't to say that Shakespeare's life was wasted. He did not answer his questions because historically they were not answerable at that time, and art is prescribed by the political situation in which it is created. But he showed the strength with which people can ask these questions, and he showed that men can't stop struggling to answer them till they have created the rational order which will give them peace. He lived on the edge of a political revolution, and his plays still work for those who live in this later time of revolution, the twentieth century.

★   ★   ★

Literature is a social act; it is the social expression of thought and uses the social medium of language. Yet a creative act comes through an individual. It is these creative acts that seal the individual with his society. A writer writes what he has experienced and learned (what else could he write about?) but he does not write about himself. What used to be called the soul is really the most public aspect of a human being. An individual only exists through society; outside society he is a monster. To say that a writer writes about 'himself' is as meaningless as to say that there could be an expression without its language. Really, the subject of all literature is society. No man is a problem to himself, but society may become his problem. You could say that literature may also sometimes be about 'nature', the 'natural scene', the 'world of plants and animals'. But these things are still written about by social man, who looks at nature as, himself, part of society – not part of nature: men cannot escape this social self. As consciousness is reflected in individuals and not in groups it could be said that part of the work of literature is to make society self-conscious. Literature is the interpretation of human life in its fullest, social sense – which includes the indissoluble union between society and individual. That is why literature is always an expression of the historical circumstances in which it is created. In literature there are no abstract statements universally true for all time – or, if there are, they are trivial until they are given content and context; otherwise they function as excuses and not reasons. After all, literature that is not trash is concerned with the problems of its times, not its anodynes.

But if this is so why does literature survive through succeeding ages ? This survival is real but seems a paradox. The intellectual analysis of the world is a scientific matter. The Greeks knew less about, for example, the physical structure of the universe than we do, and this affected their view of man. In this respect the Greeks were ignorant. We can say that the idea of gods shows the inability to understand men (and the idea of God the inability to understand history). But the truth of art lies partly in the objectivity of the standards by which it records what it cannot fully understand. Just as the objective standards of science exist independently of what scientists discover or make – so that Galileo uses the same standards as Einstein – so art uses standards. We understand what Galileo said about the universe without expecting him to say or understand everything about it. But if we did not share the same objective standards with him we could not even read his books with understanding. Greek artists wrote about men and society as objectively as they could: that is, they wrote rationally. Where there was a problem beyond their intellectual comprehension they explained it as rationally as they could. This meant the historical use of the irrational in myths. But as the Greeks lived in a progressive society even the irrational could sometimes work rationally for them. A fascist society, which is retrogressive, uses myths irrationally. The Greeks did not surrender to the irrational. they endeavoured to be rational. Like a detective who doesn't know the author of a crime, they still searched scrupulously for the clues.

However, the Greeks had (as all earlier artists had to have) a bias – because they were like a detective who, although the evidence was incomplete, still *had* to name a victim and a criminal; that is, had to distinguish between right and wrong, had to create a seemingly rational order. In doing this they were inevitably misled by the bias of a class position. The misinterpretations of the past, made in the past, are not accidental. A misinterpretation was historically necessary because accurate objective knowledge was not available. But a *particular* misinterpretation demonstrates its class origin. The world is seen in a certain way because that is the view of the onlooker from his particular social position, and that is of course a class position. Whatever the social origin of the artist his point of view was in some respects almost always decided by the ruling class. The ruling class have the surplus value to create art or to have it created for them, and so their influence over art is predominant anyway. Even more important, they control the normative values of society by their legal and economic control of the mechanical functioning of society. (I have explained this more fully in the introduction to my play *The Bundle*.) So at least on the surface art tends to reflect the views of the ruling class, to use their dictionary of meanings – and it's the ruling class that writes the dictionary.

But art includes *two* things. Firstly, rational objectivity, the expression of the need for interpretation, meaning, order – that is for a justice that isn't fulfilled in the existing social order. Doing this it tends to humanise society, make society truly self-conscious instead of self-identified. This is a truly moral function. But, secondly, it also includes a misinterpretation of experience, and this misinterpretation has a historical class origin. It distorts the first function, because it is dictated by the needs of the ruling class and its problems in running the structure it imposes on society. The Greeks would have a myth for this: someone blessed with the desire to tell the truth, but so cursed that whenever he spoke he lied. This myth wouldn't quite reconcile the poles of the problem, because of course art always tells part of the truth, and this part is profound because in describing human joy and suffering, and the nobility or decadence of social orders, artists record and transmit profound aspects of human experience: the discontent of the just with the unjust, the irreconcilability of the rational with the irrational. The value of Greek or Renaissance art is conveyed to us not merely as emotional experience but also as an intellectual imperative. What art conveys is that human beings envisage perfection, that their condition makes the search and creation of that perfection morally necessary, and that the often seemingly arbitrary or absurd events of history have meaning as part of this creation.

Human beings as a species are neither passive victims nor passive beneficiaries of history, but its creators. That is the logic of the human condition. So the art of the past – as a detail of the historical process – is not passive but conveys a human imperative; and it enables the subjectivity of the past to survive when its objectivity is superseded or destroyed. The notion that Shakespeare was a passive spectator – that aloofness is somehow insight – is completely opposed to this point of view. If he was an artist he was not passive.

Art is, therefore, not only evidence of the moral autonomy of individuals but also of the fact that they can achieve moral sovereignty only under a good government or in struggling to create such a government. This is the foundation of my socialism.

Art, it hardly needs saying, can't create a good society on its own, but it is a necessary part of its creation. It produces its interpretations of experience as technological and scientific development makes them possible, – this development is the foundation of human consciousness.

In the past art has had a two-fold function: to demonstrate the necessity of human rationality by the objectivity with which it observes and records, and at the same time to criticise the irrational imperfections of society which result from its class structure. There can be no modern art which is not socialist. Art in the society which had (Shakespeare's dream!) good government would be socialist art which had inherited its kingdom. Till then socialist art is a weapon in the struggle to create good government. It's not true that a socialist society would not need art, because all social ills would then be dealt with by social engineering. There will never be a time when sentient, conscious beings can look at the world without needing to sing or weep. We will need art as long as we are human. We don't live in the world passively (or we need not) but creatively; we create even our consciousness, in relation to the world. A socialist society will not only need to express joy but also tragedy. The world is always young and old. Even in utopia there will be untimely loss and the vicious caprice of accident, the old will die and the young still sometimes stare uncomprehendingly at the world. The art of a socialist society will have a dignity and lucidity we can't imagine. But we're able, forced, to help to make this art – so that the generations that come after us will live in peace.

*   *   *

We don't live only by concepts. A conceptual interpretation of life is not a way of life or even an image of life. The ideal only has practical significance when it's embodied in the mundane. Theatre, when it's doing what it was created to do, demonstrates order in chaos, the ideal in the ordinary, history in the present, the rational in the seemingly irrational.

Theatre is not a laboratory in the sense that a scientist's laboratory is. The good scientist is convinced of the need for abstract, objective truth. Whatever his personal motives (which may even be for money or power) the conviction of the need, the passion for the abstract and the objective is the motive of his science. An artist differs from a scientist in this way: his subjective passion for objective truth also appears intimately in his objective craft. A scientist who works for a reactionary regime is, in a broad sense, irrational; but he can still discover valid scientific truth and do good scientific work. An artist cannot create art, cannot demonstrate his objective truth, in the service of reaction or fascism; because art is not merely the discovery of new truth or new aspects of old truth – but also the demonstration of the human need for the rational. If it were impossible for scientists to discover anything further because all had been discovered, dramatists (and their audiences) would still need to create. When this need cannot be met, for example under a fascist regime, then there is no art; instead, copies of the past are made. Art isn't the discovery of particular truths in the way science is; it also demonstrates the practical working out of the human need for truth.

Brecht was against undue empathy; but there is a proper empathy in the love of truth. Drama embodies human experience into its descriptions of history. We are ourselves because we are also history. This isn't the same thing as empathy with an individual – or with all individuals in a story (as the confused teacher of Shakespeare probably supposed) – since it contains an intellectual judgement that over-rides personal responses. In the theatre we see and judge as members of society. To talk of objectivity in Brecht's sense may well be misleading. Dramatists can't treat their experiments as scientists treat theirs because the experimentation – as much as the struggle and effort outside the theatre – is an event in human life and history. Society is a surgeon operating on himself and art is part of that operation.

The human, personal motive of the artist and the scientist may well be the same. But the work of the scientist and the artist have different uses. Drama includes the artist's motive as well as the object in its portrayal of human events. But the scientist's motivation isn't part of the objectivity by which he works and judges work. It can be said that a scientific discovery is not merely made by truth but it includes that truth, which may then change society – but this still doesn't mean that the scientist's *motive* becomes part of his discovery. But the motive of the artist, as creator of art *is* and *does*. His motive for creating a work of art is demonstrated in the work itself. This is not, however, the personal motive of the artist (that he dislikes or likes this colour or sitter) but a historical motive. Just as all individuals embody in a general way the human form and the human mind, so all those who have the need to create (all men in some degree) embody the logic of the human biological and historical situation.

Practical science isn't strictly necessary. Tomorrow a law could close all laboratories and stop all experiments. But human creativity could stop only if the species were destroyed or, ironically, it were surrendered totally to technology and 'robotised'. Science isn't necessary, imperative, though it is inevitable. But 'creativity' is what we do in order to do anything else; and creativity applied to recording experience can produce art. Art is necessary even to the maintenance of the status quo. It is even more necessary for change. Unless human beings record experience creatively it doesn't become an event in history but remains inert, brute fact.

If science is something people do, art is an expression of what they are: a process in nature. It is an expression of them as a discrete part of the physical world. Science expresses the nature of the world and the rational attributes of men; art expresses the need for the rational, and so sees the individual as part of his society, which is the mode of his being. I don't want to isolate the rationality of the stage from rationality elsewhere. The objectivity of science is also the objectivity of art. But history moves, develops, because its possible for human beings to behave in certain ways – and art is an embodiment of this purpose in human activity. The scientist can abstract from society and make experiments which may have practical results in human affairs. Scientists find out the ways of development. History doesn't experiment in this way; there is a total involvement between the movement and events and people of history. Art is an aspect of history rather than of science, though of course the distinction isn't complete. That's why neither the stage nor the street can be used like the scientist's laboratory. An experiment on the street could not be discounted whatever the result; and as the stage uses the language – the truth – of the street, no experiment could be genuinely tested (that is, become art) on the stage unless it takes the same risks with reality. In art the standards of truth are impacted inside the experiment: it works within itself and proves itself, though it is still objective because it's historical and social. The scientist uses truth to discover something, the artist uses things to prove truth – to establish rationality as a focus of human experience.

Art can't be disproved, and in this it is the opposite of science.

You can't prove a work of art as you can prove a formula or test an invention. All scientific propositions are in theory capable of disproof, but how can you disprove art? A work of art incorporates the objectivity with which it was created and this objectivity is permanent: it exists over and above the specific subject of a play or painting. This means, of course, that the artist must often have been unaware of the analytical nature of his work. A specific painting or book may, therefore, often be subjected to later critical reappraisal. The portrait of a king that pleased his courtiers may later be seen as the artist's conceited flattery, and so become trivial, an object in history rather than part of the process of history; but it might also be seen as a penetrating criticism of which the king and his courtiers were unaware – and of which perhaps even the artist was not fully aware. But this means, nevertheless, that firm judgements may be made about art – though perhaps only in time. No doubt this is the reason that our understanding of the art of the past is often better than the artist's contemporaries. The truth of art may be described as 'viability'. Tyranny and injustice aren't 'viable'; they can be lived with but not expressed with concent and approval in art – that is, made normative. Viable in this context means expressing the rationality of history.

All people can potentially understand scientific truth. Scientific statements can be universally accepted except by madmen. But moral truth expressed in art works differently. I wrote earlier that historically art makes a true statement and a false statement. The first statement is about the process of history, and this can only be understood politically. The second statement is about a particular historical moment. This can be understood universally, is the subject of most aesthetics, and is indeed the only subject of art as it is still usually taught.

Just as history abandons certain classes – replacing feudalism with capitalism, for example – so art abandons certain classes. The rationality of art lies in its proof of its statements, which are the reflection or demonstration of historical purpose of shape. Art is an aspect of the logic of history, not the consecration of any particular moment of history but of the process of history. So art cannot transcend class barriers – they are indeed the substance of art. But when class barriers are transcended then art that was previously restricted in its effect can be generally understood. If there's confusion about this it's because to live means to be able, at least potentially, to respond to art. Art is an objective record and so it is theoretically observable by everyone. But class bias means the erection of subjectivity into objectivity and this creates cultural blindness. That's why the confused teacher of Shakespeare misunderstood his subject and wrongly forgave him his class bias by trying to call it wisdom.

Lear

Author's Preface

I write about violence as naturally as Jane Austen wrote about manners. Violence shapes and obsesses our society, and if we do not stop being violent we have no future. People who do not want writers to write about violence want to stop them writing about us and our time. It would be immoral not to write about violence.

*

Many animals are able to be violent, but in non-human species the violence is finally controlled so that it does not threaten the species' existence. Then why is the existence of our species threatened by its violence?

I must begin with an important distinction. The predator hunting its prey is violent but not aggressive in the human way. It wants to eat, not destroy, and its violence is dangerous to the prey but not to the predator. Animals only become aggressive – that is destructive in the human sense – when their lives, territory or status in their group are threatened, or when they mate or are preparing to mate. Even then the aggression is controlled. Fighting is usually ritualized, and the weaker or badly-placed animal will be left alone when it runs away or formally submits. Men use much of their energy and skill to make more efficient weapons to destroy each other, but animals have often evolved in ways to ensure they *can't* destroy each other.

A lot has been written on this subject and it is not my job to repeat the evidence; but it shows clearly, I think, that in normal surroundings and conditions members of the same species are not dangerous to one another, but that when they are kept in adverse conditions, and forced to behave unnaturally, their behaviour deteriorates. This has been seen in zoos and laboratories. Then they become destructive and neurotic and make bad parents. They begin to behave like us.

That is all there is to our 'innate' aggression, or our 'original' sin as it was first called. There is no evidence of an aggressive *need*, as there is of sexual and feeding *needs*. We respond aggressively when we are constantly deprived of our physical and emotional needs, or when we are threatened with this; and if we are constantly deprived and threatened in this way – as human beings now are – we live in a

constant state of aggression. It does not matter how much a man
doing routine work in, say, a factory or office is paid: he will still be
deprived in this sense. Because he is behaving in a way for which
he is not designed, he is alienated from his natural self, and this
will have physical and emotional consequences for him. He becomes
nervous and tense and he begins to look for threats everywhere.
This makes him belligerent and provocative; he becomes a threat to
other people, and so his situation rapidly deteriorates.

This is all the facts justify us in concluding: aggression is an
ability but not a necessity. The facts are often *interpreted* more
pessimistically, but that is another matter.

If we *were* innately aggressive, in the sense that it was *necessary*
for us to act aggressively from time to time, we would be condemned
to live with an incurable disease; and as the suffering caused by
aggression in a technological culture is so terrible, the question
would arise: does the human race have any moral justification for its
existence? A character in my play *Early Morning* answered no, and
he tried to kill himself. It is astonishing that many people who share
his beliefs are not forced to draw his conclusions, but can still go
about their daily business. This ability shows mental shallowness
and emotional glibness, not stoicism and spiritual strength. Their
'realism' is really only the fascism of lazy men.

Then why do we behave worse to one another than other animals?
We live in ways for which we are not designed and so our daily
existence interferes with our natural functioning, and this activates
our natural response to threat: aggression. How has this happened?
Why, in the first place, do we live in urban, crowded regimented
groups, working like machines (mostly for the benefit of other men)
and with no real control of our lives? Probably this situation could
not have been avoided. Men did not suddenly become possessors of
human minds and then use them to solve the problems of existence.
These problems were constantly posed and solved within an inherited organization or social structure, and this structure was re-
developed to deal with new problems as they arose. So there was
probably never much chance for new thinking. As men's minds
clarified they were already living in herds or groups, and these
would have evolved into tribes and societies. Like waking sleepers
they would not know dream from reality.

What problems did these half-awake, superstitious men have to
face? They were biologically so successful that they probably became too numerous for their environments and they could not go on

living as loose bands of scavengers and hunters. And the environment itself changed, sometimes suddenly and sometimes gradually but inevitably. And perhaps the relationship between earlier instincts and human awareness produced its own problems. All these changes required adaptations in social organization and created new opportunities for leadership. Habits and techniques of control would be strengthened. In critical times any non-conformity would be a danger to the group. People who are controlled by others in this way soon lose the ability to act for themselves, even if their leaders do not make it dangerous for them to do so. And then, as I shall explain, the natural feelings of opposition become moralized and work to perpetuate the very organization they basically oppose. The whole structure becomes held together by the negative biological response to deprivation and threat – it is an organization held together by the aggression it creates. Aggression has become moralized, and morality has become a form of violence. I shall describe how this happens.

Once the social structure exists it tends to be perpetuated. The organizing groups, the leaders, receive privileges. Some of these were perhaps necessary in the critical situations that created the need for leadership. But the justification for them becomes less when they are inherited by their children. At the same time they become more extensive and entrenched. They become an injustice. But the organizing group becomes self-justifying, because although its position is unjust it is the administrator of justice. At first opposition to it will not be revolutionary or even political; it will be 'meaningless' and involve personal discontents and frustrations. When public problems become private problems, as they often do for the people involved in them, they are distorted, and then people's behaviour may seem to be arbitrary and self-regarding. This can always be shown to be socially disruptive, of course. In this way an unjust society causes and defines crime; and an aggressive social structure which is unjust and must create aggressive social disruption, receives the moral sanction of being 'law and order'. Law and order is one of the steps taken to maintain injustice.

People with unjust social privileges have an obvious emotional interest in social morality. It allows them to maintain their privileges and justifies them in taking steps to do so. It reflects their fear of an opposition that would often take away everything they have, even their lives. This is one way in which social morality becomes angry and aggressive.

But there is another way. Social morality is also a safe form of obedience for many of the victims of the unjust organization. It gives them a form of innocence founded on fear – but it is never a peaceful innocence. It is a sort of character easily developed in childhood, when power relations are at their starkest. Then it is dangerous to have aggressive ideas against those in power because they can easily punish you, they are stronger and cleverer, and if you destroyed them how could you live? (In adults this becomes: We can't have a revolution because the buses wouldn't run and I'd be late for work. Or: Hitler made the trains run on time.) Our society has the structure of a pyramid of aggression and as the child is the weakest member it is at the bottom. We still *think* we treat children with special kindness and make special allowances for them, as indeed most animals do. But do we? Don't most people believe they have a right, even a duty, to use crude force against children as part of their education? Almost all organizations dealing with children are obsessed with discipline. Whenever possible we put them into uniforms and examine their minds like warders frisking prisoners. We force them to live by the clock before they can read it, though this makes no biological sense. We build homes without proper places for them. They interfere with the getting of money so mothers leave them and go to work – and some of them are no longer even physically able to feed their own children. Parents are worn out by daily competitive striving so they can't tolerate the child's natural noise and mess. They don't know why it cries, they don't know *any* of its inarticulate language. The child's first word isn't 'mummy' or 'daddy', it is 'me'. It has been learning to say it through millions of years of evolution, and it has a biological right to its egocentricity because that is the only way our species can continue.

The point is this: every child is born with certain biological expectations, or if you like species' assumptions – that it's un-preparedness will be cared for, that it will be given not only food but emotional reassurance, that its vulnerability will be shielded, that it will be born into a world waiting to receive it, and that knows *how* to receive it. But the weight of aggression in our society is so heavy that the unthinkable happens: we batter it. And when the violence is not so crude it is still there, spread thinly over years; the final effect is the same and so the dramatic metaphor I used to describe it was the stoning of a baby in its pram. This is not done by thugs but by people who like plays condemning thugs.

One way or the other the child soon learns that it is born into a strange world and not the world it evolved for: we are no longer born free. So the small, infinitely vulnerable child panics – as any animal must. It does not get the reassurance it needs, and in its fear it identifies with the people who have power over it. That is, it accepts their view of the situation, their judgement of who is right and wrong – their *morality*. But this morality – which is social morality – now has all the force of the fear and panic that created it. Morality stops being something people want and becomes what they are terrified to be without. So social morality is a form of corrupted innocence, and it is against the basic wishes of those who have been moralized in this way. It is a threat, a weapon used against their most fundamental desire for justice, without which they are not able to be happy or allow others to be happy. The aggressive response of such people has been smothered by social morality, but this only increases its tension. So they try to relieve it in extravert ways. Often they become missionaries and campaigners. They are obsessed with a need for censorship – which is only the moral justification of the peeping Tom. They find the wicked and ungodly everywhere – because these things are in themselves. Their social morality denies their need for justice, but that need is so basic it can only be escaped by dying or going mad; otherwise it must be struggled against obsessively. In this struggle pleasure becomes guilt, and the moralizing, censorious, inhuman puritans are formed. Sometimes their aggression is hidden under strenuous gleefulness, but it is surprising how little glee is reflected in their opinions and beliefs, and how intolerant, destructive and angry these guardians of morality can be.

Their morality is angry because they are in conflict with themselves. Not merely divided, but *fighting* their own repressed need for justice with all the fear and hysteria of their original panic. Because this isn't something that is done once, in childhood or later; to go on living these people must murder themselves every day. Social morality is a form of suicide. Socially moralized people must act contemptuously and angrily to all liberalism, contentment and sexual freedom, because these are the things they are fighting in themselves. There is no way out for them – it is as if an animal was locked in a cage and then fed with the key. It shakes the bars but can never get out. So other people's happiness becomes their pain, and other people's freedom reminds them of their slavery. It is as if they had created in themselves a desolate, inhospitable landscape in which they had to live out their emotional and spiritual lives. This landscape reflects, of course, the inhospitable, unjust world in which they first suffered; and it exacerbates and reinforces their

aggression and seems to give it added depths of bitterness. By calling the unjust world good they recreate it in themselves and are
condemned to live in it. They have not learned that when you are
frightened of the dark you do not make it go away by shutting your
eyes. These people are the angry, gleeful ghosts of my play, *Early
Morning*.

Not all children grow up in this way, of course. Some solve the
problem by becoming cynical and indifferent, others hide in a
listless, passive conformity, others become criminal and openly destructive. Whatever happens, most of them will grow up to act in ways
that are ugly, deceitful and violent; and the conforming, socially
moralized, good citizens will be the most violent of all, because
their aggression is expressed through all the technology and power
of massed society. The institutions of morality and order are always
more destructive than crime. This century has made that very clear.

Even if a child escapes undamaged it will still face the same
problems as a man. We treat men as children. They have no real
political or economic control of their lives, and this makes them
afraid of society and their own impotence in it. Marx has described
adult alienation very well, but we can now understand more about
it. We can see that most men are spending their lives doing things
for which they are not biologically designed. We are not designed
for our production lines, housing blocks, even cars; and these
things are not designed for us. They are designed, basically, to
make profit. And because we do not even need most of the things
we waste our lives in producing, we have to be surrounded by
commercial propaganda to make us buy them. This life is so
unnatural for us that, for straightforward biological reasons, we
become tense, nervous and aggressive, and these characteristics are
fed back into our young. Tension and aggression are even becoming
the markings of our species. Many people's faces are set in patterns
of alarm, coldness or threat; and they move jerkily and awkwardly,
not with the simplicity of free animals. These expressions are signs
of moral disease, but we are taught to admire them. They are used
in commercial propaganda and in iconographic pictures of politicians
and leaders, even writers; and of course they are taken as signs of
good manners in the young.

It is for these reasons I say that society is held together by the
aggression it creates, and men are not dangerously aggressive but
our sort of society is. It creates aggression in these ways: first, it is
basically unjust, and second it makes people live unnatural lives –
both things which create a natural, biological aggressive response in

the members of society. Society's formal answer to this is socialized morality; but this, as I have explained, is only another form of violence, and so it must itself provoke more aggression. There is no way out for our sort of society, an unjust society must be violent. Any organization which denies the basic need for biological justice must become aggressive, even though it claims to be moral. This is true of most religions, which say that justice can only be obtained in another world, and not in this. It is also true of many movements for political reform.

Moralized aggression can, of course, be mixed with ordinary kindness and decency, so can the aggression of the social institutions it maintains. But aggression is so powerful (it was after all evolved to deal with desperate situations) that it decides the character of all people and institutions it infects. So through historical times our institutions have been aggressive, and because of this they make it even easier for aggressive people to get power and authority. That is why leaders – revolutionary as well as reactionary – so often behave worse than animals. I don't say this as invective – it is a sad, historical truth.

So human aggression has important features that make it more destructive than the aggression of other animals. It *is* animal aggression, but it has to be accommodated by our human minds, and presumably it appears to us as more alarming and frightening than it does to other animals. This is true of our subjective feelings of aggression as well as of the aggression we meet from outside. We have more complicated resources to deal with this increased vulnerability. When panic and fear become unbearable it is as if we lied and said they were not there, and out of this lie we build social morality. Children are especially vulnerable in this way, as I have said, but we are all exposed to the same pressures throughout our lives. As animals we react to threat in a natural, biological way; but we must also react in more complicated ways as human beings – mentally, emotionally and morally. It is because we cannot do this successfully that we no longer function as a species. Instead we have created all the things that threaten us: our military giantism, moral hysteria, industrial servitude, and all the ugly aggressiveness of a commercial culture.

Our situation has been made much worse, at least for the time being, by our technological success. The problem can now be described in this brief, schematic way.

We evolved in a biosphere but we live in what is more and more becoming a technosphere. We do not fit into it very well and so it activates our biological defences, one of which is aggression. Our environment is changing so rapidly that we cannot wait for biological solutions to evolve. So we should either change our technosphere or use technology to change human nature. But change in our society is really decided on urgent commercial imperatives, so nothing is done to solve our main problem. But a species living in an unfavourable environment dies out. For us the end will probably be quicker because the aggression we generate will be massively expressed through our technology.

This is very over-simplified and our fate is far from being so certain. But the combination of technology and socialized morality is very ugly, and it could lead to disaster. Alternatively, governments could begin to use technology to enforce socialized morality. That is by using drugs, selection, conditioning, genetics and so on, they could manufacture people who would fit into society. This would be just as disastrous. So if we do not want either of these things we must do something else. There are signs, in the search for counter-cultures and alternative politics, that we are beginning to do so.

What ought we to do? Live justly. But what is justice? Justice is allowing people to live in the way for which they evolved. Human beings have an emotional and physical need to do so, it is their biological expectation. They *can* only live in this way, or all the time struggle consciously or unconsciously to do so. That is the essential thing I want to say because it means that in fact our society and its morality, which deny this, and its technology which more and more prevents it, all the time whisper into people's ear 'You have no right to live'. That is what lies under the splendour of the modern world. Equality, freedom and fraternity must be reinterpreted in the light of this – otherwise real revolutionary change is impossible.

We can express this basic need in many ways: aesthetic, intellectual, the need to love, create, protect and enjoy. These are not higher things that can be added when more basic needs are met. *They* are basic. They must be the way in which we express all our existence, and if they do not control our daily life then we cannot function as human beings at all. They are not weakness, but they have nothing to do with the caricatures that pass for strength in our society – the hysterical old maids who become sergeant majors, the disguised peeping Toms who become moralists, the immature social misfits who become judges. Society pays lip service to these needs, but it has no real interest in them, and they are of course incompatible with the strident competitiveness of a commercial culture. So really we deny them. Like ghosts we teach a dead religion, build a few more prisons to worship Caesar in, and leave it at that. Blake said that when we try to become more than men we become less than beasts, and that is what we have done. Our human emotions and intellects are not things that stand apart from the long development of evolution; it is as animals we make our highest demands, and in responding to them as men we create our deepest human experience.

I have not answered many of the questions I have raised, but I have tried to explain things that often go unnoticed but which must be put right if anything is to work for us. They are difficult to put right because reforms easily become socially moralized. It is so easy to subordinate justice to power, but when this happens power takes on the dynamics and dialectics of aggression, and then nothing is really changed. Marx did not know about this problem and Lenin discovered it when it was too late. The understanding of this problem must become part of contemporary socialism, otherwise change will be slower and more difficult.

There is no need for pessimism or resignation, and this play is certainly not either of these things. Lear is blind till they take his eyes away, and by then he has begun to see, to understand. (Blindness is a dramatic metaphor for insight, that is why Gloucester, Oedipus and Tiresias are blind.) Lear's new world is strange and so at first he can only grope painfully and awkwardly. Lear is old by then, but most of the play's audiences will be younger. It might seem to them that the truth is always ground for pessimism when it is discovered, but one soon comes to see it as an opportunity. Then you don't have to go on doing things that never work in the hope that they might one day – because now you know why they *can't*. Even bourgeois politics is more efficient than that.

Finally, I have not tried to say what the future should be like, because that is a mistake. If your plan of the future is too rigid you start to coerce people to fit into it. We do not need a plan of the future, we need a *method* of change.

I want to say something brief about the play. Lear did not have to destroy his daughters' innocence, he does so only because he doesn't understand his situation. When he does understand he leaves

Thomas and Susan unharmed. But I think he had to destroy the innocent boy. Some things were lost to us long ago as a species, but we all seem to have to live through part of the act of losing them. We have to learn to do this without guilt or rancour or callousness – or socialized morality. So Lear's ghost isn't one of the angry ghosts from *Early Morning*, but something different.

Apart from the ten or so main characters of the play there are about seventy other speaking parts. In a sense these are one role showing the character of a society.

Act One shows a world dominated by myth. Act Two shows the clash between myth and reality, between superstitious men and the autonomous world. Act Three shows a resolution of this, in the world we prove real by dying in it.

According to ancient chronicles Lear lived about the year 3100 after the creation. He was king for 60 years. He built Leicester and was buried under the River Soar. His father was killed while trying to fly over London. His youngest daughter killed herself when she fell from power.

(HOLINSHED and GEOFFREY OF MONMOUTH)

LEAR *was presented by the English Stage Company at the Royal Court Theatre on September 29th 1971 with the following cast:*

FOREMAN	Geoffrey Hinsliff
1ST WORKMAN	Matthew Guinness
2ND WORKMAN	Struan Rodger
3RD WORKMAN	Ron Pember
SOLDIER	Bob Hoskins
LEAR	Harry Andrews
BODICE	Carmel McSharry
FONTANELLE	Rosemary McHale
WARRINGTON	Anthony Douse
OLD COUNCILLOR	George Howe
ENGINEER	Gareth Hunt
FIRING SQUAD OFFICER	William Hoyland
BISHOP	Gareth Hunt
DUKE OF NORTH	Eric Allen
DUKE OF CORNWALL	Alec Heggie
SOLDIER A	Bob Hoskins
THE GRAVEDIGGER'S BOY	Mark McManus
THE GRAVEDIGGER'S BOY'S WIFE	Celestine Randall
CARPENTER	Oliver Cotton
SERGEANT	Bob Hoskins
SOLDIER D *at the Gravedigger's Boy's House*	Ray Barron
SOLDIER E *at the Gravedigger's Boy's House*	Geoffrey Hinsliff
SOLDIER F *at the Gravedigger's Boy's House*	Antony Milner
JUDGE	William Hoyland
USHER	Gareth Hunt
OLD SAILOR	Matthew Guinness

BEN, *a Prison Orderly*	Derek Carpenter
SOLDIER H *Guard in the Prison*	Geoffrey Hinsliff
SOLDIER I *Guard in the Prison*	Richard Howard
SOLDIER G *Guard in the Prison*	Bob Hoskins
OLD PRISON ORDERLY	Anthony Douse
WOUNDED REBEL SOLDIER	Matthew Guinness
BODICE'S AIDE (Major Pellet)	Struan Rodger
SOLDIER J *Convoy Escort*	Bob Hoskins
SOLDIER K *Convoy Escort*	Geoffrey Hinsliff
SOLDIER L *Convoy Escort*	Richard Howard
PRISONER 1	Struan Rodger
PRISONER 2	Ron Pember
PRISONER 3	Derek Carpenter
PRISONER 4, *later Prison Doctor*	William Hoyland
PRISON COMMANDANT	Gareth Hunt
SOLDIER M *Prison Guard*	Ray Barron
SOLDIER N *Prison Guard*	Matthew Guinness
SOLDIER O *Prison Guard*	Eric Allen
FARMER	Geoffrey Hinsliff
FARMER'S WIFE	Marjorie Yates
FARMER'S SON	Antony Milner
THOMAS	Alec Heggie
JOHN	Richard Howard
SUSAN	Diana Quick
SMALL MAN	Ron Pember
OFFICER	Gareth Hunt
A BOY	Ray Barron

OTHER SOLDIERS, WORKERS, STRANGERS, COURT OFFICIALS, GUARDS: Geoffrey Hinsliff, Matthew Guinness, Antony Milner, Ray Barron, Ron Pember, Eric Allen, Anthony Douse, Bob Hoskins, Richard Howard, Gareth Hunt, Derek Carpenter, Marjorie Yates, Struan Rodger.

Directed by William Gaskill   Costumes designed by Deirdre Clancy
Sets designed by John Napier   Lighting by Andy Phillips

Act One

SCENE ONE

Near the wall.
A stack of building materials – shovels, picks, posts and a tarpaulin.
Silence. Then (offstage) a sudden indistinct shout, a crash, shouts. A
FOREMAN *and* TWO WORKERS *carry on a* DEAD WORKER *and*
put him down. They are followed by a SOLDIER.

FIRST WORKER. Get some water! He needs water.

FOREMAN. He's dead.

SOLDIER. Move 'im then!

FOREMAN. Get his legs.

SOLDIER (*to* FOREMAN). Can yer see 'em? Look an' see! They're
comin' up the ditch on the other side.

> FOREMAN *goes upstage to look off.* THIRD *and* FOURTH
> WORKERS *come on.*

THIRD WORKER (*coming on*). I shouted to him to run.

FOREMAN (*coming downstage*). Go back, go back! Work!

> FOURTH WORKER *goes off again.*

THIRD WORKER. You heard me shout!

FIRST WORKER. He says he's dead.

FOREMAN. Work!

SOLDIER (*to* FIRST WORKER). You! – make yerself responsible
for 'andin' in 'is pick t' stores. (*Suddenly he sees something off
stage and runs down to the others.*) Cover 'im! Quick!

FOREMAN (*points to tarpaulin*). Take that!

> *They cover the body with the tarpaulin.* LEAR, LORD
> WARRINGTON, *an* OLD COUNCILLOR, *an* OFFICER, *an*
> ENGINEER *and* LEAR'S DAUGHTERS – BODICE *and*

FONTANELLE – *come on. The* SOLDIER, FOREMAN *and*
WORKERS *stand stiffly.* WARRINGTON *signs to them and they*
work by the tarpaulin.

BODICE (*to* FONTANELLE). We needn't go on. We can see the
end.

ENGINEER. The chalk ends here. We'll move faster now.

COUNCILLOR (*looking at his map*). Isn't it a swamp on this map?

FONTANELLE (*to* BODICE). My feet are wet.

LEAR (*points to tarpaulin*). What's that?

ENGINEER. Materials for the –

WARRINGTON (*to* FOREMAN). Who is it?

FOREMAN. Workman.

WARRINGTON. What?

FOREMAN. Accident, sir.

LEAR. Who left that wood in the mud?

ENGINEER. That's just delivered. We're moving that to –

LEAR. It's been rotting there for weeks. (*To* WARRINGTON.)
They'll never finish! Get more men on it. The officers must
make the men work!

BODICE (*shakes* ENGINEER's *hand*). Our visit has been so enjoyable
and informative.

FONTANELLE. Such an interesting day.

WARRINGTON. We can't take more men. The countryside would
be left derelict and there'd be starvation in the towns.

LEAR. Show me this body.

WARRINGTON *and the* SOLDIER *lift the tarpaulin.*

Blow on the head.

FOREMAN. Axe.

LEAR. What?

FOREMAN. An axe, sir. Fell on him.

LEAR. It's a flogging crime to delay work. (*To* WARRINGTON.)
You must deal with this fever. They treat their men like cattle.
When they finish work they must be kept in dry huts. All these
huts are wet. You waste men.

COUNCILLOR (*making a note*). I'll appoint a hut inspector.

LEAR. They dug the wall up again last night.

OFFICER. Local farmers. We can't catch them, they scuttle back home so fast.

LEAR. Use spring traps. (*To* FOREMAN.) Who dropped the axe?

WARRINGTON (*to* FOREMAN). Be quick!

FOREMAN *and* SOLDIER *push* THIRD WORKER *forward.*

LEAR. Court martial him. Fetch a firing squad. A drumhead trial for sabotage.

Quiet murmur of surprise. The OFFICER *goes to fetch the* FIRING SQUAD.

FONTANELLE. My feet are wet.

BODICE. She'll catch cold, father.

LEAR. Who was a witness?

WARRINGTON (*points to* FOREMAN). You!

FOREMAN. He dropped a pickaxe on his head. I've had my eye on him, sir. Always idle and –

LEAR (*to* THIRD WORKER). Prisoner of war?

FOREMAN. No. One of our men. A farmer.

LEAR. I understand! He has a grudge. I took him off his land.

The FIRING SQUAD *is marched in by the* OFFICER.

OFFICER. Squad as a squad – halt!

LEAR. I shall give evidence. He killed a workman on the wall. That alone makes him a traitor. But there's something else suspicious about him. Did you dig up the wall last night?

BODICE (*sighing*). It can easily be checked if he missed their roll calls.

LEAR. I started this wall when I was young. I stopped my enemies in the field, but there were always more of them. How could we ever be free? So I built this wall to keep our enemies out. My people will live behind this wall when I'm dead. You may be governed by fools but you'll always live in peace. My wall will

make you free. That's why the enemies on our borders – the
Duke of Cornwall and the Duke of North – try to stop us
building it. I won't ask him which he works for – they're both
hand in glove. Have him shot.

THIRD WORKER. Sir.

FONTANELLE (*aside to* BODICE). Thank god we've thought of
ourselves.

OFFICER. Squad as a squad to firing positions – move!

LEAR (*indicating the* FIRING SQUAD). They must work on the
wall, they're slow enough. (*Turns to* WARRINGTON.) See this is
done. I'm going down to the swamp.

BODICE. Father, if you kill this man it will be an injustice.

LEAR. My dear, you want to help me, but you must let me deal
with the things I understand. Listen and learn.

BODICE. What is there to learn? It's silly to make so much out of
nothing. There was an accident. That's all.

LEAR (*half aside to her*). Of course there was an accident. But the
work's slow. I must do something to make the officers move.
That's what I came for, otherwise my visit's wasted. And there
are saboteurs and there *is* something suspicious about this man –

BODICE. But think of the people! They already say you act like a
schoolboy or an old spinster –

LEAR. Why are they waiting? It's cruel to make him wait.

OFFICER   } Sir – you're –
WARRINGTON } Move, sir.

LEAR *moves out of the* FIRING SQUAD'*s way.*

BODICE (*loudly*). Listen to me. All of you notice I disassociate
myself from this act.

LEAR. Be quiet, Bodice. You mustn't talk like that in front of me.

FONTANELLE. And I agree with what my sister says.

LEAR. O my poor children, you're too good for this world. (*To the
others.*) You see how well they'll govern when I'm dead.
Bodice, you're right to be kind and merciful, and when I'm
dead you *can* be – because you will have my wall. You'll live

inside a fortress. Only I'm not free to be kind or merciful. I must build the fortress.

BODICE. How petty it is to be obstinate over nothing.

LEAR. I have explained and now you must understand!

BODICE. It is small and petty to make –

LEAR. I have explained.

BODICE. Small and petty! All these things are in your head. The Duke of Cornwall is not a monster. The Duke of North has not sworn to destroy you. I have proof of what I say.

LEAR. They're my sworn enemies. I killed the fathers therefore the sons must hate me. And when I killed the fathers I stood on the field among our dead and swore to kill the sons! I'm too old now, they've fooled me. But they won't take my country and dig my bones up when I'm dead. Never.

FONTANELLE (to BODICE). This is the moment to tell him.

BODICE. I'm going to marry the Duke of North and my sister's going to marry the Duke of Cornwall.

FONTANELLE. He's good and reliable and honest, and I trust him as if we'd been brought up together.

BODICE. Good lord! – how can they be your friends if you treat them like enemies? That's why they threatened you: it was political necessity. Well, now that's all in the past! We've brought them into your family and you can pull this absurd wall down. There! (Slight laugh.) You don't have to make your people slaves to protect you from your sons-in-law.

LEAR. My sons-in-law?

FONTANELLE. Congratulate us, father, give us your blessing.

BODICE. I'm marrying North.

FONTANELLE. And I'm marrying Cornwall.

LEAR (points to THIRD WORKER). Tie him straight! He's falling!

BODICE. So now you don't have to shoot him. Our husbands could never allow you to, anyway.

FONTANELLE. I know you'll get on with my husband. He's very understanding, he knows how to deal with old people.

LEAR. Straighter!

BODICE. You'll soon learn to respect them like your sons.

LEAR. I have no sons! I have no daughters! (*Tries to be calmer.*) Tell me – (*Stops, bewildered.*) – you are marrying North and you are marrying –. No, no! They've deceived you. You haven't met them. When did you meet them? Behind my back?

FONTANELLE. We sent each other photographs and letters. I can tell a man from his expression.

LEAR. O now I understand! You haven't met them. You're like blind children. Can't you see they only want to get over the wall? They'll be like wolves in a fold.

BODICE. Wall, wall, wall! This wall must be pulled down!

FONTANELLE. Certainly. My husband insists on that as part of the marriage contract.

BODICE (*to* OFFICER). I order you not to shoot this man. Our husbands will shoot anyone who shoots him. They offer us peace, we can't shoot innocent men because we think they're their spies!

LEAR. Shoot him!

BODICE. No!

LEAR. This is not possible! I must be obeyed!

WARRINGTON. Sir, this is out of hand. Nothing's gained by being firm in little matters. Keep him under arrest. The Privy Council will meet. There are more important matters to discuss.

LEAR. My orders are not little matters! What duke are you marrying? Who have you sold me to?

BODICE. If the king will not act reasonably it's your legal duty to disobey him.

WARRINGTON. Ma'am, you make this worse. Let me –

LEAR (*takes pistol from the* OFFICER *and threatens the* FIRING SQUAD). Shoot him!

BODICE. There, it's happened. Well, the doctors warned us, of course. (*Loudly.*) My father isn't well. Warrington, take the king back to his camp.

FONTANELLE. He shouldn't have come out today. This mud's too much for him. My feet are wringing.

LEAR. My enemies will not destroy my work! I gave my life to these people. I've seen armies on their hands and knees in blood, insane women feeding dead children at their empty breasts, dying men spitting blood at me with their last breath, our brave young men in tears –. But I could bear all this! When I'm dead my people will live in freedom and peace and remember my name, no – venerate it! . . . They are my sheep and if one of them is lost I'd take fire to hell to bring him out. I loved and cared for all my children, and now you've sold them to their enemies! (*He shoots* THIRD WORKER, *and his body slumps forwards on the post in a low bow.*) There's no more time, it's too late to learn anything.

BODICE. Yes, you'll ruin yourself. Our husbands can't let you terrorize these people – they'll be *their* people soon. They must protect them from your madness.

LEAR. Work! Get your men to work! Get them on the wall!

> WORKERS, SOLDIERS and FOREMAN *go out. They take the two bodies with them.*

I knew it would come to this! I knew you were malicious! I built my wall against *you* as well as my other enemies! You talk of marriage? You have murdered your family. There will be no more children. Your husbands are impotent. That's not an empty insult. You wrote? My spies know more than that! You will get nothing from this crime. You have perverted lusts. They won't be satisfied. It *is* perverted to want your pleasure where it makes others suffer. I pity the men who share your beds. I've watched you scheme and plan – they'll lie by you when you dream! Where will your ambition end? You will throw old men from their coffins, break children's legs, pull the hair from old women's heads, make young men walk the streets in beggary and cold while their wives grow empty and despair – I am ashamed of my tears! You have done this to me. The people will judge between you and me.

LEAR *goes out. The* ENGINEER *and the* OLD COUNCILLOR
follow him.

WARRINGTON. I'm sorry, ma'am. If you'd spoken another time –
FONTANELLE. You should have taken him away when you were
told –
BODICE. You were caught out. Well, learn your lesson. As it
happens, no harm's done. Go and keep in with him. We'll let
you know what must happen next.

WARRINGTON *and the others go out.* BODICE *and*
FONTANELLE *are left alone.*

We must go to our husbands tonight.
FONTANELLE. Happiness at last! I was always terrified of him.
BODICE. We must attack before the wall's finished. I'll talk to my
husband and you talk to yours. The four of us will sit in the
Council of War. We must help each other. Goodbye.
FONTANELLE. Goodbye.

The daughters go out.

SCENE TWO

Parade ground.
A saluting stand. LEAR, OLD COUNCILLOR, WARRINGTON,
BISHOP, MILITARY AIDES. *Marching, march music, and parade
commands are heard during the scene.* LEAR *stands with both arms
stretched out in a gesture of salute and blessing.*

LEAR. Greetings to the eighth regiment! (*Still saluting. To*
WARRINGTON.) You will command my right flank and circle
them on the right. Then I attack the centre. That's how I
crushed the fathers. (*Still saluting.*) I salute my loyal comrades!
WARRINGTON. We could refuse this war. We're old, sir. We
could retire and let these young men choose what to do with

their own lives. Ask your daughters to let you live quietly in the country.

LEAR (*still saluting*). How could I trust myself to them? My daughters are proclaimed outlaws, without rights of prisoners of war. They can be raped – or murdered. Why should they be held for trial? Their crimes aren't covered by my laws. Where does their vileness come from?

WARRINGTON. I've given you advice it was my duty to give. But I'm proud you've rejected it.

LEAR (*still saluting*). Greetings to my glorious ninth!

WARRINGTON. I have two letters from your daughters, sir. They both wrote in secret and told me not to let anyone know, especially each other.

LEAR. Give them to me.

WARRINGTON. No, sir. They ask me to betray you and then each other. They'll both make me head of the army and let me share their bed.

LEAR. They live in their own fantasies! They chose their husbands well, they should be married to my enemies! Have the war ceremonies taken place? It doesn't matter. (*He takes the letters from* WARRINGTON. *He reads part of one.*) 'He is mad. If he won what security would you have?' (*He reads from the other.*) 'He would turn on you as he turned on us.' (*Salutes as before.*) Greetings to my friends the ninth! (*Still saluting.*) Warrington, if I'm killed or fall into their hands you must take my place and build the wall.

WARRINGTON. Sir. This fry won't take you. Your army is paraded!

BISHOP. Our prayers go with you into war, sir. God blesses the righteous. He has nothing to do with women who make war.

COUNCILLOR. I feel confidence in my bones. That's never failed me. If only I were a young man!

LEAR. The trumpet! I smell victory!

Cheers and trumpet. They go out.

SCENE THREE

Daughters' War Council.
Table, chairs, map. BODICE, FONTANELLE, NORTH, CORNWALL.
BODICE *knits.*

NORTH. We share the command between us.

CORNWALL. Yes.

NORTH. We must guess how Lear will attack.

BODICE (*knitting*). He'll send Warrington round the right and
attack the centre himself.

CORNWALL. Are you sure, sister?

BODICE. He always has and he's set in his ways.

> CORNWALL, NORTH *and* BODICE *study the map.* BODICE
> *knits at the same time.*

FONTANELLE (*aside*). I'm bitterly disappointed in my husband.
How dare he! A civil servant wrote his letters and an actor posed
for his photographs. When he gets on top of me I'm so angry I
have to count to ten. That's long enough. Then I wait till he's
asleep and work myself off. I'm not making do with that for
long. I've written to Warrington and told him to use all his
men against Bodice and leave my army alone – that'll finish
her – and then I paid a young, blond lieutenant on my husband's staff to shoot him while they're busy fighting. Then I'll
marry Warrington and let him run the country for me.

NORTH (*studying the map*). They can't get round these mountains.

CORNWALL. No.

BODICE (*aside*). I'm not disappointed in my husband. I expected
nothing. There is some satisfaction in listening to him squeal
on top of me while he tries to get his little paddle in. I lie still
and tell myself while he whines, you'll pay for this, my lad. He
sees me smiling and contented and thinks it's his virility.
Virility! It'd be easier to get blood out of a stone, and far more
probable. I've bribed a major on his staff to shoot him in the

battle – they're all corrupt – and I've written to Warrington and told him to use all his force against hers. She'll be crushed and then I'll marry Warrington and run the country through him. So I shall have three countries: my father's, my husband's and my sister and brother-in-law's.

NORTH. Till tomorrow.

CORNWALL. Yes. (*Goes to* FONTANELLE.) Let's go to bed. I need your body before I risk death.

FONTANELLE. My darling. (*Aside.*) I'll get him drunk. He's such a frightened little boy, fighting terrifies him. He'll fidget and mawl all night. I'd rather mop up his vomit.

NORTH (*to* BODICE). Let me take you to bed, my dear. I must feel you on me when I go to the field.

BODICE. Yes, North. (*Aside.*) He must prove himself a man before he plays with his soldiers. He'll fuss and try all night, but he won't be able to raise his standard. I'll help him and make it worse. By the morning he won't know which side he's fighting on. And that'll make it easier for the major.

FONTANELLE. Sleep well.

BODICE. And you.

They all go out.

SCENE FOUR

Prison area.

THREE SOLDIERS (A, B *and* C) *upstage.*

SOLDIER A. 'Ow long they goin' a keep us 'ere? The war's over. They wan'a send us 'ome.

SOLDIER B. They'll think a some reason. (*Indicates offstage.*) Watered 'im yet?

SOLDIER A. No point.

BODICE, FONTANELLE *and an* OFFICER *hurry on downstage.*

BODICE. Is our father taken yet?

OFFICER. He got away.

FONTANELLE (*stamps her foot*). Damn! That's spoiled everything!

CORNWALL *comes on.*

(*Aside.*) My husband! Damn! Damn! Damn! Has the lieutenant dared to betray me?

CORNWALL (*kisses* FONTANELLE). A great victory! They fought like devils but we beat them!

BODICE (*aside*). If I hadn't told him father's plans he'd be lying dead under his army by now.

NORTH *comes in.*

(*Aside.*) Damn it! My husband!

NORTH (*kisses* BODICE). Your enemies are routed!

FONTANELLE (*to* CORNWALL. *Prying*). What are our losses? Are your staff all safe?

NORTH. I lost one major. He was talking to one of Cornwall's lieutenants before the fighting –

CORNWALL. A young blond man called Crag.

FONTANELLE. Yes, I knew him.

CORNWALL. – the first shell fell between them and blew their heads off.

BODICE (*aside*). One can't allow for everything.

NORTH. Warrington's in the cage.

BODICE (*aside*). Now I must be careful. He didn't attack my sister's men, so I couldn't risk him talking about my letter. I had his tongue cut out.

CORNWALL. Let's go and see what he has to say for himself.

FONTANELLE. Wait ... (NORTH *and* CORNWALL *stop.*) He was shouting insults about you and I didn't want our troops to be upset. So I let them cut his tongue out. I thought that was best.

CORNWALL. O, my men would have laughed at him.

BODICE (*aside*). I see my sister thinks like me, I must never trust her.

NORTH. It doesn't matter, he's going to be killed anyway.

BODICE. I'll see to that for you. Go and thank our armies. (*Aside.*) He could still make signs. It's better if he dies in silence.

NORTH. Yes, Cornwall, let's go together.

CORNWALL *and* NORTH *go out with the* OFFICER.

BODICE. I'm glad they've gone. Men are squeamish after a war. (*To* SOLDIER A.) Private, you look strong and capable, would you like to go up in the world?

SOLDIER A. Yessam.

FONTANELLE. Good teeth, too.

BODICE. Get rid of them.

SOLDIER A *flicks his head and* SOLDIERS B *and* C *go out.*

Fetch him out.

SOLDIER A *fetches* WARRINGTON *on stage. He is dishevelled, dirty and bound.*

SOLDIER A. Yer wan' 'im done in in a fancy way? Thass sometimes arst for. I once 'ad t' cut a throat for some ladies t' see once.

FONTANELLE. It's difficult to choose.

BODICE (*sits on her riding stick and takes out her knitting*). Let him choose. (*Knits.*)

SOLDIER A. I once give a 'and t' flay a man. I couldn't manage that on me own. Yer need two at least for that. Shall I beat 'im up?

FONTANELLE. You're all talk! Wind and piss!

SOLDIER A. Juss for a start. Don't get me wrong, thass juss for a start. Get it goin' and see 'ow it goes from there.

FONTANELLE. But I want something –

BODICE (*knitting*). O shut up and let him get on with it. (*Nods at* SOLDIER A *to go on.*)

SOLDIER A. Thankyermum. Right, less see 'ow long it takes t' turn yer inside out.

FONTANELLE. Literally?

SOLDIER A (*hits* WARRINGTON). O, 'e wants it the 'ard way.
(*Hits him.*) Look at 'im puttin' on the officer class! (*Hits him.*)
Don't pull yer pips on me, laddie.

FONTANELLE. Use the boot! (SOLDIER A *kicks him.*) Jump on
him! (*She pushes* SOLDIER A.) Jump on his head!

SOLDIER A. Lay off, lady, lay off! 'Oo's killin' 'im, me or you?

BODICE (*knits*). One plain, two pearl, one plain.

FONTANELLE. Throw him up and drop him. I want to hear him
drop.

SOLDIER A. Thass a bit 'eavy, yer need proper gear t' drop 'em –

FONTANELLE. Do something! Don't let him get away with it. O
Christ, why did I cut his tongue out? I want to hear him
scream!

SOLDIER A (*jerks* WARRINGTON'*s head up*). Look at 'is eyes, Miss.
Thass boney-fidey sufferin'.

FONTANELLE. O yes, tears and blood. I wish my father was
here. I wish he could see him. Look at his hands! Look at
them going! What's he praying or clutching? Smash his
hands!

> SOLDIER A *and* FONTANELLE *jump on* WARRINGTON'*s
> hands.*

Kill his hands! Kill his feet! Jump on it – all of it! He can't hit
us now. Look at his hands like boiling crabs! Kill it! Kill all of
it! Kill him inside! Make him dead! Father! Father! I want to
sit on his lungs!

BODICE (*knits*). Plain, pearl, plain. She was just the same at
school.

FONTANELLE. I've always wanted to sit on a man's lungs. Let me.
Give me his lungs.

BODICE (*to* SOLDIER A). Down on your knees.

SOLDIER A. Me?

BODICE. Down! (SOLDIER A *kneels.*) Beg for his life.

SOLDIER A (*confused*). 'Is? (*Aside.*) What a pair! – O spare 'im,
mum.

BODICE (*knits*). No.

SOLDIER A. If yer could see yer way to. 'E's a poor ol' gent, lonely ol' bugger.

BODICE. It can't be pearl? I think there's an error in this pattern book.

FONTANELLE. O let me sit on his lungs. Get them out for me.

BODICE. I shall refuse his pardon. That always gives me my deepest satisfaction. Hold him up.

SOLDIER A *sits* WARRINGTON *upright.*

FONTANELLE. Look at his mouth! He wants to say something. I'd die to listen. O why did I cut his tongue out?

SOLDIER A. 'E's wonderin' what comes next. Yer can tell from 'is eyes.

BODICE (*pulls the needles from her knitting and hands the knitting to* FONTANELLE). Hold that and be careful.

SOLDIER A. Look at 'is eyes!

BODICE. It's my duty to inform you –

SOLDIER A. Keep still! Keep yer eyes on madam when she talks t'yer.

BODICE. – that your pardon has been refused. He can't talk or write, but he's cunning – he'll find some way of telling his lies. We must shut him up inside himself. (*She pokes the needles into* WARRINGTON'*s ears.*) I'll just jog these in and out a little. Doodee, doodee, doodee, doo.

FONTANELLE. He can see my face but he can't hear me laugh!

BODICE. Fancy! Like staring into a silent storm.

FONTANELLE. And now his eyes.

BODICE. No ... I think not. (*To* SOLDIER A.) Take him out in a truck and let him loose. Let people know what happens when you try to help my father. (*To* FONTANELLE.) Let me sit on his lungs! You old vulture! Go and flap round the battlefield.

FONTANELLE. Don't make fun of me. You're so stupid. You don't understand anything.

BODICE. I don't think I'd like to understand you. (*Takes her*

knitting from FONTANELLE.) You've let my knitting run!
(*Starts to go.*) Come on, we've won the war but we can't dilly-
dally, there's still part of the day left. I must see what my
husband's up to.

> BODICE *and* FONTANELLE *go out.* SOLDIER A *starts to take*
> WARRINGTON *out.*

SOLDIER A. It's all over. Walking offal! Don't blame me, I've got
a job t' do. If we was fightin' again t'morra I could end up
envyin' you anytime. Come on then, less 'ave yer. Yer'll live if
yer want to.

> *They go out.*

SCENE FIVE

Woods.
A large empty plate and jug on the bare stage. Further down, a piece
of bread. LEAR *and the* OLD COUNCILLOR *come in. They are*
ragged, tired, dirty and frightened.

COUNCILLOR. I've studied people, sir. Your daughters aren't
bad. Put yourself in their hands. They'll respond to your trust.
LEAR. Never. (*Stops.*) A jug and a plate. Empty!
COUNCILLOR. At least there are people about! I thought this was
the end of the world. Wait here, sir, and I'll look.
LEAR. No, don't leave me!
COUNCILLOR. There might be a village and I can get some food.
I'll be careful, sir. Sit down and rest.

> OLD COUNCILLOR *goes out.* LEAR *finds the bread on the*
> *ground.*

LEAR. Bread! Someone was eating this and they dropped it and
ran away. (*He eats it.*) That's all there is.

> LEAR *sits down. He is very tired.* WARRINGTON *comes on*
> *upstage. He is crippled and his face looks as if it's covered with*

bad plastic surgery. He carries a knife awkwardly. He's already seen LEAR *and comes on creeping towards him from behind.*

My daughters have taken the bread from my stomach. They grind it with my tears and the cries of famished children – and eat. The night is a black cloth on their table and the stars are crumbs, and I am a famished dog that sits on the earth and howls. I open my mouth and they place an old coin on my tongue. They lock the door of my coffin and tell me to die. My blood seeps out and they write in it with a finger. I'm old and too weak to climb out of this grave again.

WARRINGTON *sees someone coming and goes out.*

(*Looking off.*) Is this one of my daughters' men?

The GRAVEDIGGER'S BOY *comes on. He carries bread and water.*

No, there's no blood on him. – Who are you?
BOY. I live near here.
LEAR. Is that bread?
BOY. Yes.
LEAR. Is it poisoned?
BOY. No.
LEAR. Then my daughters didn't send him. They'd never miss a chance to poison good bread. Who's it for?
BOY. There's a man who roams round here. He's wild. They say he was wounded in the war.
LEAR. I'm hungry. I know you have no pity to sell, there's always a shortage of that in wartime, but you could sell me some bread. I can pay. (*Looks round.*) My friend keeps my money.
BOY. Take it. It's not much. (LEAR *eats.*) Have you come far?
LEAR. No.
BOY. Where are you going?
LEAR. I shan't know till I get there.
BOY. Was that your friend with the stick? He's left you, he wanted a horse to take him to town.

LEAR. The traitor! Give him a bad horse and let him break his neck!

BOY. I can't leave you out here on your own. I think you'd better come to my place for the night. Then you can think what to do.

LEAR. Your place? Have you any daughters?

BOY. No.

LEAR. Then I'll come. No daughters! Where he lives the rain can't be wet or the wind cold, and the holes cry out when you're going to tread in them.

The BOY *leads* LEAR *out.*

SCENE SIX

The GRAVEDIGGER'S BOY's *house.*
Wooden house upstage. A few steps to the front door. A well. A bench with bedding on it.
LEAR *and the* BOY *are sitting on the ground.*

BOY. My father was the village gravedigger. I liked to help him when I was a boy, and he taught me the work. He didn't want to be buried in a graveyard – you wouldn't want to be buried where you work.

The BOY'S WIFE *comes from the house with three bowls of soup. She gives the bowls out and sits by the* BOY. *The three eat.*

So when he died I found this place and started to dig his grave. And when I got down I struck a well. I thought, there's water here and some land, why do I want to dig graves all my life? So I live here and built this farm. (*Nods at bowl.*) It's good.

LEAR (*eating. To himself. The* BOY's WIFE *stares at him*). The mouse comes out of his hole and stares. The giant wants to eat the dragon, but the dragon has grabbed the carving knife.

BOY. My wife keeps pigs. I've got two fields and I catch things. No one minds out here. Any more?

LEAR *shakes his head. The* WIFE *takes the bowls inside.*

Now the nights are hot we've started to sleep outside. You can sleep inside if you like.

LEAR. I can't sleep on my own since I lost my army.

BOY. Then sleep out here. (*Indicates well.*) The well went dry in the summer. I had to dig down again. But it's all right now, I'm down to the spring.

LEAR (*to himself*). My daughters turned a dog out of its kennel because it got fond of its sack.

BOY. The pigs don't cost anything, I let them grub round all day and lock them up at night. They fatten themselves and I just have to slaughter them. Would you like a walk? I'll show you where we keep them. And then we must get to bed. I'm up early in the mornings. (*They stand. He calls into the house.*) Won't be long. Can you fetch the spare blanket? (*To* LEAR.) Take my arm.

LEAR. No. I once knew a man who was drowned on a bridge in a flood.

> LEAR *and the* BOY *go out. After a moment* WARRINGTON *comes on, still holding the knife. He has been watching* LEAR *and he now stares after him. He sees a movement through the doorway and hides. The* WIFE *comes out of the house with a blanket. She cries quietly, persistently and evenly, as if out of habit. She sees* WARRINGTON.

WIFE. Go away! (*She throws the blanket at him.*) Beggars, scroungers, filthy old men!

> *She looks round for something to throw. She runs into the house, crying loudly.* WARRINGTON *looks round in terror. He hides down the well. The* WIFE *comes out of the house with a soup bowl ready to throw. She can't see* WARRINGTON. *She sits down and cries loudly and bitterly.*
> *The* BOY *runs in.*

BOY. What is it? Are you all right?

WIFE (*crying*). Your wild man was here!

BOY. What did he do? Are you all right?

> LEAR *walks in.*

LEAR. There's no one here.

WIFE (*crying*). Of course not! He ran away.

BOY. Don't cry.

WIFE (*crying*). I'm trying to stop.

BOY. He only wanted his food. I'll go up and feed him in the morning. Look, come and lie down. You're shivering. (*He spreads the blanket and pillow for her.*) Let me cover you up.

> She lies down. She cries more quietly.

That's better. (*To* LEAR.) It's because she's carrying.

LEAR. Poor woman.

BOY (*taking* LEAR *to the other side of the stage*). We'd all better go to sleep, we don't want to disturb her. You can sleep here. (*He spreads a blanket and pillow.*) You'll be fine here. Good night.

> BOY *goes back to his* WIFE *and lies beside her.* LEAR *sits on his blanket.*

LEAR (*to himself*). It is night. My daughters empty their prisons and feed the men to the dead in their graveyards. The wolf crawls away in terror and hides with the rats. Hup, prince! Hup rebel! Do tricks for human flesh! When the dead have eaten they go home to their pits and sleep. (*He lies down in an awkward pose and sleeps.*)

WIFE (*crying*). Hold me. Stop me crying.

BOY (*holding her*). You must take things easy now. You work too hard.

WIFE. Don't say that! It's not true!

BOY. All right, I won't.

WIFE. But you don't believe me.

BOY. Yes I do.

WIFE. You don't. I can see you don't. Why can't I make you happy?

BOY. I am happy.

WIFE. You're not. I know you're not. You make me happy – my father said I'd be unhappy here, but I'm not, you've made me so happy – why can't I make you happy? Look at the way you brought that man here! The first one you find! Why? I'm so afraid something will happen.

BOY. Does he matter to you?

WIFE. Of course he matters! And he's a tramp!

BOY. I'll make him wash.

WIFE. You see! You don't understand! Who is he?

BOY. I don't know. He told me he was an officer, but that's not true. Who'd take their orders from him!

WIFE. And he talks to himself. I'm afraid of him.

BOY. That's only a habit. He's lonely. You'll be all right, I thought you'd like someone to help you. He can look after the pigs.

WIFE. I knew it! You're going to ask him to stay!

BOY. What else can I do? He can't look after himself. He's a poor old man – how can I throw him out? Who'd look after him then? I won't do it!

WIFE. O you're a fool! Can anyone come who likes? Don't you have any sense of responsibility?

BOY. Responsibility!

LEAR. . . . When he saluted I saw blood on his hand . . .

WIFE. Listen!

LEAR. . . . I slept in the morning because all the birds were dead . . .

WIFE. . . . He's stopped.

BOY. O go to sleep. Please. For the child's sake.

Silence. They all sleep. WARRINGTON *comes out of the well. He still carries the knife. He goes to the* BOY *and his* WIFE *and peers down to see who they are. He crosses to* LEAR *and stops.*

Peers. Throws himself on LEAR, *roars, and hits him with the knife.* LEAR *jumps up.*

LEAR (*still dreaming*). My daughters – help me! There! Guards! (*Grabs* WARRINGTON *and stares at his face.*) What's this? . . . No! No!

The BOY *runs to* LEAR *and* WARRINGTON *runs out.*

A ghost!
BOY. He's gone! He ran!
LEAR. A ghost!
WIFE. It's the wild man! I saw him!
BOY. A light! (*The* WIFE *runs into the house.*) He's bleeding! Water! Cloth! (*To* LEAR.) Your arm! It's cut.
LEAR. He's dead! I saw his face! It was like a stone! I shall die!

The WIFE *comes out with a light.*

BOY. Water –
WIFE. Bring him inside! It's not safe out here!
BOY (*helping* LEAR *into the house*). Yes. Fetch the blanket. Quick. He's bleeding.
LEAR. I'll die! I've seen a ghost. I'm going to die. That's why he came back. I'll die.
BOY. The steps.

BOY *takes* LEAR *into the house. His* WIFE *picks up the blankets and follows them in.*

SCENE SEVEN

Same.
The next afternoon. There is no one there. The BOY *comes in. Takes off his hat and hangs it up on the side of the house. His* WIFE *comes in from the opposite side. She carries a pig pole and an empty swill bucket.*

WIFE. Is he still asleep?

BOY. I don't know. I just got back.

WIFE. You haven't asked him about last night.

BOY. Not yet. (*He kisses her.*) You're better.

WIFE. Yes. (*She takes the pole and bucket to the side of the house.*) The well's dirty, I saw it this morning when I did the washing.

BOY. O lord! I'll go down later on.

The CARPENTER *comes in. He is tall and dark and carries a wooden box.*

Hello.

CARPENTER. Hello.

BOY. How are you?

CARPENTER. Fine. A bit busy.

BOY (*points to box*). What is it?

CARPENTER. Something I made.

BOY. It's early, but I'll go and shut the pigs up.

The BOY *goes out.*

WIFE. What is it?

CARPENTER. A cradle. (*He gives it to her.*)

WIFE. O.

CARPENTER. He doesn't mind.

WIFE. It's beautiful.

The CARPENTER *sits and looks at her. Slight pause.*

He's got someone staying here. An old man. You haven't seen him in the village?

CARPENTER. No. Who is he? I'll try and find out.

WIFE. He just brought him here to look after the pigs. Why? It's so silly, so silly . . .

CARPENTER (*after another slight pause*). Any jobs I can do?

WIFE. The door wants mending, but he'll do that.

CARPENTER. No, I left my tools in the cart down on the road. I'll fix it.

BOY (*off*). I-yoo! I-yoo! I-yoo! (*Two or three pigs squeal.*)

> LEAR *comes out of the house.*

LEAR (*puzzled*). I've slept all day. It's evening. (*Sees* CARPENTER.) Who's that?

WIFE. A man from the village.

LEAR. O. (*He sits on the cradle.*)

CARPENTER. ⎤ Not on that!
WIFE.   ⎦ You'll break it!

LEAR (*stands*). Where's your husband?

WIFE. He'll be here. I suppose you'll go away now after last night.

LEAR (*confused*). I don't know. I dreamed –

> The BOY *comes in.*

BOY. How are you? I thought I heard you up. Let me see your arm.

WIFE. John brought this.

BOY (*looks at the cradle*). O that's very clever. For the child. Thanks. (*The* CARPENTER *stands.*) You needn't go.

CARPENTER. Your wife wants me to fix her door.

> The CARPENTER *goes out. The* BOY *looks at* LEAR's *cut.*

WIFE (*picking up the cradle*). It's not deep.

BOY. It needs washing.

> The WIFE *goes into the house with the cradle.*

LEAR. Who is he?

BOY. Village carpenter. He makes coffins and cradles and mends chairs, anything. He's very good. Don't worry about him, he's always hanging round. He's in love with my wife.

LEAR. Last night I saw a ghost.

BOY (*amused*). My father said there aren't any, and he should know. It was this wild man.

LEAR. I see, I see . . . then it was all in my dream. (*Slight pause.*) I should have spent my life here.

BOY (*looking at the cut*). I'm sorry about this.

LEAR (*still confused and puzzled*). I've been cut before. It's almost gone. I was worse when I came here. You've looked after me well. I slept like a child in this silence all day. It's so long since I slept like that, I'd forgotten ... And now I shall get well again. It's so simple and easy here. (*Becoming angry.*) But where shall I go now, how can I live, what will become of me?

BOY. Stay here. You can look after my pigs. I can't pay you but you can eat and sleep with us.

LEAR. No. I'd get you into trouble. No, no. I must go away.

BOY. Listen, how many men were you in charge of?

LEAR. A few.

BOY. Well they won't come all this way for one old man who was in charge of a few other men. So stay.

LEAR. I could have a new life here. I could forget all the things that frighten me – the years I've wasted, my enemies, my anger, my mistakes. I've been too trusting, too lenient! I'm tormented by regrets – I must forget it all, throw it away! Yes! – let me live here and work for you.

BOY. Good. You'll be a real help to me when you've settled in. I'll be able to clear some more fields. You needn't worry about the soldiers. They're too busy looking for the king to worry about you. Did you know they're pulling his wall down?

LEAR. The wall?

BOY. Up and down, up and down. The king was mad. He took all the men from this village. But I hid. They'd worked with their hands all their lives but when they started on the wall their hands bled for a week.

LEAR. No.

BOY. You died of work or they shot you for not working. There was a disease –

LEAR. They tried to stop that.

BOY. – 'Wall death'. Their feet used to swell with the mud. The stink of it even when you were asleep! Living in a grave! He should come here – I'd go back to my old job and dig a grave for him! We used to dig his wall up at nights, when they were

working near here. (*Sighs.*) Let's talk about something else.
(LEAR *stops listening to him.*) My wife will be all right. She'll be
a bit cold at first, but she'll soon be glad to have you helping
us ... We're supposed to be a bad match. I know her father
didn't want us to marry. He's never come to see us. I asked him.
I don't like that, it makes you feel bad. He's a priest, he taught
her everything. She's very clever, but she can't understand
how I live. I've got my house, my farm, my wife – and every
night I tell her I love her. How could I be unhappy? She's
afraid it will change, she'd like to put a fence round us and shut
everyone else out.

    His WIFE *comes out of the house with a long rope. She fixes it
across the back of the stage as a long clothes line. Short silence.*

LEAR. I remember some of my dream. There was a king and he
had a fountain in his garden. It was as big as the sea. One night
the fountain howled and in the morning the king went to look
at it. It was red. The servants emptied it and under the sea they
found a desert. The king looked in the sand and there was a
helmet and sword.

    The WIFE *goes into the house.*

So the king –
BOY. I know that. A clown told it to us at the fair.

    LEAR *stares at him. The* WIFE *comes out of the house with a
basket of washing.*

WIFE. I want some more water but it's dirty.
BOY (*stands*). I'll go down.

    The WIFE *takes some pegs from the wall and starts to peg out a
line of white sheets. The* BOY *climbs into the well and goes out of
sight.*

LEAR (*to* WIFE). I'll do that. You mustn't work too hard.

She doesn't answer, but LEAR *helps her. They hang the sheets so that the bottoms just clear the ground.*

WIFE (*pegging*). Who is the wild man? You recognized him last night.

LEAR (*holding up a sheet*). No. I was dreaming.

WIFE (*taking the sheet*). When are you going?

LEAR (*picking up pegs*). Your husband's asked me to work for him.

WIFE (*pegging*). You're not stopping here. I won't have you.

LEAR (*handing her pegs*). He needs me. He said so.

WIFE (*taking the pegs*). I'm not having any dirty old tramps about. I'm carrying. I mustn't let myself get upset.

LEAR (*adjusting a sheet. Becoming angry*). You don't hang them straight.

WIFE (*pegging*). I could easily make him send you away.

LEAR. Straight.

WIFE (*pegging*). I don't want to have to do that. I'm not arguing and shouting any more, it upsets him too much. Please go – and don't tell him I made you.

LEAR (*holding up a sheet*). Where can I go?

WIFE (*taking the sheet*). Anywhere. You're free. You've got the whole world.

LEAR. He asked me to stay! No, I won't go! (*He crosses to the well.*) He said I could stay. He won't break his word. I'm too old to look after myself. I can't live in ditches and barns and beg for scraps and hire myself to peasants! No, I won't be at everyone's call! My daughters sent you! *You* go! It's you who're destroying this place! We must get rid of you! – (*He stops short and stares at the bucket.*)

WIFE. What is it?

LEAR. Blood.

WIFE. What?

LEAR. Blood. That's blood in the water. I've seen it before. (*Calls down the well.*) What are you doing? Where are you?

BOY (*off*). What?

WIFE. That's where he was hiding! (*Calls down well.*) He hid
down there last night – (*To* LEAR.) – and then he came up and
tried to kill you and ran away!

LEAR (*afraid*). No. There's too much blood . . . He came back and
he's down there now . . .

> Silence. *A* SERGEANT *and* THREE SOLDIERS (D, E *and* F)
> come on. They all carry rifles.

SOLDIER D. Don't run. I don't like breakin' women's legs.

SERGEANT. Turn it over inside.

> SOLDIERS D *and* E *go into the house.*

'Oo else yer got knockin' around?

LEAR. No one. You want me. We can go now.

> *He starts to go.* SOLDIER F *stops him.*

No, no! We must go.

SOLDIER F. 'Oo else? Shouldn't lie your age, time yer knowd
better.

SERGEANT. Come on, darlin', yer must a 'ad some one t' put yer
in that class.

SOLDIER F. Couldn't a bin 'im.

> SOLDIER D *comes out of the house.*

SOLDIER D. 'E'd 'ave t' use a carrot.

SOLDIER F. 'E would, the dirty ol' toe rag.

WIFE. Go away –

SOLDIER D (*to* SERGEANT). Empty.

WIFE. – he's gone.

SERGEANT. 'Oo'd leave a nice little lay like you?

> SOLDIER E *comes from behind the house.*

SOLDIER E. Pigs out the back.

LEAR. I look after them!

SERGEANT. We know there's a young fella.

LEAR. There's no one else. Take me away.

BOY (*off*). He's here! I've got him!

The SOLDIERS *stare. They are puzzled.*

LEAR. We can go. The girl didn't know who I am. I'll report you for –

SOLDIER F *puts his hand over* LEAR's *mouth. Silence.*

BOY (*off*). His neck's broken.

SOLDIER D *points to the well.*

SERGEANT (*threatens* LEAR *with his rifle*). Tell 'im somethin'.

LEAR (*speaking down the well*). Yes.

BOY (*off*). He's dead. I'll bring him up. Pull the rope.

The SERGEANT *pulls the rope. The* SOLDIERS *take the* WIFE *and hide behind the sheets with her.*

(*Off. Nearer.*) Steady.

LEAR *goes upstage, sits on the steps or the bench and watches. The* SERGEANT *goes behind the sheets. The* BOY *comes out of the well, carrying* WARRINGTON. WARRINGTON *is dripping wet.*

He fell down. He must have died straight away. My God! – he's breathing. There's bubbles on his mouth! Look! Help me!

He puts WARRINGTON *down. A pool forms round him. The* BOY *looks at* LEAR. *Stops. Suddenly he panics and shouts.*

Cordelia!

The SERGEANT *and* SOLDIERS E *and* F *come from behind the sheets.*

Cordelia!

SOLDIER E *shoots him. He staggers upstage towards the sheets. His head is down. He clutches a sheet and pulls it from the line.* CORDELIA *stands behind it. Her head is down and she covers*

her face with her hands. SOLDIER D *is preparing to rape her.
The* BOY *turns slowly away and as he does so the sheet folds
round him. For a second he stands in silence with the white sheet
draped round him. Only his head is seen. It is pushed back in
shock and his eyes and mouth are open. He stands rigid. Suddenly a huge red stain spreads on the sheet.*

SERGEANT. Kill the pigs.

SOLDIER E *runs off.*

SOLDIER F (*peering down at* WARRINGTON). Chriss look at this!
SERGEANT (*to* SOLDIER D). Do that inside.
LEAR. She's pregnant.
SOLDIER D. It can play with the end.
SOLDIER F (*poking* WARRINGTON's *mouth with the end of his
rifle*). Look at this blowin' bubbles!

Off, squealing starts as the pigs are slaughtered. SOLDIER D
takes the WIFE *into the house. The* BOY *suddenly drops dead.*

SERGEANT. Drop 'im down the 'ole.

The SERGEANT *and* SOLDIER F *drop* WARRINGTON *down the
well.*

SOLDIER F. 'Ere's another one.
SERGEANT. Up!

They drop the BOY *down the well. He points to* LEAR.

An' run 'im down t' the truck.

The SERGEANT *goes into the house.*

SOLDIER F. Some jammy bastards 'ave all the fun. I don't fancy
old grandads.

Off, the pig squealing stops.

LEAR (*stands*). O burn the house! You've murdered the husband,
slaughtered the cattle, poisoned the well, raped the mother,

killed the child – you must burn the house! You're soldiers –
you must do your duty! My daughters expect it! O burn the
house! Burn the house! Burn the house!

SOLDIER F. Shut it an' move.

> SOLDIER F *takes* LEAR *outside.* SOLDIER E *comes on from
> behind the house.*

LEAR (*going*). O burn it down! Burn it!

> *There is blood on* SOLDIER E's *face, neck, hands, clothes and
> boots. In the house* CORDELIA *gives a high, short gasp.*

SOLDIER E (*muttering contentedly*). An' I'll 'ave 'er reekin' a pig
blood. Somethin' t' write 'ome t' tell mother.

> *The* CARPENTER *follows him on. He carries his tool pack. He
> takes a cold chisel from it.*

(*Sees* CARPENTER.) Yes? (*A fraction later he calls towards the
house.*) Sarge!

> *The* CARPENTER *kills him with a blow from the cold chisel.*

CARPENTER (*looks towards the house*). Are there more of you?

> *The* CARPENTER *picks up* SOLDIER D's *rifle and goes into the
> house. Slight pause. Three rifle shots from inside the house.
> Silence.*

Act Two

SCENE ONE

Courtroom.
NORTH *and* CORNWALL *enter and talk quietly together while the court assembles. There is a* JUDGE, USHER, CLERK *and other Officials.*

CORNWALL. Our wives will condemn him and have his life.
NORTH. Yes.
CORNWALL. I don't think we should let them have their way in too many things.
NORTH. Bodice is a good woman. But she's had to bear her troubles on her own too long. Perhaps it's too late for her to trust anyone.
CORNWALL. That's true of both of them. We'll put him in a safe prison. He'll die without us.

BODICE *and* FONTANELLE *come on. The* JUDGE *goes to them.*

BODICE. You've studied your instructions?
JUDGE. Indeed, ma'am.
BODICE. This is a political trial: politics is the higher form of justice. The old king's mad and it's dangerous to let him live. Family sentiment doesn't cloud our judgement. I've arranged to call the people who upset him most.
FONTANELLE. I'm a witness.
BODICE. Let him rattle on and condemn himself. Goad him if it helps – but not too openly.
JUDGE. I understand ma'am.

The JUDGE *takes his place.* LEAR *is brought in under guard.*

BODICE (*to* FONTANELLE). He's deteriorated. I must put the gaoler on the Honours List.

JUDGE. You are the late king?

LEAR. You know who I am. I gave you your job.

JUDGE. And these ladies are your daughters.

LEAR. No.

JUDGE. They are your daughters.

LEAR. No.

JUDGE. Don't you recognize them?

LEAR. I've never seen them.

JUDGE. Sit. (LEAR *sits*.) The late king says his daughters –

LEAR. They're not my daughters!

> BODICE *pushes* FONTANELLE. FONTANELLE *goes to the witness stand.*

FONTANELLE. I will tell the truth.

JUDGE. Ma'am, try to make the late king remember you.

FONTANELLE. Father, once you found a white horse on a battle-field. You gave it to me and it broke its leg on the ice. They tied it to a tree and shot it. Poor little Fontanelle cried.

LEAR. Poor horse.

FONTANELLE. Another time I asked you how high the wall would be. You held me over your head and said you still couldn't see over the top.

LEAR. I was always exact. – Take me back to my prison. We are freer there.

> FONTANELLE *shrugs and goes back to her seat beside* BODICE. BODICE *smiles at her. An* OLD SAILOR *is led to the witness stand.*

OLD SAILOR. I will tell the truth. I can't see. I was a sailor and the sea blinded me. I have a little sight, but in a mist. I showed you how to sail. Your voice hasn't changed. You came back when you were king and showed me your daughters. I could see in those days. These are your daughters, sir.

LEAR. Are you taken care of?

OLD SAILOR. I've been blind seven years, sir. They say I have clear eyes, but they don't see for me.

LEAR. Are you well looked after, sir?

OLD SAILOR. Yes, sir. I have a good daughter.

LEAR. Go home and watch her. They change faster than the wind at sea.

> *The* OLD SAILOR *is led away. The* OLD COUNCILLOR *goes to the witness stand.*

COUNCILLOR. I will tell the truth. (*Takes out his notebook.*) Sir, you know me.

LEAR. Through and through.

COUNCILLOR (*looks in notebook*). I helped you to escape on –

LEAR. You ran after me to be saved.

COUNCILLOR. Now you shouldn't say –

LEAR. And when you saw that I was finished you ran back here.

COUNCILLOR. I did my duty as a man of conscience –

LEAR. Convenience!

COUNCILLOR. Sir, when I saw that –

LEAR. I would be caught –

COUNCILLOR. – you were mentally disturbed –

LEAR. – you betrayed me! Is there no honour between old men? You've been corrupted by your children!

BODICE. Give him my mirror! (*Aside to* JUDGE.) Madmen are frightened of themselves!

> *The* USHER *goes towards her but* BODICE *walks past him and takes the mirror to* LEAR.

LEAR. How ugly that voice is! That's not my daughter's voice. It sounds like chains on a prison wall. (BODICE *puts the mirror in his hand and walks back to her chair.*) And she walks like something struggling in a sack. (LEAR *glances down briefly at the mirror.*) No, that's not the king.

JUDGE. Take the oath first.

LEAR. You have no right to sit there!

JUDGE. Take the oath.

LEAR. I gave you your job because you were corrupt!

JUDGE. Take the oath.

LEAR. The king is always on oath! (*He stares down at the mirror.*) No, that's not the king . . . This is a little cage of bars with an animal in it. (*Peers closer.*) No, no, that's not the king! (*Suddenly gestures violently. The* USHER *takes the mirror.*) Who shut that animal in that cage? Let it out. Have you seen its face behind the bars? There's a poor animal with blood on its head and tears running down its face. Who did that to it? Is it a bird or a horse? It's lying in the dust and its wings are broken. Who broke its wings? Who cut off its hands so that it can't shake the bars? It's pressing its snout on the glass. Who shut that animal in a glass cage? O god, there's no pity in this world. You let it lick the blood from its hair in the corner of a cage with nowhere to hide from its tormentors. No shadow, no hole! Let that animal out of its cage! (*He takes the mirror and shows it round.*) Look! Look! Have pity. Look at its claws trying to open the cage. It's dragging its broken body over the floor. You are cruel! Cruel! Look at it lying in its corner! It's shocked and cut and shaking and licking the blood on its sides. (USHER *again takes the mirror from* LEAR.) No, no! Where are they taking it now! Not out of my sight! What will they do to it? O god, give it to me! Let me hold it and stroke it and wipe its blood! (BODICE *takes the mirror from the* USHER.) No!

BODICE. I'll polish it every day and see it's not cracked.

LEAR. Then kill it. Kill it. Kill it. Don't let her torment it. I can't live with that suffering in the world.

JUDGE. See the king's madness.

LEAR. My daughters have been murdered and these monsters have taken their place! I hear all their victims cry, where is justice?

BODICE. Yes! I've locked this animal in its cage and I will not let it out!

FONTANELLE (*laughing and jumping up and down in her seat*).
   Look at his tears!
LEAR. Cruelty! Cruelty! See where they hauled it up by its hair!
BODICE (*to* CLERK). Get it all down!
CLERK. Ma'am.
JUDGE. The court is adjourned.

   LEAR *is taken quickly away, and the court goes.*

LEAR (*going*). Its blood's on the steps where the prisoners come!

   The JUDGE *goes to* BODICE *and* FONTANELLE.

JUDGE. That went better than I expected, ma'am.
BODICE. It went as I planned. There's to be a death sentence but
   it's not yet decided. Good day.

   The JUDGE *bows and goes.* BODICE *and* FONTANELLE *are
   alone.*

FONTANELLE. It *was* – till your husband interfered.
BODICE. And yours! Keep him on a tighter leash! Well, they must
   be brought to sense. Men are always obstinate, it's their form of
   maturity. I've bad news. My spies have found agitators and
   malcontents in every village. There's going to be serious
   fighting – civil war.
FONTANELLE. Good! If it's there let's root it out. Meet it head
   on. Did you know this riffraff is commanded by a woman?
   Called Cordelia.
BODICE (*aside*). Yes, my sister has her own spies. Power goes to
   her head. The head must be squeezed. As it happens, her spies
   are in my pay so she can never know more than I know. But
   from now on I shall trust her even less. If things go well her
   days are numbered. (*To* FONTANELLE.) Well, we'd better go
   and see to our husbands. This campaign needs proper prepara-
   tion.
FONTANELLE. Then we can't leave it to them!

BODICE. And the army must be purged. Victory is bad for soldiers, it lowers their morale.

They go out together.

SCENE TWO

LEAR's *cell.*
Bare, empty. A stone shelf for sitting on. SOLDIERS G *and* H *bring* LEAR *in.* SOLDIER H *drops a roll of sacking on the floor.* SOLDIER G *stands by the door. They ignore* LEAR.

SOLDIER G. Not a bad way t' earn yer livin' if it weren't for the smell.

SOLDIER H. It won't last.

SOLDIER G. Nah, they'll send us up the front with the rest.

SOLDIER H. Cross laddie 'ere off.

SOLDIER G *marks a list and the* TWO SOLDIERS *go out.*

LEAR. I must forget! I must forget!

The GHOST OF THE GRAVE DIGGER'S BOY *appears. His skin and clothes are faded. There's old, dry blood on them.*

GHOST. I heard you shout.

LEAR. Are you dead?

GHOST. Yes.

LEAR. There's an animal in a cage. I must let it out or the earth will be destroyed. There'll be great fires and the water will dry up. All the people will be burned and the wind will blow their ashes into huge columns of dust and they'll go round and round the earth for ever! We must let it out! (*Calls, bangs on the wall.*) Here! Pull your chain! Here! Break it! (*There is banging from the other side of the wall.*) What? It's here! A horse!

GHOST. No. It's other prisoners.

LEAR. Help me!

GHOST. What animal is it? I've never seen it!

LEAR. Where are my daughters! They'd help me!

GHOST. I can fetch them.

LEAR. My daughters? You can fetch them here?

GHOST. Yes.

LEAR. Fetch them! Quickly! (*The* GHOST *whistles softly.*) Where are they?

GHOST. You'll see them. Wait. (*Whistles softly again.*)

> FONTANELLE's GHOST *appears.*

LEAR. Fontanelle!

> GHOST *whistles.* BODICE's GHOST *appears.*

Bodice!

GHOST. Let them speak first.

> *The* DAUGHTERS' GHOSTS *move slowly at first, as if they'd been asleep.*

FONTANELLE. Do my hair ... Father comes home today.

BODICE. I must put on my dress.

FONTANELLE. O you dress so quickly! Do my hair. (BODICE *attends to her hair.*)

LEAR. My daughters!

BODICE. They're burying soldiers in the churchyard. Father's brought the coffins on carts. The palls are covered with snow. Look, one of the horses is licking its hoof.

FONTANELLE. This morning I lay in bed and watched the wind pulling the curtains. Pull, pull, pull ... Now I can hear that terrible bell.

LEAR. Fontanelle, you're such a little girl. (*He sits on the stone shelf.*) Sit here.

FONTANELLE. No.

LEAR. On my knees. (*He sits her on his knees.*) Such a little girl.

BODICE (*listening*). Father! I must get dressed! I must get dressed. (*She struggles frantically into her dress.*)

LEAR. That's better.

FONTANELLE. Listen to the bell and the wind.

LEAR (*wets his finger and holds it in the air*). Which way is it
blowing? (BODICE *gets into the dress and comes down to him. He
points at her.*) Take it off!

BODICE. No.

LEAR. Take it off. Your mother's dress!

BODICE. She's dead! She gave it to me!

LEAR (*pointing*). Take it off!

BODICE. No!

LEAR. Yes, or you will always wear it! (*He pulls her to him.*) Bodice!
My poor child, you might as well have worn her shroud.

> BODICE *cries against him.* BEN, *a young orderly, comes in with
> a small jug and plate. He sets them on the floor.*

BEN. Don't 'ang it out, grandad. They'll be round for the empties
in a minute. Don't blame me if it ain't 'ow yer like it. I ain't the
chef, I'm only the 'ead waiter.

> BEN *goes out. The* DAUGHTERS' GHOSTS *sit on the floor
> beside* LEAR *and rest their heads on his knees. He strokes their
> hair.*

BODICE. Where are we?

LEAR. In a prison.

BODICE. Why?

LEAR. I don't know.

BODICE. Who put us here?

LEAR. I don't know.

FONTANELLE. I'm afraid.

LEAR. Try not to be.

BODICE. Will we get out?

LEAR. Yes.

BODICE. Are you sure?

LEAR. O yes.

BODICE. If I could hope! But this prison, the pain –

LEAR. I know it will end. Everything passes, even the waste. The fools will be silent. We won't chain ourselves to the dead, or send our children to school in the graveyard. The torturers and ministers and priests will lose their office. And we'll pass each other in the street without shuddering at what we've done to each other.

BODICE. It's peaceful now.

FONTANELLE. And still.

LEAR. The animal will slip out of its cage, and lie in the fields, and run by the river, and groom itself in the sun, and sleep in its hole from night to morning.

> THREE SOLDIERS (G, H and I) *come in. They are methodical and quiet.*

SOLDIER H. Watch careful an' take it all in.

SOLDIER I. Corp.

SOLDIER H. Under the sack an' in the corners. (SOLDIER G *shows him how to search.*) Can yer remember it? Five times a day. Yer skip the personal.

SOLDIER I. Corp.

SOLDIER H. Less see yer try.

SOLDIER I (*searching in the corners*). When yer off?

SOLDIER G. Tmorra. Least it's out a this 'ole.

SOLDIER I. I'll stay out a the fightin' any day!

SOLDIER H. Yer don't know nothin' about it. When there's a war on yer all end up fightin'.

SOLDIER I (*finishes his search*) Corp.

SOLDIER H. So yer're ready t' mark yer list.

SOLDIER I. Corp. (*Goes to mark his list.*)

SOLDIER H. An' did yer look under the beddin'?

SOLDIER I. Corp.

SOLDIER H. Then look under the beddin'.

SOLDIER I (*looks under the bedding*). Corp.

SOLDIER H. An' now yer can mark yer list.

SOLDIER I. Corp. (*Marks his list.*)

SOLDIER H. Nignogs! . . . (*When* SOLDIER I *has finished*.) An' on t' the next one.

The THREE SOLDIERS *go out*.

BODICE. Listen. (*She stands*.)

LEAR. Where are you going?

BODICE. Mother's dead. I must serve tea. They're ringing the bell.

LEAR. Stay here.

FONTANELLE. They're waiting. There's a long line behind the coffins. They're standing so still!

LEAR. Stay here and they can't begin. We can stay here together!

GHOST. They must go! You can't stop them!

LEAR. But my mind! My mind!

The DAUGHTERS *go*.

Listen! The animal's scratching! There's blood in its mouth. The muzzle's bleeding. It's trying to dig. It's found someone! (*He falls unconscious on his sack*.)

An OLD ORDERLY *comes in*.

OLD ORDERLY. Sing away, I won't 'urt you. I come for the plate. (*He sees it's untouched*.) O. Shall I come back? Writin' petitions an' appeals an' retainin' yer self respect an' keepin' yer mind occupied – thass all right, but yer must eat. Well, yer know yer own stomach. (*Reassuringly*.) I ain' on the staff. (*Slight pause*.) They're sendin' the young filth up the front. Let 'em rot. Waste a good bullets. I come in 'ere thousands a years back, 'undreds a thousands. I don't know what I come in for. I forgot. I 'eard so many tell what they come in for it's all mixed up in me 'ead. I've 'eard every crime in the book confessed t' me. Must be a record. Don't know which was mine now. Murder? Robbin'? Violence? I'd like t' know. Juss t' put me mind t' rest. Satisfy me conscience. But no one knows now. It's all gone. Long ago. The records is lost. 'Undreds a years back. (*Points to plate.*) Shall I wait? (*No answer.*) The customer knows what 'e wants.

The OLD ORDERLY *takes the plate and mug and goes out.*

LEAR. I shouldn't have looked. I killed so many people and never looked at one of their faces. But I looked at that animal. Wrong. Wrong. Wrong. It's made me a stupid old man. What colour's my hair?

GHOST. White.

LEAR. I'm frightened to look. There's blood on it where I pulled it with these hands.

GHOST. Let me stay with you, Lear. When I died I went somewhere. I don't know where it was. I waited and nothing happened. And then I started to rot, like a body in the ground. Look at my hands, they're like an old man's. They're withered. I'm young but my stomach's shrivelled up and the hair's turned white. Look, my arms! Feel how thin I am. (LEAR *doesn't move.*) Are you afraid to touch me?

LEAR. No.

GHOST. Feel.

LEAR (*hesitates. Feels*). Yes, thin.

GHOST. I'm afraid. Let me stay with you, keep me here, please.

LEAR. Yes, yes, poor boy. Lie down by me. Here. I'll hold you. We'll help each other. Cry while I sleep, and I'll cry and watch you while you sleep. We'll take turns. The sound of the human voice will comfort us.

SCENE THREE

Rebel field post.
CORDELIA *and some* REBEL SOLDIERS. PETE *nurses a* WOUNDED REBEL SOLDIER *called* TERRY. LEWIS *stands upstage as look-out.* SOLDIER I *sits with his hands tied behind his back and no cap. Beside him is a* CROUCHING REBEL SOLDIER *with a rifle. Some of*

the other REBEL SOLDIERS *carry rifles. They wear simple, utilitarian clothes, not uniforms. There is a tense silence.*

LEWIS (*looks off*). They're coming.

CORDELIA (*relaxes a little and goes to the* WOUNDED REBEL SOLDIER). Is he all right?

PETE. There's no drugs, no equipment, nothing.

The CARPENTER *comes on with two more* REBEL SOLDIERS. *They carry rifles and bundles.*

CARPENTER. What was the firing?

CORDELIA. Some scouts found us. It's all right, we got them. What did you bring?

CARPENTER. Tea, spuds, two blankets. They won't take money. They want to join us.

CORDELIA. How many?

CARPENTER. Up to twenty.

CORDELIA. Will they bring their own supplies?

CARPENTER. Yes.

CORDELIA. We'll pick them up when we move through. We're almost ready.

CARPENTER (*indicates* SOLDIER I). One of the scouts?

CORDELIA. Yes. The rest were shot. I wanted to talk to him first. Terry was hit.

CARPENTER. O . . .

The two REBEL SOLDIERS *who have just arrived drink tea quickly. The other* REBEL SOLDIERS *carry their bundles off-stage. A* REBEL SOLDIER *hands a mug of tea to the* CARPENTER.

CORDELIA (*to* SOLDIER I). How far did you come?

SOLDIER I. 'Ard t' say. We never come straight an' the maps is US. I was born in the city. These fields are China t' me.

CORDELIA. How long did you march?

SOLDIER I. O I can tell yer that. We moved off at first light.

CARPENTER (*sips his tea*). They've reached the river.

SOLDIER I. Yeh, we come over a river. On a rope – that was a giggle. The farmers'd burned the real bridge. My life!

CORDELIA. What are your supplies like?

SOLDIER I. Nothin'. They used t' be regular. Now everythin's burned. We come through this town. Same thing – burned. Nothin' t' loot. A nice place once.

CORDELIA. Why d'you fight us?

SOLDIER I. I'm more afraid a me own lot than I am a yourn. I'd make a run for it but I'd get a bullet in me back. Not that I'm knockin' your lads! After all, I'm one a you if yer like t' look at it. If I lived out in the sticks I'd be fightin' with you lot, wouldn't I?

CORDELIA *and the* CARPENTER *walk away.*

CARPENTER. Let him join us.

CORDELIA. He's a child, he crawls where he's put down. He'd talk to anyone who caught him. To fight like us you must hate, we can't trust a man unless he hates. Otherwise he has no use. (*To* CROUCHING REBEL SOLDIER.) We've finished.

CROUCHING REBEL SOLDIER *and* LEWIS *start to take* SOLDIER I *out. Another* SOLDIER *takes* LEWIS's *place as look-out.*

SOLDIER I. 'Ello, we goin' then?

The three go out. CARPENTER *looks at the* WOUNDED REBEL SOLDIER.

CARPENTER. Where?

PETE. Stomach.

WOUNDED SOLDIER. It's all right, don't whisper. I won't be a nuisance. We said we'd die quietly, if we could. Don't scream or ask for anything. It upsets the others and holds them up . . .

CORDELIA. You must rest before we –

WOUNDED SOLDIER. Yes, yes. Don't treat me like a child because I'm dying. Let me drink some water.

PETE. No.

WOUNDED SOLDIER. It doesn't matter about my stomach. It'll
help my throat. (CARPENTER *gives him some water*.) Yes. Now
go and get ready.

They leave him and get ready to move.

CORDELIA (*to the* LOOK-OUT). Tell them to start moving. Keep
off the road.

The LOOK-OUT *goes out.*

WOUNDED SOLDIER. When it's dark I'll pretend my wife's come
to meet me and they're coming up the road. I put our girl on my
shoulder and she pulls my hair and I say ah . . .

PETE. More tea?

CARPENTER. No.

PETE empties the tea can and packs it.

WOUNDED SOLDIER. She sees a bird and asks me what it is and
I say it's a wader but I don't know . . . Who'll tell my wife I'm
dead?

Off, a single shot. No one reacts.

It's dark, there are the stars . . . look . . .

LEWIS and the CROUCHING SOLDIER *come back. They pick
up their things.*

CORDELIA. When we have power these things won't be necessary.

Everyone goes off except the WOUNDED SOLDIER.

WOUNDED SOLDIER. The stars . . . Look . . . One . . . Two . . .
Three . . .

Silence.

SCENE FOUR

HQ.

BODICE *sleeps slumped forward over a desk. On the desk a map,
documents, pen, ink, teacher's bell. By the desk,* BODICE's *knitting
bag full of documents. Off, a knock.* BODICE *hears and moves but
doesn't sit up. Off, a second knock.* BODICE *sits up and rings the bell
once. An* AIDE *comes in.*

AIDE. Your sister's here now, ma'am.

BODICE. What time is it?

AIDE. Two.

BODICE. Let her in.

AIDE *lets* FONTANELLE *in and goes out.*

FONTANELLE. Your aide says our husbands have run away!

BODICE. They met the Chiefs of Staff this afternoon. The army
thinks we'll lose the war.

FONTANELLE. Impossible. We're fighting peasants.

BODICE. The army thinks –

FONTANELLE. They can't think! Our husbands ran our campaign,
that's why we lost. But if they're gone now, we'll win!

BODICE. You silly woman, haven't you learned anything yet? I
had to send troops to bring them back. They're downstairs now.

FONTANELLE. Why?

BODICE. Why? We need their armies!

FONTANELLE. O – they'll fight for us!

BODICE. They wouldn't break a grasshopper's leg for us. Why
d'you think I put up with my husband for so long?

FONTANELLE. Put up with him?

BODICE. O don't waste your hypocrisy on me. You tried to kill
yours once. My spies told me and they don't lie. They're the
only moral institution in this country.

FONTANELLE (*shrugs*). Well, I don't bother any more. He's
stopped slobbering over me and I sleep with whom I like.

BODICE. It must be getting difficult to find someone.

FONTANELLE (*after a pause, in a small voice*). Well I don't wake them up in the middle of the night to ask them to hold my wool. Is that why you sleep alone?

BODICE. At least they'd get to sleep first. Sign these before you go.

FONTANELLE. What are they?

BODICE. Various warrants. We'll have to run the country between us – but you're no good at office work, it's a waste of time you trying.

FONTANELLE. I'll only sign what doesn't conflict with my conscience. (*Picks up a document.*) What's this?

BODICE. Father's death warrant.

FONTANELLE. Where's the pen?

BODICE (*as* FONTANELLE *signs*). There are a number of old matters it's politically dangerous to leave open. They should have been closed long ago, but it's been left to us, of course!

FONTANELLE. Where is he?

BODICE. They're bringing a batch of prisoners to HQ. They had to evacuate the prisons. The warrants will be carried out when they arrive. Sign the others.

A signal is tapped on the door. BODICE *rings the bell once.* TWO PLAINCLOTHES SPIES *bring the* DUKES OF CORNWALL *and* NORTH *in. They have been questioned but not marked. Their jackets, belts and laces have been removed. They look flushed.* BODICE *stands.*

No – be silent! Not one word! There's nothing to explain. My spies have learned more about you than you know yourselves, and none of it came as a surprise to me.

FONTANELLE. Burn them!

BODICE. Be quiet! You will be kept in cells until we need you to be seen in public, or for any other reason. (NORTH *opens his mouth to speak.*) Be quiet! While you are out of your cells you will at all times be accompanied by my plainclothes spies. If you misbehave in any way you will be instantly shot. (NORTH

opens his mouth to speak.) Will you be quiet! – We would explain
it away as an assassination by the enemy.

FONTANELLE. Burn them! I'm superstitious, they'll bring us bad
luck.

BODICE. Take them downstairs.

> The TWO PLAINCLOTHES SPIES *take the* DUKES OF NORTH
> *and* CORNWALL *out.*

FONTANELLE. And what will you do about the war?

BODICE (*rings the bell once*). You'd better go back to bed. You
mustn't keep your chauffeur waiting.

> FONTANELLE *goes towards the door and meets the* AIDE
> *coming in.*

FONTANELLE. Major Pellet, don't let my sister overwork you.

AIDE. We're very busy, ma'am.

FONTANELLE. If she bullies you let me know.

AIDE. Ma'am.

> FONTANELLE *goes out.* BODICE *hands him the warrants.*

BODICE. Hand these to the adjutant. Morning will do.

AIDE. Yes, ma'am.

> The AIDE *goes out.* BODICE *looks at the map.*

BODICE. War. Power. (*Off,* FONTANELLE *laughs briefly, and then
the* AIDE *laughs briefly.*) I'm forced to sit at this desk, work with
my sister, walk beside my husband. They say decide this and
that, but I don't decide anything. My decisions are forced on
me. I change people's lives and things get done – it's like a
mountain moving forward, but not because I tell it to. I started
to pull the wall down, and I had to stop that – the men are
needed here. (*She taps the map with the finger tips of one hand.*)
And now I must move them here and here – (*She moves her
index finger on the map.*) – because the map's my straitjacket and
that's all I can do. I'm trapped. (*Off, a clock strikes rapidly.
Silence. She thinks about her life, but not reflectively. She is*

trying to understand what has happened to her.) I hated being a girl, but at least I was happy sometimes. And it was better when I grew up, I could be myself – they didn't humiliate me then. I was almost free! I made so many plans, one day I'd be my own master! Now I have all the power . . . and I'm a slave. Worse! (*Rings the bell once.*) Pellet! – I shall work. I shall pounce on every mistake my enemy makes! (*Rings the bell once.*) War is so full of chances! I only need a little luck. (*Rings the bell twice.*) Pellet! Pellet! (*Picks up the map and starts to go.*) Are you asleep?

    She goes out.

SCENE FIVE

Road.
Prison convoy on a country road. LEAR *and* FOUR PRISONERS *chained together by the neck and blindfolded.* LEAR *is also gagged. They are led and guarded by* THREE SOLDIERS (J, K *and* L). *Everyone is tired and dirty. They talk nervously and quietly, all except* LEAR. *Continuous heavy gun fire in the distance.*

SOLDIER J (*looking at a map*). Useless bloody map!

SOLDIER K (*looks round*). We're lost!

SOLDIER J. Shut up! (*To* PRISONERS.) Hup hup!

FIRST PRISONER (*quietly*). Can't go anymore.

SECOND PRISONER. Lean on me.

SOLDIER K. Hup.

THIRD PRISONER (*to* SECOND PRISONER). Let 'im go. 'E knows when e's 'ad enough.

SOLDIER L. Hup.

SECOND PRISONER. No. They'll shoot him.

SOLDIER K. We're 'eadin' back the way we come.

SOLDIER J. 'Alt! (*The* PRISONERS *stop immediately.*) Down. (*They sit. To* SOLDIER K.) Go 'an 'ave a little reccy. You're good at directions.

SOLDIER K *goes out. The* PRISONERS *pass round a water can.*
They don't remove their blindfolds.

FOURTH PRISONER. I'm next.

SOLDIER J (*crouches and studies map*). They must a issued this for
the Crimea.

SECOND PRISONER (*gives water to* FIRST PRISONER). I'll hold
it.

SOLDIER L. I tol' yer t' wrap it.

SOLDIER J. Wha' direction's the firin' comin' from?

SOLDIER L. Moves about.

SECOND PRISONER. Enough.

FIRST PRISONER. Thank you.

SECOND PRISONER. I'll try to look where we are. Keep in front
of me.

FOURTH PRISONER. Here. (*The water can is passed to him. It's
almost empty.*) Bastards! It's empty! (*Drinks.*)

THIRD PRISONER. Leave some. (*Takes the water can.*)

SOLDIER L (*sees* SECOND PRISONER *trying to look*). Oi wass your
game!

SOLDIER J. Wass up?

SECOND PRISONER. Nothing. Nothing.

SOLDIER L. I saw yer look.

SECOND PRISONER. No.

SOLDIER J. 'E look?

SOLDIER L. Yeh! Any more out a you and yer'll look through a 'ole
in yer 'ead. I got the enemy breathin' up me arse. I ain' messin'
about with you, sonny.

The TWO SOLDIERS *go back to the map.*

SOLDIER J (*looking off*). Wass keepin' 'im?

SOLDIER L. Don't tell me 'e's gone an' got lost now. Why don't we
run for it?

SOLDIER J (*indicates* PRISONERS). What about these darlin's?

SOLDIER L. Leave 'em, kill 'em.

SOLDIER J. Give it another minute. Best t' stick t' orders as long as yer can.

SOLDIER L (*grumbling nastily*). I ain' cartin' this garbage round much longer, we ain' safe ourselves. (*Suddenly calls after* SOLDIER K, *low and intense*.) Billy? (*Silence.*) 'E don't 'ear. Reckon 'e's scarpered?

SOLDIER J. Billy? Nah.

THIRD PRISONER (*removes gag from* LEAR's *mouth and holds the water can against it*). 'Ere, drink this an' be quiet.

LEAR (*after drinking a mouthful*). More.

FOURTH PRISONER. It's gone.

LEAR. I can't see.

THIRD PRISONER. Our eyes are covered.

LEAR. Where are we?

SOLDIER L. Joker. 'Oo unplugged 'is gob?

LEAR (*loudly and serenely*). Why do they pull me about like this? Why do they waste their time on me. If they let me I'd go away quietly. How could I harm them? They're young, why do they waste their life leading an old man on a rope?

The distant guns sound louder.

SOLDIER L. 'Ark at it! (*Calls as before.*) Billy?

SOLDIER J. Leave it.

SOLDIER L. I'll go an' look for 'im.

SOLDIER J. O no you don't.

LEAR. I've lost my boy.

SOLDIER L (*to* PRISONERS). I ain' warnin' yer. Keep 'im quiet.

LEAR. There are so many voices! I must find him. I had a terrible pain in my head and he stopped it and now I must help him. He's lost. He needs me. What will they do to him if I'm not there to call them off? Boy! Boy! Hey!

SOLDIER L. All right, bloody 'ush!

LEAR (*stands*). Here! Here!

FOURTH PRISONER. Stop him! My neck!

SOLDIER J. E's bloody mad!

FOURTH PRISONER. Kick him!

SOLDIER L (*runs to* LEAR *and gags him*). I said stow it, grandad.
Now bloody talk t' yerself. (*He goes back to* SOLDIER J, *who is
still by the map.*) Get yer rifle. They've 'ad long enough.

SOLDIER J. Give 'em a little bit longer. (*He kneels in front of the
map.*) We must be on 'ere somewhere.

> *Pause.* LEAR *makes sounds through his gag. Slowly* SOLDIERS
> J *and* L *raise their hands over their heads – they look like
> Moslems about to pray.* SOLDIER K *comes on with his hands
> above his head. They stay like this in silence for a few moments.
> The* CARPENTER, LEWIS, PETE *and other* REBEL SOLDIERS
> *come on. They are quick, quiet and tense.*

CARPENTER. This them?

SOLDIER K. Yeh.

> LEWIS *goes upstage as Look Out. A* REBEL SOLDIER *picks up*
> SOLDIERS J *and* L's *rifles.*

CARPENTER. Anyone in charge?

SOLDIER J. 'Ere.

CARPENTER. Where were you wanting to get to?

SOLDIER J. HQ. Evacuating that lot.

CARPENTER. You haven't got an HQ left.

FOURTH PRISONER (*takes off his blindfold*). We're free . . . (*The*
PRISONERS *hesitate awkwardly.*) Can we take the chains
off?

CARPENTER. No. Not till the political officers have been through
you. (*Points to* SOLDIERS J, K *and* L.) Tie them up.

> *The* THREE SOLDIER'S *hands are tied behind their backs. The*
> CARPENTER *goes to the side of the stage, whistles, and gestures
> to someone to come on.*

FOURTH PRISONER. You can undo me. I'm a political prisoner.
On your side. I shall have influence when things are changed.
I'll put in a word for you soldiers. You've saved my life.

FONTANELLE *and a* REBEL SOLDIER *come on from the direction of the* CARPENTER's *whistle. Her hands are tied behind her back. She is dirty and dishevelled and her clothes are torn.*

CARPENTER. Tie her on the end.

PETE (*tying* FONTANELLE *on to the chain of* PRISONERS). Can they take their blindfolds off?

CARPENTER. If you like.

The PRISONERS *remove their blindfolds.* THIRD PRISONER *takes* LEAR's *off.*

LEAR. Undo this chain. My hands are white. There's no blood in them. My neck's like old leather. You'd have a job to hang me now. I don't want to live except for the boy. Who'd look after him?

FONTANELLE. Don't tie me up with him! (*Cries with anger.*) O God, how foul . . .

LEAR. Who's crying? (*Still serenely. He doesn't recognize her.*) Stop that, child. Ask them quietly. You're a woman, you should know how to do that. Some of them are kind, some of them listen.

FONTANELLE. You stupid, stupid, wicked fool!

LEAR. You mustn't shout. No one will listen to that. They all shout here.

CARPENTER. Who is he? I've seen him before.

SOLDIER J. Don't know any of 'em from Adam. That one thinks 'e's king.

CARPENTER. It'd be safer to be Jesus Christ.

Off, a whistle.

LEWIS. We're off. (*He whistles back.*)

PETE. On your feet. (*The* PRISONERS *stand.*)

FONTANELLE. Don't take me like this. The people will throw stones at me and shout. They hate me. I'm afraid. I'll faint and

scream. I've never been humiliated, I don't know how to
behave. Help me. Please.

LEAR. Don't ask them for favours. Walk with us. Be gentle and
don't pull.

CARPENTER. Watch that old one. He's a trouble maker.

LEAR. We'll go decently and quietly and look for my boy. He was
very good to me. He saved my mind when I went mad. And to
tell you the truth I did him a great wrong once, a very great
wrong. He's never blamed me. I must be kind to him now.
Come on, we'll find him together.

They go out in the direction from which the PRISONERS *came
on.*

SCENE SIX

LEAR's *second cell.*
It is darker than the first cell. LEAR, FONTANELLE *and the*
PRISONERS *from the chain gang (except* FOURTH PRISONER*) are
sitting on the ground. A bare electric bulb hangs from the ceiling. It
is unlit. Off, a sudden burst of rifle shots.*

FIRST PRISONER (*jumps up*). They're starting again!

SECOND PRISONER. No. They said last week it was only once.
They got rid of the undesirables then. (*Trying to sound calm.*)
We mustn't panic.

The OLD ORDERLY *comes on with a bucket and puts it down
upstage.*

THIRD PRISONER. Yeh, they're still feedin' us. They wouldn't
waste grub . . .

SECOND PRISONER (*to* OLD ORDERLY). What are they doing?

OLD ORDERLY. Never noticed.

FIRST PRISONER. We heard shooting.

OLD ORDERLY. Could 'ave. My 'earin' went 'undred a years back.

THIRD PRISONER. Why are they keepin' us 'ere? We should a bin out by now.

OLD ORDERLY. No orders, no papers, no forms, nothing comes through – no one knows what to do.

The OLD ORDERLY *goes out. Everyone eats except* LEAR *and* FIRST PRISONER. *They watch each other hungrily while they eat.* FONTANELLE *only eats a little.* LEAR *sits on the ground. He is still calm and remote.*

SECOND PRISONER (*jostling at the bucket*). Steady!

The GRAVEDIGGER'S BOY'S GHOST *comes on. He is white and thin.*

LEAR. Where have you been? Are you in pain?

GHOST. What? I don't know. I'm so cold. See how thin I am. Look at my legs. I think my chest's empty inside. Where have you been?

LEAR. Some men took us out of the town and along a road and some more men stopped us and brought us back again. I was lonely without you and worried, but I knew I'd find you. (LEAR *and the* GHOST *sit and lean against each other.*)

GHOST. Tell me what you saw. This city's like a grave. I tried to follow you but when we got out in the open the wind was too strong, it pushed me back.

LEAR. There was so much sky. I could hardly see. I've always looked down at the hills and banks where the enemy was hiding. But there's only a little strip of earth and all the sky. You're like my son now. I wish I'd been your father. I'd have looked after you so well.

The COMMANDANT, OLD ORDERLY *and* THREE SOLDIERS (M, N *and* O) *come in. The* SOLDIERS *carry rifles.*

COMMANDANT. What's that food bucket doing here?

OLD ORDERLY. They're always fed at this time. It's on standin' orders.

COMMANDANT. You old fool. (*Reads from a list.*) Evans.

THIRD PRISONER. Yeh.

COMMANDANT. M413. Leave that. L37 Hewit.

SECOND PRISONER. Yes.

COMMANDANT. H257 Wellstone.

FIRST PRISONER. Yes.

COMMANDANT. Outside.

SOLDIER M. Get fell in sharp.

SECOND PRISONER. We're on the wrong list.

SOLDIER N. Tell me that outside.

THIRD PRISONER. We're politicals.

SECOND PRISONER. I was on your side. That's why I'm here.

COMMANDANT. It's all been cleared up. You're transferees. Outside, there's good lads.

SECOND PRISONER. No.

> SOLDIERS M *and* N *run* SECOND PRISONER *out. He shouts* '*No!*' *once more before he goes.* COMMANDANT *and* SOLDIER O *take* FIRST *and* THIRD PRISONERS *outside. The* OLD ORDERLY *picks up some scraps of food from the floor and drops them in the bucket.* LEAR *goes to the bucket to feed.*

OLD ORDERLY. Throw their muck anywhere.

FONTANELLE. For as long as I can remember there was misery and waste and suffering wherever you were. You live in your own mad world, you can't hear me. You've wasted my life and I can't even tell you. O god, where can I find justice?

LEAR. They didn't leave much.

> *Off, a burst of rifle shots.*

OLD ORDERLY. Do this, run there, fetch that, carry this. Finished? (*He picks up the bucket.*) No one can put a foot right today. Job like this upsets the whole place. (*Starts to go.*) Work. Work. Work.

The OLD ORDERLY *goes out.* FONTANELLE *goes to* LEAR.

FONTANELLE. Talk to them! Say you know something the government ought to know. Promise them something. Anything. Make them – negotiate! – put us on trial! O father, you must think!

LEAR. He's taken the bucket. I always scrape it.

FONTANELLE. Bodice is still fighting. She'll beat them, she always does. Help me, father. If Bodice saves us I'll look after you. I understand you now. Take everything back. God knows I don't want it. Look, let me help you. Father, think. Try. Talk to them, argue with them – you're so good at that. Sit down. (*She brushes hair from his face.*) We mustn't shout at each other. I do love you. I'm such a stupid woman. Yes (*She laughs.*) – stupid, stupid! But you understand me. What will you say to them?

LEAR. All the sky.

FONTANELLE. Remember! Remember!

LEAR. And a little piece of earth.

The CARPENTER, COMMANDANT, OLD ORDERLY, FOURTH PRISONER *and* SOLDIERS M, N *and* O *come in.* FOURTH PRISONER *wears a crumpled, dark-blue striped suit.*

COMMANDANT (*to* SOLDIERS, *indicating the cell*). Keep this one separate for the family.

FONTANELLE. Are you putting us on trial?

CARPENTER. Your father's case is still open. But yours has been closed.

FONTANELLE (*calmer*). If I appealed it would go to you?

CARPENTER. Yes.

FONTANELLE. My sister will punish you if you do anything to us!

CARPENTER. We've got her. We're bringing her here.

Off, a burst of rifle shots.

FONTANELLE (*agitated again*). Let me swallow poison. You don't care how I die as long as you get rid of me. Why must you hurt me?

CARPENTER (*shakes his head*). No. I can't stay long and I must see it finished. I have to identify the body.

> SOLDIER N *shoots* FONTANELLE *from behind. She falls dead immediately.*

COMMANDANT. Will you wait in my office? It's warmer.

CARPENTER. Thank you.

> *The* COMMANDANT *and* CARPENTER *go out wearily.* SOLDIERS M *and* N *follow them.* LEAR, GHOST, FOURTH PRISONER *and* SOLDIER O *are left.* SOLDIER O *helps* FOURTH PRISONER *to erect a trestle table.*

FOURTH PRISONER. Bring this here.

> SOLDIER O *helps* FOURTH PRISONER *to put* FONTA-NELLE's *body on the table. They move quietly and efficiently.* FOURTH PRISONER *switches on the bare electric light over the table. He has turned his white shirt-cuffs back over his jacket sleeves. The* GHOST *cringes away.* LEAR *stares at* FOURTH PRISONER. *Slowly he stands. He begins to see where he is.*

GHOST. It's beginning.

LEAR. What?

GHOST. Quickly, Lear! I'll take you away! We'll go to the place where I was lost!

LEAR. No. I ran away so often, but my life was ruined just the same. Now I'll stay. (*He stares at* FOURTH PRISONER.)

FOURTH PRISONER (*efficiently*). I'm the prison medical doctor. We met in less happy times. I said I was in good standing with the government. My papers confirmed that. I'm just waiting for more papers and then I'll be given a post of more obvious trust and importance. We're ready to begin.

LEAR. What are you doing?

FOURTH PRISONER. A little autopsy. Not a big one. We know what she died of. But I handle this routine work methodically.

Otherwise they think you can't be trusted with bigger things. My new papers will open up many new opportunities for me.

LEAR. Who was she?

FOURTH PRISONER. Your daughter.

LEAR. Did I have a daughter?

FOURTH PRISONER. Yes, it's on her chart. That's her stomach and the liver underneath. I'm just making a few incisions to satisfy the authorities.

LEAR. Is that my daughter . . .? (*Points.*) That's . . .?

FOURTH PRISONER. The stomach.

LEAR (*points*). That?

FOURTH PRISONER. The lungs. You can see how she died. The bullet track goes through the lady's lungs.

LEAR. But where is the . . . She was cruel and angry and hard . . .

FOURTH PRISONER (*points*). The womb.

LEAR. So much blood and bits and pieces packed in with all that care. Where is the . . . where . . .?

FOURTH PRISONER. What is the question?

LEAR. Where is the beast? The blood is as still as a lake. Where . . .? Where . . .?

FOURTH PRISONER (*to* SOLDIER O). What's the man asking? (*No response.*)

LEAR. She sleeps inside like a lion and a lamb and a child. The things are so beautiful. I am astonished. I have never seen anything so beautiful. If I had known she was so beautiful . . . Her body was made by the hand of a child, so sure and nothing unclean . . . If I had known this beauty and patience and care, how I would have loved her.

The GHOST *starts to cry but remains perfectly still.*

Did I make this – and destroy it?

BODICE *is brought in by* SOLDIERS M *and* N. *She is dirty and dishevelled, but she has tried to clean herself and tidy her hair. She tries to sound eager and in control.*

BODICE. In here? Yes. Thank you. Did my letter go to the government?

SOLDIER M. Wait 'ere.

BODICE. Yes. Thank you. I must see someone in authority. I want to explain my letter, you see. (*Sees* LEAR.) O, yes, they've put us together. That must be a friendly sign. Now I know they mean to act properly!

FOURTH PRISONER. Pass me my forms. (SOLDIER O *hands him some forms.*)

BODICE (*brightly trying to show interest*). What are you doing?

LEAR. That's your sister.

BODICE. No!

LEAR. I destroyed her.

BODICE. Destroyed? No, no! We admit nothing. We acted for the best. Did what we had to do.

LEAR. I destroyed her! I knew nothing, saw nothing, learned nothing! Fool! Fool! Worse than I knew! (*He puts his hands into* FONTANELLE *and brings them out covered with dark blood and smeared with viscera. The* SOLDIERS *react awkwardly and ineffectually.*) Look at my dead daughter!

BODICE. No! No!

LEAR. Look! I killed her! Her blood is on my hands! Destroyer! Murderer! And now I must begin again. I must walk through my life, step after step, I must walk in weariness and bitterness, I must become a child, hungry and stripped and shivering in blood, I must open my eyes and see!

The COMMANDANT *runs in shouting and pointing at the* SOLDIERS.

COMMANDANT. You! – You! – What is this? Get it under control!

FOURTH PRISONER. I tried to stop them – saboteurs! – don't let this stop my petition –

The CARPENTER *comes in.*

BODICE. Thank god! At last! I wrote to your wife. She's sent you to me. She accepts my offer to collaborate. I was against the fighting. I can show you minutes. My father's mad, you can see that – and my sister drove him on!

CARPENTER. The government found no extenuating circumstances in your case.

BODICE. O – but you haven't been told everything. You must acquaint yourself with the facts. No, I don't expect you to let me go. I'm culpable by association. I've been foolish. I accept that. Now there must be a term of imprisonment. I fully accept it.

CARPENTER. You were sentenced to death.

BODICE. No! You have no right! I will not be dealt with by your – committee! I have a right to justice in court! O you are cruel when you get a little power – when you have the power I had you beg people to accept your mercy so that god will not judge you! (*Falls down.*) Please. Please. Please.

CARPENTER. Be quick.

> SOLDIER N *moves behind* BODICE *with a pistol. She sees him and fights furiously.* SOLDIERS M *and* O *join in. They can't see to aim.* SOLDIER O *fixes a bayonet.* BODICE *bites* SOLDIER M.

SOLDIER M. Bitch!

> SOLDIER M *throws her to the ground again. She writhes away and screams.*

'Old 'er still!

> SOLDIER N *kicks her.* SOLDIERS M *and* N *pinion her with their boots. She writhes and screams.*

'Old 'er! 'Old 'er!

> SOLDIER O *bayonets her three times. Slight pause. She writhes. He bayonets her once again. She gives a spasm and dies.*

CARPENTER. Thank you. I'm sorry. You're good lads.

SOLDIER O. . . . Blimey.

COMMANDANT (*to* SOLDIERS). Clear up, lads.

> *The* CARPENTER *starts to go. The* COMMANDANT *stops him. While the* COMMANDANT *and the* CARPENTER *talk,* SOLDIERS *remove* FONTANELLE, BODICE *and the trestle table and turn off the light.*

(*He tries to force the* CARPENTER.) We should finish everything. There's still the old man.

CARPENTER. You know I can't. My wife says no. She knew him.

COMMANDANT. I've been having a word with the prison MO. Very reliable man, sir. (*He beckons* FOURTH PRISONER *over.*) About the old one.

FOURTH PRISONER. If he has to be kept alive –

CARPENTER. I've already explained that –

FOURTH PRISONER. I follow, sir. Then he could be made politically ineffective.

CARPENTER. What does that mean?

FOURTH PRISONER. Madmen often harm themselves.

CARPENTER. But not killed. That's too obvious.

FOURTH PRISONER. Only harmed.

CARPENTER. Well, anything happens in a war.

COMMANDANT. Good.

> *The* COMMANDANT *and* CARPENTER *go out.*

FOURTH PRISONER. This is a chance to bring myself to notice.

> FOURTH PRISONER *goes upstage into the dark.*

SOLDIER M. She bit me. What yer do for snake bite?

SOLDIER N (*looks*). I'd burn that.

SOLDIER O. Thass only a dose a rabbies.

> FOURTH PRISONER *comes downstage with a heap of equipment. The* GHOST *stands and watches silently.* LEAR *is immobile. He is completely withdrawn.*

FOURTH PRISONER. Right. (*He goes to* LEAR.) Good morning. Time for your drive. Into your coat. (LEAR *is put into a strait-jacket. He doesn't help in any way.*) Cross your arms and hold your regalia. Now the buttons. This nasty wind gets in everywhere. You've been inside too long to trust yourself to fresh air. (LEAR *is seated on a chair.*) Get settled down. (*His legs are strapped to the chair legs.*) And last your crown. (*A square frame is lowered over his head and face.* FOURTH PRISONER *steps back. Then* LEAR *speaks.*)

LEAR. You've turned me into a king again.

FOURTH PRISONER (*produces a tool*). Here's a device I perfected on dogs for removing human eyes.

LEAR. No, no. You mustn't touch my eyes. I must have my eyes!

FOURTH PRISONER. With this device you extract the eye undamaged and then it can be put to good use. It's based on a scouting gadget I had as a boy.

SOLDIER N. Get on. It's late.

FOURTH PRISONER. Understand, this isn't an instrument of torture, but a scientific device. See how it clips the lid back to leave it unmarked.

LEAR. No – no!

FOURTH PRISONER. Nice and steady. (*He removes one of* LEAR's *eyes.*)

LEAR. Aahh!

FOURTH PRISONER. Note how the eye passes into the lower chamber and is received into a soothing solution of formaldehyde crystals. One more, please. (*He removes* LEAR's *other eye.*)

LEAR. Aaahhh!

FOURTH PRISONER (*looking at the eyes in the glass container*). Perfect.

LEAR (*jerking in the chair*). Aaahhh! The sun! It hurts my eyes!

FOURTH PRISONER (*sprays an aerosol into* LEAR's *eye sockets*). That will assist the formation of scab and discourage flies. (*To* SOLDIERS.) Clean this up with a bucket and mop.

FOURTH PRISONER *starts to leave.*

LEAR. Aaahhh! It hurts!

FOURTH PRISONER. Keep still. You make it worse.

FOURTH PRISONER *goes out.*

SOLDIER M. Less get away an' shut the door.

SOLDIER N. 'E'll 'ave the 'ole bloody place up.

SOLDIER O. O lor.

The THREE SOLDIERS *go out.* LEAR *and the* GHOST *are left.*

LEAR. Aaahhh! The roaring in my head. I see blood. (*Spits.*) Blood in my mouth. (*Jerks.*) My hands – undo my hands and let me kill myself.

GHOST. Lear.

LEAR. Who's that! What d'you want? You can't take my eyes, but take the rest! Kill me! Kill me!

GHOST. No – people will be kind to you now. Surely you've suffered enough.

LEAR. You. (*The* GHOST *starts to unfasten* LEAR.) Tell me the pain will stop! This pain must stop! O stop, stop, stop!

GHOST. It will stop. Sometimes it might come back, but you'll learn to bear it. I can stay with you now you need me.

LEAR. Wipe my mouth. There's blood. I'm swallowing blood.

GHOST. Stand. Please. (LEAR *stumbles to his feet.*) Walk as if you could see. Try. We'll go back to my house. It's quiet there, they'll leave you in peace at last.

LEAR (*stumbling forward*). Take me away! This pain must stop! Ah! (*Stumbling out.*) Take me somewhere to die!

LEAR *stumbles out with the* GHOST.

SCENE SEVEN

Near the wall.
Open fields.
A FARMER, *his* WIFE *and* SON *hurry on. They cross upstage. They carry bundles.*

SON. Doo come. Thass late.
FARMER'S WIFE. Don't fret. Goo on, we'll keep up.
> LEAR *stumbles on downstage with the* GHOST. LEAR *now carries a stick.*
LEAR. Where are we, where are we? The wind's stinging my eyes. They're full of dust.
GHOST. We're near the wall. It'll be easier to walk along the top. Stop. There's some people here. Shall we hide in the scrub?
LEAR. No. I must beg.

> LEAR *takes out a bowl and begs.*

Alms! I'm not a criminal, I wasn't blinded by a judge. Alms!

The FARMER, *his* WIFE *and* SON *come down to* LEAR.

FARMER. Good day, father. (*He looks at the bowl. His* SON *makes a gesture of refusal.*) We ont got no bait for yoo. We're poor people off the land. Thass my wife an' my littl' ol' boy by me here.
LEAR. Can I rest in your house? I'm so tired.
FARMER. Yoo'd be welcome an' more, but thass gone. See, sir, when the ol' king went mad they stop buildin' his wall, an' a great crowd a people come up these parts. The ol' king cleared a good strip a land both sides his wall. Rare land that was. So we took a plow an' built ourselves homes.
FARMER'S WIFE. An' now they're buildin' the wall again, count a the govermin's changed.
FARMER. So the soldier boys turned us out on our land. Now everyone's off to the work camp to work on the wall. We'd best move sharp, do there'll be no more room.

FARMER'S WIFE. The women as well.

FARMER. An' the boy's off to be a soldier.

FARMER'S WIFE. We can't bait en an' dress en n' more.

LEAR. But they'll kill him in the army.

FARMER'S WIFE. We must hope they won't.

SON. Thass late. T'ent time t' natter. Doo come.

The SON *goes out.*

FARMER'S WIFE. We're speedin', boy.

The FARMER *and his* WIFE *go out after their* SON.

LEAR. I could learn to endure my blindness with patience, I could never endure this! (*Calls.*) Children! Ah!

LEAR *falls down on to his knees.*

FARMER'S WIFE (*off*). The poor gentleman's toppled over.

The FARMER *and his* WIFE *and* SON *hurry on.*

LEAR. I am the King! I kneel by this wall. How many lives have I ended here? Go away. Go anywhere. Go far away. Run. I will not move till you go!

FARMER'S WIFE. Do stand, sir.

LEAR. I've heard your voices. I'd never seen a poor man! You take too much pity out of me, if there's no pity I shall die of this grief.

SON. That ol' boy's a great rambler.

LEAR. They feed you and clothe you – is that why you can't see? All life seeks its safety. A wolf, a fox, a horse – they'd run away, they're sane. Why d'you run to meet your butchers? Why?

SON. I'll see you in the camp.

The FARMER'S SON *goes out.*

FARMER'S WIFE. Tent decent leavin' en out here on his own, dad.

FARMER. Poor man. If yoo take en someplace they'll beat en an' chain en. Let en be, he's at home in the fields. Let en bear his cross in peace.

The FARMER *and the* FARMER'S WIFE *go out.*

LEAR (*stumbles to his feet*). Men destroy themselves and say it's their duty? It's not possible! How can they be so abused? Cordelia doesn't know what she's doing! I must tell her – write to her!

GHOST. No, no, no! They never listen!

LEAR. I can't be silent! O my eyes! This crying's opened my wounds! There's blood again! Quick, quick, help me! My eyes, my eyes! I must stop her before I die!

LEAR *stumbles out on the* GHOST's *arm.*

Act Three

SCENE ONE

The GRAVEDIGGER'S BOY'S *house.*
More dilapidated, but obviously lived in. The stage is empty for a
moment. THOMAS *and* JOHN *come in.*

THOMAS (*calls*). We're home! (*Stretches and yawns happily.*) I'm all in.

> JOHN *draws water from the well and washes himself.* SUSAN
> *comes to the door with* LEAR. THOMAS *embraces her.*

SUSAN. Have you been busy?
LEAR. No news from the village?
THOMAS. No.
LEAR. None? (THOMAS *starts to lead* LEAR *to a bench.*) Cordelia should have answered my last letter. It was stronger than the others. I thought she'd have to answer –
THOMAS (*calming him*). I know, I know.
JOHN. I'll eat in the village tonight with my girl's family.
SUSAN (*slightly annoyed*). You should have told me. (*To* THOMAS.) It won't be long.
THOMAS. I'm starving!

> SUSAN *goes into the house with* THOMAS. JOHN *throws his*
> *water away. A* SMALL MAN *comes in. He is dirty and frightened*
> *and in rags.*

SMALL MAN. I was lookin' – for someone. Could you give us some water?

> JOHN *nods to a pitcher by the well. The* SMALL MAN *drinks*
> *noisily.*

JOHN. You're off the road.

SMALL MAN (*sees* LEAR). Ah, sir. It was you I was lookin' for, sir.
They said – (*He stops.*) You knew me when I was a soldier, sir.
Small dark man. Black hair.

LEAR. What's your name?

SMALL MAN. O yes. McFearson.

JOHN. How did you get in that state?

> THOMAS *comes out of the house. He puts his hand on* LEAR's
> *shoulder.*

SMALL MAN. On the road. Thass why I'm 'ungry.

LEAR. Yes, I think I remember you. If you're hungry you'd better
stay to dinner.

SMALL MAN. Thank you, thanks.

LEAR. Give him John's. He's going down to the village. Take him
into the house.

> THOMAS *takes the* SMALL MAN *into the house.* THOMAS *turns
> in the doorway.*

THOMAS (*to* LEAR). He can't stay. Apart from anything else there
isn't enough food.

LEAR. I'll tell him.

> THOMAS *goes on into the house. The* GHOST *has come on. He
> looks thinner and more wasted.*

GHOST. D'you know who he is?

LEAR. A soldier.

> JOHN *turns to watch* LEAR.

GHOST. That's right, a deserter. I suppose the fool didn't keep out
of sight, moved by day, asked everyone where you were. It
won't take them long to follow him. Get rid of the lot of them!
Then we'll be safe.

> *The* SMALL MAN *comes out of the house.*

SMALL MAN. Didn't want to get under the lady's feet. It's good of

you to let me – (*He stops.*) I thought, for old time's sake . . . The
'ole regiment said you was one a the best.

JOHN (*putting on his jacket*). I'm off.

> JOHN *goes and the* SMALL MAN *immediately sits down on the
> bench.*

SMALL MAN. Good old days, really. (*Laughs.*) Only yer never
know it at the time. Nice 'ere, nice place. You're very well fixed
– considerin'.

LEAR. Yes.

SMALL MAN. Mind you, yer must be hard pressed. Not a lot t' do
everythin'. Juss the two men an' the girl, is it? (*No reply.*) An'
you must take a fair bit a lookin' after. An' why shouldn't yer be
looked after? Yer deserve it. Yes. I was a batman – as I suppose
yer remember.

LEAR. I'm sorry. I was thinking about something else. I've written
to Cordelia, but she doesn't answer. Yes, there's just the four of
us. They moved in when the house was empty, and they've
looked after me since I came back. I thought I'd die but they
saved me. But tell me about your life. I'd like to know how
you've lived and what you've done.

SMALL MAN. O nothin'. Not t' interest your class a person. Not
worth tellin'.

LEAR. But you've fought in great wars and helped to make great
changes in the world.

SMALL MAN. What?

> THOMAS *comes out of the house and the* SMALL MAN *jumps up.*

O – this your place?

THOMAS. Where've you come from?

SMALL MAN. Well, my wife dies so I was on me own. I says t'
meself – travel! See the world while it's still there. New bed
every night, a new life every mornin' –

THOMAS. But why are you in that state?

SMALL MAN. Well. (*Sits.*) Yes, why shouldn't I tell yer. I wasn't goin' t' tell yer – the truth upsets people. But you're men of the world. I got beaten up. These thugs, they'd feed their own kids to a guard dog t' keep it quiet –

THOMAS. He's lying –

SMALL MAN. I take an oath – as I stand 'ere –

THOMAS. You're lying!

LEAR. Of course he's lying! Did it take you that long to find out?

THOMAS. Anyone could have sent him! He might be dangerous!

SMALL MAN. No, no, that's not true. Dangerous! (*Half laughs.*) God knows I couldn't 'urt a fly.

THOMAS. Then who are you? Tell me!

SMALL MAN. No! I came t' see 'im, not you!

THOMAS. Who are you?

SMALL MAN. Nobody! I'm from the wall a course – are you stupid? I ran away! I couldn't work. Anyone can see I'm sick. I spit blood. So they put me in a punishment squad. And then the black market . . . (*He stops.*) But if yer can't work they don't feed yer! So I ran. God knows what I was doin'. I must a bin off me 'ead. It's too late now.

THOMAS. But why did you come here?

SMALL MAN. I 'id in the trees but they was everywhere. – What made me what? They're all afraid in the camps so news travels fast. Thass 'ow we 'eard a you.

SUSAN (*off*). It's ready.

SMALL MAN. When I come here I said – say it ain't true, juss talk, an' they give yer up? O Chriss, I didn't know what t' think. Thass why I said yer knew me. You bein' blind I thought –

LEAR. What did you hear in the camp?

SMALL MAN. Yer wan'a get rid a the army an' blow up the wall, an' shut the camps an' send the prisoners home. Yer give money to a deserter.

THOMAS. Did you?

SMALL MAN. An' I was goin t' die on the wall.

JOHN *comes in.*

JOHN. There's soldiers coming up the hill.

LEAR. Take him in the woods.

THOMAS. Lear! –

LEAR. No! Tell me all that later. Hide him. Warn Susan. He hasn't been here.

> SMALL MAN *whimpers.* THOMAS *hurries with him into the house.*

Sit down. (JOHN *and* LEAR *sit. Pause. He talks to fill the silence, so that they will seem at ease.*) Your young girl will be waiting in the village.

JOHN. Yes. I'm late again. Something always happens, and she gets upset . . .

LEAR. Will you marry her?

JOHN (*listening*). They're coming.

LEAR. Have you asked her? She might not have you.

JOHN. No, not yet.

> *An* OFFICER *and* THREE SOLDIERS (P, Q, *and* R) *come in.*

There's some soldiers here, Lear.

LEAR (*nods*). Is there anything you want? Water or food?

OFFICER. Who else is here?

LEAR. There's a woman in the house and another man somewhere.

OFFICER. Who else?

LEAR. No one.

OFFICER (*to* SOLDIERS). Look round. (SOLDIERS P *and* Q *go into the house. To* JOHN.) Have you seen anyone?

LEAR. He was at work, he's just got back.

SOLDIER R (*offering to go*). Scout round the woods, sir?

OFFICER (*irritated*). You'll never find him in there.

> SUSAN *comes out of the house and stands still.*

(*To* LEAR.) A man was asking for you in the village. Small, dark man.

LEAR. Well, he'll turn up if they told him where I am. I'll let you know.

SOLDIERS P *and* Q *come out of the house.*

SOLDIER P (*shakes his head*). Dead.
OFFICER (*to* LEAR). Very well. This place will be watched in
   future.

   The OFFICER *and* THREE SOLDIERS *leave.*

JOHN. They've gone.
LEAR. Go and see them off.

   JOHN *goes out.* SUSAN *goes upstage and calls.*

SUSAN. Tom! (*To* LEAR.) They can't do anything to us. We didn't
   ask him to come. I'll give him some food to take with him. If
   he's caught he can say he stole it.

   THOMAS *comes in.* SUSAN *goes to him.*

THOMAS. What happened? What did they say?
LEAR. I don't know. I didn't listen. They were just soldiers. No
   rank.
THOMAS. We must get rid of him quick. If he's caught here now
   we're for it.

   BEN, *the young orderly, comes in. He is dirty, dishevelled,
   ragged and breathless. They stare at him.*

BEN. There were soldiers out on the road. I 'ad t' crawl the last bit
   on me 'ands an' knees.

   The SMALL MAN *comes in and watches.*

   (*Goes to* LEAR.) I looked after you in the cage, sir. They put me
   on the wall for floggin' snout t' cons.
LEAR. Yes. You fed me in prison. You can stay here.
THOMAS. No!
LEAR. He can stay.
THOMAS. But we'll all be responsible. They'll say we encourage
   them! They'll blame us for everything! It's insane!
LEAR. Where else can he go? *You* go if you're afraid!

THOMAS. How can you be so obstinate, how can you be such a fool?

BEN (*to* LEAR). Yeh, you ain' some prisoner no one's ever 'eard of, they can't mess you about.

LEAR. No, you mustn't say that. I'm not a king. I have no power. But you can stay. You're doing no harm. Now I'm hungry, take me inside. I'll write to Cordelia again. She means well, she only needs someone to make her see sense. Take me in. I came here when I was cold and hungry and afraid. I wasn't turned away, and I won't turn anyone away. They can eat my food while it lasts and when it's gone they can go if they like, but I won't send anyone away. That's how I'll end my life. I'll be shut up in a grave soon, and till then this door is open. (*He smiles.*)

LEAR *and the others go towards the house.*

SMALL MAN (*following them. He speaks half to himself*). Thass all very well. But yer never seen 'is sort on the wall. We can't let everyone in. We 'ave t' act fly.

The SMALL MAN *follows the others into the house.*

SCENE TWO

Same.
Months later. Many strangers have gathered to listen to LEAR.
THOMAS *leads him out of the house and down to the audience and turns* LEAR *to face them. As* LEAR *comes down a few* STRANGERS *say 'Good morning' and* LEAR *smiles at them and says 'Good morning'.*
THOMAS *stands at* LEAR's *side and* JOHN *stands a little way back. The* STRANGERS *watch with respect.*

LEAR (*to the audience*). A man woke up one morning and found he'd lost his voice. So he went to look for it, and when he came to the wood there was the bird who'd stolen it. It was singing beautifully and the man said 'Now I sing so beautifully I shall be rich and famous'. He put the bird in a cage and said 'When I open my mouth wide you must sing'. Then he went to the king and said 'I will sing your majesty's praises'. But when he opened his mouth the bird could only groan and cry because it was in a cage, and the king had the man whipped. The man took the bird home, but his family couldn't stand the bird's groaning and crying and they left him. So in the end the man took the bird back to the wood and let it out of the cage. But the man believed the king had treated him unjustly and he kept saying to himself 'The king's a fool' and as the bird still had the man's voice it kept singing this all over the wood and soon the other birds learned it. The next time the king went hunting he was surprised to hear all the birds singing 'The king's a fool'. He caught the bird who'd started it and pulled out its feathers, broke its wings and nailed it to a branch as a warning to all the other birds. The forest was silent. And just as the bird had the man's voice the man now had the bird's pain. He ran round silently waving his head and stamping his feet, and he was locked up for the rest of his life in a cage.

The STRANGERS *murmur.*

A STRANGER. Tell me, Lear –
THOMAS. Later. He must rest now.

> THOMAS *leads* LEAR *to one side. The* STRANGERS *break up into groups and talk. A few leave.*

I want you to send Ben back to the wall.
LEAR. Why?
THOMAS. Hundreds of people come to hear you now. The government can't let this go on, and they could crush us like that! We need support. We must infiltrate the camps.

> BEN *has been watching intensely. He comes over to them.*

BEN. Has he told you? I'll give myself up. They'll put me in a punishment squad. I'll be beaten and starved and worked like an animal. I may not survive – but at least I'll use what time I've got left. I'll help them to organize and be ready. I can bring them hope. You must give me a message to take –

LEAR. If I saw Christ on his cross I would spit at him.

BEN. What?

LEAR. Take me away.

THOMAS. You haven't listened!

BEN. Listen to us!

LEAR. Take me away!

> THOMAS *leads* LEAR *towards the house. Some of the* STRANGERS *meet him and take him inside.* BEN *and* THOMAS *look at one another in silence.* SUSAN *puts an arm round* THOMAS *to comfort him.*

THOMAS. You look tired.

SUSAN. No.

THOMAS (*sitting down with her*). Don't work too hard.

SUSAN. I'm not.

THOMAS (*presses her*). And don't run round after all these people. They can look after themselves.

SUSAN. O I don't mind them. But when we have our baby –

THOMAS. You don't have to worry about that. They'll all help.

SUSAN. Only it's a small house. Sometimes I'd like to speak to you and there are so many people –

THOMAS. Speak about what? You can always speak to me.

SUSAN. O I don't know. I meant . . . (*She is silent.*)

THOMAS (*thinking about* LEAR. *After a slight pause*). We talk to people but we don't really help them. We shouldn't let them come here if that's all we can do. It's dangerous to tell the truth, truth without power is always dangerous. And we *should* fight! Freedom's not an idea, it's a passion! If you haven't got it you fight like a fish out of water fighting for air!

> The STRANGERS *who left hurry on quickly.*

STRANGERS (*quietly and intensely*). Soldiers. Soldiers.

THOMAS *stands.*

THOMAS. What is it?

The OLD COUNCILLOR, *an* OFFICER *and* SOLDIERS P, Q *and* R *come on.*

OFFICER (*reads from a form*). Rossman – (BEN *comes forward.*) – and – (*He points at the* SMALL MAN *as he tries to slip away.*) – grab him – (SOLDIERS P *and* Q *stop the* SMALL MAN.) – Jones –

SMALL MAN. Thass not me! I'm Simpson!

OFFICER. – I'm taking you into custody as absentees from your work camps.

LEAR *is led from the house. He stands on the steps surrounded by* STRANGERS.

LEAR. Who is it? What d'you want?

OFFICER. You're harbouring deserters.

LEAR. I don't ask my friends who they are.

BEN. Let them take me!

SOLDIER R. Shut it!

OFFICER. I'm returning them under guard to the area military commandant.

SMALL MAN (*tries to go to* LEAR *but the* SOLDIERS *stop him*). For god's sake what d'you want me for? Yer can see I'm ill! What work can I do? I'm in everyone's way. For god's sake leave me alone.

OFFICER. You're not going back to work. Certain economic offences have been made capital with retrospective effect. You were found guilty of dealing on the unauthorized market. The revised sentence is mandatory.

SMALL MAN (*bewildered*). I don't understand that.

OFFICER. You're a social liability. You're going back to be hanged.

SMALL MAN (*vaguely*). Yer can't . . . I've already been dealt with. It's on me records, sir. I don't understand.

LEAR. Take me to him. (LEAR *is led to the* OFFICER. *He puts his hand on the* OFFICER's *arm. Quietly.*) You're a soldier, how many deaths are on your conscience? Don't burden yourself with two more. Go back and say you can't find them.

COUNCILLOR. Lear, every word you say is treason.

LEAR. Who's that? Who's there?

COUNCILLOR. I was your minister –

LEAR. Yes – I know you!

COUNCILLOR. Out of respect for your age and sufferings Cordelia has tolerated your activities, but now they must stop. In future you will not speak in public or involve yourself in any public affairs. Your visitors will be vetted by the area military authorities. All these people must go. The government will appoint a man and woman to look after you. You will live in decent quietness, as a man of your years should.

LEAR. Are you in their new government?

COUNCILLOR. Like many of my colleagues I gave the new undertaking of loyalty. I've always tried to serve people. I see that as my chief duty. If we abandon the administration there'd be chaos.

LEAR. Yes, yes – but you won't hang this man for money?

SMALL MAN. The records must be wrong . . . That's it!

OFFICER. Take him down to the road.

SMALL MAN (*bewildered. Whimpers*). No.

LEAR (*to* COUNCILLOR). Stop them.

COUNCILLOR. It isn't my concern at all. I came to speak to *you*.

LEAR. I see. Savages have taken my power. You commit crimes and call them the law! The giant must stand on his toes to prove he's tall! – No, I'm wrong to shout at you, you have so much to do, things to put right, all my mistakes, I understand all that . . . But he's a little swindler! A petty swindler! Think of the crimes you commit every day in your office, day after day till it's just routine, think of the waste and misery of that!

COUNCILLOR. I was sent to talk to you as an old friend, not to be insulted, Lear. He'll be taken back to the wall and hanged. And – as you are interested in my views – I think he should be.

LEAR. O I know what you think! Whatever's trite and vulgar and hard and shallow and cruel, with no mercy or sympathy – that's what you think, and you're proud of it! You good, decent, honest, upright, lawful men who believe in order – when the last man dies, you will have killed him! I have lived with murderers and thugs, there are limits to their greed and violence, but you decent, honest men devour the earth!

SOLDIERS P *and* Q *start to take the* SMALL MAN *out.*

SMALL MAN. No – stop them!

LEAR. There's nothing I can do! The government's mad. The law's mad.

SMALL MAN (*throws himself at* LEAR). Then why did yer let me come 'ere? O god, I know I'm bad sometimes and I don't deserve to – O god, please!

LEAR. There's nothing I can do!

SMALL MAN. Then I should a stayed an' be shot like a dog. I lived like a dog, what did it matter? It'd be finished now. Why've I suffered all this?

The SMALL MAN *is taken out crying. The* OFFICER, OLD COUNCILLOR, BEN *and* SOLDIERS *go with him.* LEAR *starts to push the* STRANGERS *out.*

LEAR. Send them away!

JOHN. You'll fall!

LEAR (*stumbling up and down. Flailing with his stick*). Send them away! The government's given its orders. Power has spoken. Get out! What are you doing here? What have I been telling you? There's nothing to learn here! I'm a fool! A fool! Get out!

SUSAN (*turning away*). O god.

LEAR. Send them away! Throw them out!

THOMAS. They're going. (*He talks as quietly as he can to the* STRANGERS.) Wait in the village. I'll talk to him.

LEAR. Get out! Get out! I said get rid of them!

The STRANGERS *go.* LEAR, SUSAN, THOMAS *and* JOHN *are left.*

THOMAS. They've gone.

LEAR. Get out! All of you! Leave me alone!

THOMAS. No! I must know what to tell them. We're not backing out now.

LEAR. O go away! Go! Go! Go! Who is this stupid man who keeps talking to me?

JOHN (*pulls* THOMAS). Come on.

THOMAS. Sit! I'll go if you sit!

LEAR. O go . . . Go.

LEAR *sits.* THOMAS, JOHN *and* SUSAN *go into the house.*

What can I do? I left my prison, pulled it down, broke the key, and still I'm a prisoner. I hit my head against a wall all the time. There's a wall everywhere. I'm buried alive in a wall. Does this suffering and misery last for ever? Do we work to build ruins, waste all these lives to make a desert no one could live in? There's no one to explain it to me, no one I can go to for justice. I'm old, I should know how to live by now, but I know nothing, I can do nothing, I am nothing.

The GHOST *comes in. It is thinner, shrunk, a livid white.*

GHOST. Look at my hands! They're like claws. See how thin I am.

LEAR. Yes, you. Go with the rest. Get out. It's finished. There's nothing here now, nothing. Nothing's left.

GHOST. There's too much. Send these people away. Let them learn to bear their own sufferings. No, that hurts too much. That's what you can't bear: they suffer and no one can give them justice.

LEAR. Every night my life is laid waste by a cry. I go out in the dark but I never find who's there. How do most men live? They're hungry and no one feeds them, so they call for help and

no one comes. And when their hunger's worse they scream –
and jackals and wolves come to tear them to pieces.

GHOST. Yes. That's the world you have to learn to live in. Learn
it! Let me poison the well.

LEAR. Why?

GHOST. Then no one can live here, they'll have to leave you alone.
There's a spring hidden in the wood. I'll take you there every
day to drink. Lie down. Look how tired you are. Lie down.

> LEAR *lies down.*

Cordelia will come tomorrow and you can tell her you know
how to keep silent at last.

> *It's dark.* LEAR *sleeps on the bench.* JOHN *comes out of the
> house with a bundle. He crosses the stage.* SUSAN *comes to the
> door. He sees her and stops.*

SUSAN. Why are you taking your things?

JOHN. Come with me.

SUSAN. No.

JOHN. I love you. Your husband doesn't any more. He's full of
Lear.

SUSAN (*angrily*). He does love me!

JOHN. I see. (*Slight pause.*) I was used to saying nothing, but you
came out so I told you. How beautiful you are. There's nothing
to say, you know all about me. I'll wait in the village. If you
don't come I'll marry the girl down there. But I'll wait a few
days, or I'll always be sorry.

> JOHN *goes.* SUSAN *sits on the steps and starts to cry, quietly and
> methodically.* THOMAS *comes in the doorway behind her.*

THOMAS. Stop crying.

SUSAN. Take me away.

THOMAS. I can't leave him now. It'd be cruel.

SUSAN (*still crying*). I know he's mad. You shouldn't keep me
here when I'm like this.

THOMAS (*calmly and quietly*). There's been enough tears for one day. Stop crying and come inside.

> THOMAS *goes back into the house.* SUSAN *stops crying and follows him in.*

SCENE THREE

Woods.

LEAR *is alone. He wears outdoor clothes. He gropes on his hands and knees. Off, the pigs start to squeal angrily.* LEAR *stands. The* GHOST *comes in. Its flesh has dried up, its hair is matted, its face is like a seashell, the eyes are full of terror.*

GHOST. I frighten the pigs. They run when they see me.

LEAR. I was collecting acorns for them. (*He stands.*)

GHOST. The soldiers are moving into the village. They're sealing you off. Will you send the people away?

LEAR. No.

GHOST. I thought you'd forget all this: crowds, wars, arguments. . . . We could have been happy living here. I used to be happy. I'd have led you about and watched you grow old, your beautiful old age . . .

LEAR. We buried your body here. And Warrington's. It's beautiful under the trees. I thought I might think of something to tell Cordelia out here. I don't know . . . They're coming to bury me and I'm still asking how to live. Can you hear the wind?

GHOST. No. My mind goes. You hear very well when you're blind.

LEAR. Yes.

GHOST. Can you hear an owl on the hill?

LEAR. Yes.

GHOST. But not the fox.

LEAR. No.

GHOST. No. (*He starts to cry.*)

LEAR (*listens to him crying*). Why?

GHOST. Because I'm dead. I knew how to live. You'll never know.
It was so easy, I had everything I wanted here. I was afraid
sometimes, like sheep are, but it never haunted me, it would
go . . . Now I'm dead I'm afraid of death. I'm wasting away,
my mind doesn't work . . . I go away somewhere and suddenly
I find myself standing by the house or out in the fields . . . It
happens more now . . .

   CORDELIA *and the* CARPENTER *come in.*

CORDELIA. Lear. (*She holds* LEAR'*s hand for a moment.*) I've
brought my husband.

LEAR. You've been to the house? Did it upset you?

CORDELIA. No. I wanted to see it.

LEAR. Are you well?

CORDELIA. Yes. And you? D'you need anything?

LEAR. No.

CORDELIA. I came because the cabinet wants you to be tried.
There could only be one sentence. Your daughters were killed.
And it's clear there's no real difference between you and them.

LEAR. None.

CORDELIA. You were here when they killed my husband. I
watched them kill him. I covered my face with my hands, but
my fingers opened so I watched. I watched them rape me, and
John kill them, and my child miscarry. I didn't miss anything.
I watched and I said we won't be at the mercy of brutes anymore, we'll live a new life and help one another. The government's creating that new life – you must stop speaking against
us.

LEAR. Stop people listening.

CORDELIA. I can't. You say what they want to hear.

LEAR. If that's true – if only some of them want to hear – I must
speak.

CORDELIA. Yes, you sound like the voice of my conscience. But if
you listened to everything your conscience told you you'd go

mad. You'd never get anything done – and there's a lot to do, some of it very hard.

GHOST. Tell her I'm here. Make her talk about me.

LEAR. Don't build the wall.

CORDELIA. We must.

LEAR. Then nothing's changed! A revolution must at least reform!

CORDELIA. Everything *else* is changed!

LEAR. Not if you keep the wall! Pull it down!

CORDELIA. We'd be attacked by our enemies!

LEAR. The wall will destroy you. It's already doing it. How can I make you see?

GHOST. Tell her I'm here. Tell her.

CARPENTER. We came to talk to you, not listen. My wife wants to tell you something.

LEAR. She came like the rest! And she'll listen like the rest! I didn't go out of my way to make trouble. But I will not be quiet when people come here. And if you stop them – that would be easy! – they'll know I'm here or was here *once*! I've suffered so much, I made all the mistakes in the world and I pay for each of them. I cannot be forgotten. I am in their minds. To kill me you must kill them all. Yes, that's who I am. Listen, Cordelia. You have two enemies, lies *and* the truth. You sacrifice truth to destroy lies, and you sacrifice life to destroy death. It isn't sane. You squeeze a stone till your hand bleeds and call that a miracle. I'm old, but I'm as weak and clumsy as a child, too heavy for my legs. But I've learned this, and you must learn it or you'll die. Listen, Cordelia. If a god had made the world, might would always be right, that would be so wise, we'd be spared so much suffering. But we made the world – out of our smallness and weakness. Our lives are awkward and fragile and we have only one thing to keep us sane: pity, and the man without pity is mad.

The GHOST *starts to cry as* CORDELIA *speaks.*

CORDELIA. You only understand self-pity. We must go back, the government's waiting. There are things you haven't been told. We have other opponents, more ruthless than you. In this situation a good government acts strongly. I knew you wouldn't co-operate, but I wanted to come and tell you this before we put you on trial: we'll make the society you only dream of.

LEAR. It's strange that you should have me killed, Cordelia, but it's obvious you would. How simple! Your law always does more harm than crime, and your morality is a form of violence.

CORDELIA (to CARPENTER). The sooner it's finished now the better. Call a cabinet for the morning.

CORDELIA and the CARPENTER go out.

GHOST. Why didn't you tell her I was here? She wanted to talk about me. She couldn't forget me. I made love to her in that house night after night, and on this grass. Look at me now! I've turned into this – I can't even touch her!

LEAR. Where are you going?

GHOST. I can watch her go.

The GHOST goes out. THOMAS and SUSAN come on. They have dressed up a little because of the visitors.

THOMAS. We waited till they went. Shall I take you back?

LEAR. Listen, I must talk to you. I'm going on a journey and Susan will lead me.

THOMAS. Yes, go into hiding! Don't let them get their filthy hands on you.

LEAR. Tomorrow morning we'll get up and have breakfast together and you'll go to work, but Susan will stay with me. She may not be back tomorrow evening, but she'll be back soon, I promise you. You're fond of me and I've been happy with you. I'm lucky. Now I have only one more wish – to live till I'm much older and become as cunning as the fox, who knows how to live. Then I could teach you.

Off, distant squealing of angry pigs, further off than at the end of Act One, Scene Seven.

THOMAS. The pigs!
SUSAN. What is it?

　　SUSAN *and* THOMAS *run off.* LEAR *stands by himself.*

THOMAS (*off*). They've gone mad!
SUSAN (*off*). Quick!
THOMAS (*off*). That way!
SUSAN (*off*). Look out!
THOMAS (*off*). Berserk! Wup-wup-wup-wup-wup-wup-wup!
SUSAN (*off*). Wup-wup-wup! Mad!

　　The GHOST *stumbles in. It is covered with blood. The pig squeals slowly die out. A few more isolated calls of 'wup'.*

GHOST. The pigs! I'm torn! They gored me! Help me, help me! I'll die!
LEAR (*holds him*). I can't!
GHOST. Lear! Hold me!
LEAR. No, too late! It's far too late! You were killed long ago! You must die! I love you, I'll always remember you, but I can't help you. Die, for your own sake die!
GHOST. O Lear, I am dead!

　　The GHOST'S *head falls back. It is dead. It drops at* LEAR'S *feet. The calls and pig squeals stop.*

LEAR. I see my life, a black tree by a pool. The branches are covered with tears. The tears are shining with light. The wind blows the tears in the sky. And my tears fall down on me.

SCENE FOUR

The wall.
A steep earth bank. A stack of tools at the bottom of the bank. Clear daylight. SUSAN *leads* LEAR *on. He has no stick.*

SUSAN. This is the wall.
LEAR. Where are the tools?
SUSAN. On the ground in front of you.
LEAR. You were angry with me.
SUSAN. I was, but I'm not now.
LEAR (*kisses her*). Goodbye. Go back alone.
SUSAN. I can't! Who'll look after you. My husband would be angry.
LEAR. No. He'll understand now.

> SUSAN *goes out.* LEAR *goes to the tools. He finds a shovel.*

A shovel. (*He climbs the wall.*) It's built to last. So steep, and my breath's short. (*He reaches the top.*) The wind's cold, I must be quick. (*He digs the shovel in.*) Work soon warms you up.

> *He throws a shovel of earth down the side and digs the shovel in again. A* BOY *comes on and stares at* LEAR. LEAR *throws another shovel of earth down. The* BOY *goes out in the direction he came.*

This will be three. (*He digs the shovel in again.*) The tool's got no edge. No one cares for it.

> *A group of* WORKERS *come on and stare at* LEAR. *He leaves the shovel stuck in the earth. He takes off his coat and folds it neatly. A junior officer comes in. It is the* FARMER'S SON. *He watches.* LEAR *lays his folded coat on the ground and turns back to the shovel.*

FARMER'S SON. Oi, I know yoo, boy. What yoo up to now?

The FARMER'S SON *aims his pistol.*

LEAR (*spits on his hands and grips the shovel*). I'm not as fit as I was. I can still make my mark.

LEAR *digs the shovel into the earth. The* FARMER'S SON *fires.* LEAR *is killed instantly. He falls down the wall. The shovel stays upright in the earth. Some of the* WORKERS *move toward the body with curiosity.*

FARMER'S SON. Leave that. They'll picken up. Off now.

The WORKERS *go quickly and orderly. One of them looks back. The* FARMER'S SON *shepherds them off, and marches off after them.* LEAR's *body is left alone on stage.*

END

The Sea

A Comedy

The Sea was presented by the Royal Court Theatre and Michael Codron on 22 May 1973 with the following cast:

WILLY CARSON	Simon Rouse
EVENS	Alan Webb
HATCH	Ian Holm
HOLLARCUT	Mark McManus
VICAR	Jeremy Wilkin
CARTER	Anthony Langdon
THOMPSON	Simon Cord
LOUISE RAFI	Coral Browne
ROSE JONES	Diana Quick
JESSICA TILEHOUSE	Gillian Martell
MAFANWY PRICE	Susan Williamson
JILLY	Adrienne Byrne
RACHEL	Barbara Ogilvie
DAVIS	Margaret Lawley

Ladies and men.

Directed by William Gaskill
Designed by Deirdre Clancy

ONE	Beach
TWO	Shop
THREE	Beach
FOUR	House
FIVE	Shop
SIX	Beach
SEVEN	Cliff
EIGHT	Beach

There is an interval after Scene Five.

East Coast, 1907

SCENE ONE

Beach.

Empty stage. Darkness and thunder. Wind roars, whines, crashes and screams over the water. Masses of water swell up, rattle and churn, and crash back into the sea. Gravel and sand grind slowly. The earth trembles.

WILLY. Help. Aaahhh – (*The sound is drowned by water.*) Help. Colin. Shout. Oh, god, make him shout.

The tempest grows louder.

WILLY. Help – (*The sound is drowned by water again.*)

A drunken man comes on singing.

EVENS. I don't know why – I sing'ss song – 'Ss day'ss short – an' ss—
WILLY. Help. Help.
EVENS. Wha'?
WILLY. Here. In the water. A man's in the water.

Thunder.

EVENS. 'Ss too late f'ss thass. 'Ss sea 'sl finish all'ss thass. Have'ss drink. Lil'ss drink. Here'ss, take'ss bottle . . .
WILLY. Help me. Our boat turned over. I can't find him.
EVENS. I sing 'ss song – 'Ss day'ss short – an'ss —
WILLY. You bastard. Colin. Colin.
EVENS. Wah'? I don' know why'ss – 'Ssing'ss song – 'Ss some'ss in'ss wasser?

The storm is worse. Thunder. The wind screams. HATCH, *a middle-aged man, comes on with a torch.*

HATCH. What are you up to?

EVENS. Oh god, 'ss draper. Have'ss drink, ol' pal. Tha'ss bottle —
HATCH. Filthy beast.
EVENS. I'm off. (*Going*) Wha'ss night! Dear o' lor'.
HATCH. I know what's going on here.
WILLY. Help. Help.
HATCH. I know who you are. You thought you wouldn't be seen
    out here.
WILLY. Colin. For god's sake shout.

EVENS *goes out singing.*

EVENS. (*Going*) I ssing'ss my song – 'ss day'ss short –
WILLY. Oh god.

WILLY *comes out of the water. He is soaked. His hair and clothes
are plastered down. He stands on the edge of the sea crying and
pleading.* HATCH *catches him in his torch.* WILLY *is heard shouting
above the storm.*

WILLY. Help us.
HATCH. Go back.
WILLY. Are you all mad? Where am I?
HATCH. I knew you were coming. We'll fight you, you filthy
    beast.

WILLY *turns and goes back into the sea.*

WILLY. Colin. Colin.

Heavy guns fire some way off.

HATCH. The guns! They've brought the guns up! Hurrah!
WILLY. What?
HATCH. Hurrah the guns! The army knows you're here. The
    whole country's turning out. We'll smash you.

HATCH *goes out with his torch. The storm grows.*

WILLY. Colin. Don't die. Not like this. Shout.

WILLY *runs through the water.*

SCENE TWO

Draper's Shop.

Counter. Shelves with rolls of material and piles of clothes. Two wicker chairs for customers. On the counter various haberdasheries, a wooden till, and a display dummy cut off at the waist and neck.

MRS RAFI (ageing) and her companion MRS TILEHOUSE (forties, retiring but determined) are in the shop. HATCH, the draper, is serving them. He is fortyish, with oiled hair and a rather flat face. Very pale blue eyes.

HATCH. Art serge is coming in now, Mrs Rafi. Very fashionable for winter curtains.

MRS RAFI ignores him and goes on examining a specimen on the counter.

MRS RAFI. Does this wear?

HATCH. Embosseds don't wear as well as Utrechts, of course.

MRS RAFI. Show me this in blue.

HATCH. We don't carry any blues, I'm afraid. I can show you a faded pink or the club green.

MRS RAFI (*to him as she looks through a bulky catalogue*). Blue, blue.

HATCH. Have you seen the moquettes? (*He tries to show her a place in the catalogue.*)

MRS RAFI. Don't jolly me along. I wouldn't be comfortable with an artificial material. I want velvet.

HATCH. Velvet does hang best. It gives the wear and it keeps its lustre.

MRS RAFI. At that price it should.

HATCH (*to* MRS TILEHOUSE). Have you seen our Indian Dhurries, Mrs Tilehouse? New in this week. You'll appreciate the superb colourings. You can carry them off.

MRS RAFI. I'm not interested in this new-fangled craze to support the trading efforts of the Empire by getting the east coast into native dress. I came to choose curtains, and I want Utrecht velvet – which I suppose comes from Birmingham. Your catalogue is full of interesting items but none of them are in your shop. You offer only shoddy! How can you attract a discriminating and rewarding class of client? Look, your catalogue lists blue – (*She hands him the catalogue.*) – at the bottom of page one three two one in the right hand column.

HATCH (*holding catalogue*). All you see here is available against special order, Mrs Rafi. Blue isn't asked for. (*To MRS TILEHURST.*) There isn't the demand for it. Not at the price, Mrs Tilehouse.

MRS TILEHOUSE (*nods sympathetically*). There wouldn't be.

MRS RAFI. I suppose it would be wholly optimistic of me to ask to see an example?

Silently HATCH *takes a blue sample from a drawer and hands it to her. She studies it.*

MRS RAFI. I take it delivery is appalling.

HATCH. The suppliers quote two weeks to the nearest railway station. Very reasonable, I think.

MRS RAFI. If you could rely on it.

MRS TILEHOUSE. My new work-basket came within the week.

MRS RAFI (*looking in the catalogue*). Nottingham lace, Guipure d'Art, Turkish carpets, Japanese Nainsooks: I suppose they all come in two weeks from the warehouse in Birmingham. The art has gone out of shopping. (*She sighs. She picks up the sample.*) Is this accurate?

HATCH. I believe so.

MRS RAFI. Most samples are sent out to deliberately deceive customers. I have no doubt about it, you could add it to the Articles of Religion. Well, it's a handsome material. I'll say that. It will look well at Park House. I want a hundred and sixty-two yards in three-yard lengths. I'll have it made up at

Forebeach. I can supervise the work there. (*She puts the sample in her bag.*) I'll take this piece of evidence.

MRS TILEHOUSE. Louise, would it be better to have one room made up first? So that you get the sight of it.

MRS RAFI. Why? The downstairs curtains are shabby, even you remarked on it. This material is suitable. I've already enlarged my impression of this small piece into the entire scene – and I can tell you it looks very well.

HATCH. I'll send a copy of the order up to Park House. (*A bit too firmly.*) Then you'll have your own reminder.

MRS RAFI. I'm obliged. Now gloves. What have you to offer me in that line?

HATCH. Only what you saw last week, Mrs Rafi.

MRS RAFI. Nothing new? But you undertook to obtain further examples for me to see.

HATCH. Not in yet.

MRS RAFI. I suppose on gloves they quote immediate delivery. Well, you'd better show me the ones I saw last week. I must have gloves and if that's all you offer I shall have to make do with them – until I can drive into Forebeach and select from a more convenient range.

HATCH *produces two boxes of gloves.*

MRS TILEHOUSE. I liked these on you, Louise. They go with anything.

MRS RAFI. Jessie, please don't try to hustle me into a purchase. You know it makes me cross. One uses one's hands to point and emphasize and gesture. People are judged by what they have on their hands. They're important.

HATCH. Gazelle. Five shillings and five and eleven. Buck. Close grained, hard wearing. Doe. Feel the softness, Mrs Rafi. Washable kid. Two and six. Natural beaver. These have white tips, which many ladies prefer for the few pence extra. Then we have the military style – that's coming in now. At three shillings.

MRS RAFI (*trying on a pair of gloves*). It says six and three-quarters in the cuff. Why can't I get into them?

HATCH. Perhaps if you tried a slender man's —

MRS RAFI. I've always worn a lady's habit. Seven at the most. And these come from Birmingham. Isn't that a centre of precision engineering? One should at least be entitled to expect them to manufacture gloves to size. (*She tries another pair.*) Six and three-quarters again and a completely different fit. (*She gets a glove on with difficulty.*) They support the hand comfortably, but will they stand wearing? (*She thumps her hand on the counter.*) No. Gone at the seams. There you are, they give under the slightest emphasis. (*Takes the glove off.*) I'm an emphatic woman and I must have gloves that accommodate themselves to my character. I'm not having those. Thank heavens I found out in time. (*She picks up another pair.*) Now these have style. I could wear this cuff. Tap on the window.

MRS TILEHOUSE. What?

MRS RAFI. Quickly.

MRS TILEHOUSE *taps on the window.*

MRS RAFI. Louder.

MRS TILEHOUSE *taps louder.* MRS RAFI *waves broadly but genteelly and calls by opening her mouth wide and whispering.*

MRS RAFI. A moment.

The doorbell clangs. WILLY *comes in.*

MRS RAFI. It is Mr Carson? I'm Mrs Rafi. Howdyoudo.

WILLY. Howdyoudo.

MRS RAFI. This is a terrible tragedy. Colin was engaged to my niece. My companion, Mrs Jessica Tilehouse.

WILLY. Howdyoudo.

MRS TILEHOUSE. Howdyoudo. Oh terrible. I knew Colin well.

So courteous. He always had a kind word, even for those in
the background.

MRS RAFI. The coroner's wife called to tell me the details after
breakfast. You must feel low. You can imagine the state my
poor niece is in.

WILLY. I've just been at your house. I tried to see her but they
told me to come back later.

MRS RAFI. Please treat my house as your home. I was devoted to
Colin.

MRS TILEHOUSE. *He* was one for whom the future seemed all
brightness. Oh dear.

MRS RAFI. Are you staying long?

WILLY. Till the inquest.

MRS TILEHOUSE. Oh dear.

MRS RAFI. You must tell me exactly what happened. I was going
to complain to the Chief-of-Staff about the battery opening
fire. But the coroner's wife tells me you'd strayed into their
target area. How can that be? It's marked on the charts.
Who was the navigator?

WILLY. Oh. We both looked after that. It was a small boat. The
storm swept us off course. The guns didn't sink us. We'd
already turned over.

MRS TILEHOUSE. Such a night. Thank heavens I didn't know
you were out in it. I would have had no sleep. I assure you.
I would have been tormented by the vision of – (*She stops in
sudden realization and deep embarrassment. She almost panics.*)
Not that my sufferings would have mattered. Of course.
Compared to you. I would gladly, gladly have watched the
whole night through if —

MRS RAFI (*drops a pair of gloves on the counter*). I shan't take
these after all, Hatch. My umbrella handle lodges itself in
the cuff. Send these others back to the manufacturers. Tell
them they are not up to the standard one should be entitled
to expect. Mr Carson, perhaps you'll drive back to Park
House for luncheon. My pony and trap is outside.

WILLY. Will they find the body?

MRS TILEHOUSE. Oh dear. This terrible sea, this terrible life.

MRS RAFI. Everything is washed up. Our coast is known for it. You throw a handkerchief into the sea one day and pick it up the next. See Mr Evens. He's peculiar, but he knows the water round here. He'll tell you where anything will come out, and when. Jessie, you must walk. Pony can't manage three.

WILLY. I'll walk.

MRS RAFI. Come along.

MRS RAFI and WILLY go out. The doorbell clangs.

MRS TILEHOUSE. Mr Hatch, who was on coastguard duty last night?

HATCH. Why?

MRS TILEHOUSE. Surely it will come out at the inquest? Why was nothing seen by the town lookout?

HATCH. You'd need second sight to see anything last night. (*He is putting the gloves away.*) I was on duty.

MRS TILEHOUSE. Dear me, and the town pays you ten shillings a year to watch —

HATCH. I watch, Mrs Tilehouse. More than the town's ten shillings is worth.

The doorbell clangs. HOLLARCUT comes in. He is a quiet, blond young man.

HOLLARCUT. Oh.

HATCH. Morning, Billy. Wait out the back, lad.

HOLLARCUT starts to go through behind the counter.

MRS TILEHOUSE. Morning, Hollarcut. Were you on duty last night?

HOLLARCUT. No, Mrs Tilehouse.

MRS TILEHOUSE. Not? But surely on such a night? I thought all the coastguards would have gone to their posts.

HATCH. That's not in my copy of the Regulations, Mrs Tilehouse.

HOLLARCUT. An' I can't read mine.

HOLLARCUT *goes out behind the counter.*

HATCH. This material, Mrs Tilehouse. A hundred and sixty-two yards. Will she change her mind? Last time she ordered cushions she wouldn't even look at them. Now I have to send cash with every order, and they'll only take back against bona fide complaints. I've had a letter from the suppliers. It's signed by the managing director.

MRS TILEHOUSE. You're in business, Mr Hatch. You have to do what the customer wants.

HATCH (*goes to door*). Very good, Mrs Tilehouse. Good day.

MRS TILEHOUSE. I think I'll look at those Indian Dhurries.

HATCH. We're closed for lunch. Allow me. (*He opens the door for her.*) Good day, m'am. Much obliged.

MRS TILEHOUSE *goes out.* HATCH *locks the door behind her. He stands looking through the window.*

HATCH. Bit longer, lads. The old buzzard's still there . . . (*Turns back into the shop, smacking his hands together.*) She's gone.

HOLLARCUT, THOMPSON *and* CARTER *come out of the back of the shop.* THOMPSON *is a thinnish man with dark hair. Early middle age.* CARTER *is heavier and older.*

THOMPSON. My life. I was sweatin' back there. I was certain-shar Mrs Rafi'd come through. Juss the sort a notion she'd git took in her hid. She give me the sack doo she find me here.

HATCH. Did you follow him?

HOLLARCUT. I bin on his tail all mornin'. Then I seen him come here an goo off with that ol' bat. Tent no use followin' him now. She see you comin' afore yoo started.

HATCH. What did he do?

HOLLARCUT. Nothin' t' remark on.

HATCH. Clever.

THOMPSON. What yoo make on him then, Mr Hatch?

HATCH. Look at the facts. He lands in the middle of the storm
    when no one's going to see him. He arranges to meet that
    devil Evens out on the beach.

HOLLARCUT. Right.

HATCH. And Mr Bentham's dead. They've started with murder
    and they'll do worse.

THOMPSON. Oh lor'.

HATCH. That boat didn't go down by accident.

HOLLARCUT. You may depend on it.

CARTER. We must take this to the magistrates, lads. It's too big
    for us.

HATCH. They wouldn't believe us, Mr Carter. You coastguards
    don't believe me half the time, in spite of all my warnings.

THOMPSON. Thass a rum ol' do.

CARTER. You hear tell a such queer ol' gooins on. Tell the truth,
    I on't know what I doo believe n'more . . .

HOLLARCUT (to HATCH). They do believe sometime. (To
    THOMPSON.) Don't yoo, Wad?

THOMPSON. Oh I believe sometime right enough. Oh ah.

HATCH. They come from space. Beyond our world. Their world's
    threatened by disaster. If they think we're a crowd of weak
    fools they'll all come here. By the million. They'll take our
    jobs and our homes. Everything. We'll be slaves working all
    our lives to make goods for sale on other planets.

THOMPSON. An' the women folk? They after that?

HATCH. No. They come from a higher stage of progress. Their
    intellects run more on science and meditation. They build
    formal gardens for a hobby.

THOMPSON. Chriss.

HATCH. Listen, where's the world's weak spot? Here. (HOLLAR-
    CUT and THOMPSON grunt assent.) They know there's no
    leadership, no authority, no discipline in this town. So it's up
    to us. All these ships in distress are really secret landings

from space. We won't go out to help them, we'll go and drive
them off. Run them down.

CARTER. What if they're sailors in distress?

HATCH. They aren't sailors, they aren't even real storms. These
people come millions of miles – they know how to whip up
a storm when they get here. We might lose a few innocent
men. (*Shrugs.*) That's a risk, but *they're* guilty, not us. Now
go and wait outside Park House, Billy. Follow him when he
leaves.

HOLLARCUT. Right.

HATCH. They'll have arranged times to hover overhead invisibly.
You watch and you'll see him make signs in a prearranged
code. It could be anything: a scratch, a wave, or he'll pretend
to tie his shoe. Keep it all in your head. I'll go through it
with you later.

HOLLARCUT, THOMPSON *and* CARTER *go out. The doorbell
clangs.* HATCH *bolts the door behind them. He goes to the till, takes
out the money and puts it into a little canvas bank-bag. He looks up
into the air and makes a small ritualised gesture of defiance. He
speaks in an almost business-like voice.*

HATCH. St George for England.

SCENE THREE

Beach.
*An old hut with an old bike leaning against it. An empty shopping
bag hangs from the handle bars. A few washed up wooden spars and
boxes smoothed by water.*

Bright, sunny, fresh. A wind from the sea. WILLY *is just coming on.
His jacket collar is turned up and his hands are in his pockets. He
looks round, goes to the hut and taps on the door. No answer. It is
padlocked. He tries the padlock.* EVENS *comes on behind him and
watches. He is old, weathered and bearded.*

EVENS. It's locked.

WILLY. Oh. Hello. I'm a friend of Mrs Rafi.

EVENS. Yes.

WILLY. I was on the boat that turned over last night.

EVENS. A boat?

WILLY. Yes.

EVENS. Last night?

WILLY. Yes.

EVENS. It was rough.

WILLY. My friend drowned

EVENS. Oh. You want to know where he'll come up.

WILLY. Well yes.

EVENS (*shrugs wearily*). Depends where he went down.

EVENS *goes into the hut.* WILLY *stands silently. When* EVENS *comes out again he is surprised to see* WILLY *still there.*

EVENS. Oh. I'll think about it. (*He is turning to go back into the hut.*) I'm sorry about the accident.

WILLY. You live here?

EVENS. Yes.

WILLY. It must be nice.

EVENS. . . . Sometimes. It gets cold. The wind.

WILLY *sits down on a box and starts to cry into his hands.* EVENS *looks at him for a moment and then goes slowly into the hut.* WILLY *cries a bit longer before he speaks.*

WILLY (*trying to stop*). So stupid – doing this – coming here and . . .

EVENS (*inside the hut*). Is there a proper place?

WILLY (*trying to stop*). . . . last night . . .

HATCH *comes on.* HOLLARCUT *follows a little way behind and stands watching.*

HATCH. It didn't take you long to get out here. You've got to get rid of the body before anyone sees the marks. Wait till it comes in and tow it out to sea or bury it in the sand. I'm watching you —

EVENS *comes out of the hut.*

HATCH. – yes, and you, Evens. You're both under surveillance. (*Yells back to* HOLLARCUT.) Did you see him cry, Billy?

HOLLARCUT. Ay.

HATCH. That was a sign. Crying: bad news. That's us. Those devils are up there watching. He's telling them we're onto him.

WILLY (*trying to stop crying*). What's the matter with him?

EVENS. He's harmless.

HATCH. Oh, we know how to handle you, Evens. This isn't your sort of sea. This is real sea where you drown. It's not governed by your fancy, twisted laws of gravity. You'll find out. (*Yells back to* HOLLARCUT.) They're afraid of our sea, Billy. They're not immune to wetness. It soaks in and melts their insides. You watch: they're terrorized of it.

HOLLARCUT. They en't worth a sermon, Mr Hatch. Give the word an' I'll kick their bloody hids off.

HATCH. Not yet. We'll make a study of them first. Learn their ways. Break their code. You keep the watching going. Goodbye, Mr Evens. We'll settle our account shortly.

HATCH *and* HOLLARCUT *go out.*

EVENS (*normally*). It's nice now. I hope the weather lasts.

WILLY. Do they often come here?

EVENS. No. They're as timid as mice. You coming, the storm, the boat – they're excited.

WILLY. Aren't they dangerous?

EVENS (*shrugs*). Yes, to themselves.

WILLY. Why d'you live here?

EVENS. Isn't it what everyone wants?

WILLY. No.

EVENS. Perhaps not. We're into the spring tides now. He'll be

washed up where the coast turns in. (*Points.*) You see?
People are cruel and boring and obsessed. If he goes past that
point you've lost him. He should come in. He's hanging
round out there now. He could see us if he wasn't dead.
My wife died in hospital. She had something quite
minor. I sold up. They hate each other. Force. Make. Use.
Push. Burn. Sell. For what? A heap of rubbish. Don't
believe what they say: I don't understand the water. I
know the main currents, but luck and chance come into it.
It doesn't matter how clear the main currents are, you have to
live through the details. It's always the details that make the
tragedy. Not anything larger. They used to say tragedy
purified, helped you to let go. Now it only embarrasses.
They'll make a law against it. He should come out in the
middle of next week. Don't count on it. There might be a
flood. Then everything goes by the board. A man was drowned
at sea and the next day a flood washed him miles inland and
left him in his own garden hanging up in the apple tree. All
the apples were washed off and went bobbing away in the
water. His wife and children were stranded up on the roof
watching him. They sat there three days.

HOLLARCUT *throws a lump of driftwood against the side of the
house.*

HOLLARCUT (*off*). Let yoo know I'm still watchin'.
WILLY. Couldn't you have him certified?
EVENS. The town doctor's madder than he is.

EVENS *takes out a half-bottle of whisky. He removes the cap and
holds the bottle out towards* HOLLARCUT.

EVENS. Drink?
HOLLARCUT (*off*). Is it poisoned?
EVENS. Yes.
HOLLARCUT. No ta then.

EVENS *drinks from the bottle. He holds it towards* WILLY.

EVENS (*looks round*). I don't have a cup.

WILLY. No thanks.

EVENS (*calls to* HOLLARCUT). Come and sit by the house, lad. Out of the wind.

HOLLARCUT *comes and sits down by the house.*

HOLLARCUT. Juss so's I see yoo better.

EVENS. What's old Hatch been telling you?

HOLLARCUT. Thass right, he say yood start in with yoor questions. On't took you long, hev it!

EVENS. You know he's mad.

HOLLARCUT (*evenly*). So you say.

EVENS. You're not that stupid, lad.

HOLLARCUT. He on't normal like me, or Wad, or my ma. But how'd I know he can't fathom out things I can't? Thass a rum ol' world. Yoo hev t'be a bit daft in the hid to know what doo goo on in en. Ask me it on't pay t'be too level-hided. I know it on't pay *me*.

EVENS. It's hard work talking to you.

HOLLARCUT (*contentedly*). I never ask yoo t' start. I on't interfere. I'm quite content sittin' here listenin'. You think I'm soft in the hid. Well there on't much goo' by I miss. I'll surprise the lot on yer one day.

EVENS (*drinks*). It keeps the wind out.

EVENS *puts the whisky bottle down on a box.*

WILLY. I met you on the beach last night.

EVENS. Oh?

HOLLARCUT. Thass right, when yoo was up t'yoor tricks in the water.

WILLY. You were drunk.

EVENS. Was I? I am sometimes.

HOLLARCUT. If they put yoo through a wringer they could start a brewery.

WILLY. You had a lantern.

HOLLARCUT. Signal for yoo t' come ashore.

EVENS (*sudden irritation*). You said you wouldn't talk.

HOLLARCUT. Juss let yoo know I'm listenin'.

WILLY (*calmly*). Why were you drunk?

HOLLARCUT. Cause he drunk too much. (*Laughs.*) There, I told yoo: I hev a sharp wit when I like. I hev em in stitches in our kitchen some nights when I hev my sprits up. My ma doo laugh. She hev all the neighbours in. She goo hollerin' arter 'em down the road. That make me laugh even more. We doo enjoy ourselves. Then we hev a singsong.

EVENS. I drink to keep sane. There's no harm in the little I drink. Li Po: you who are sated with life, now drink the dregs.

HOLLARCUT. Ah, code-talk now. We're on to that.

EVENS. Who drowned?

WILLY. From this town. Colin Bentham.

EVENS. Oh.

WILLY. He was going to marry Mrs Rafi's niece.

EVENS. I knew him. He came here when he was a boy. All the time. He used to play by the hut and swim. I remember the sea last night.

> Mad woman in a grey bed
> She struggles under the sheets
> Threshing her grey hair.

WILLY. If you hadn't been drunk.

EVENS. I answered that question long ago: *if* he hadn't gone to sea.

WILLY. He wanted to get here quickly, not go round on land.

EVENS. Why?

Silence. WILLY *stands.*

HOLLARCUT. Where yoo gooin?

EVENS. Hatch told you to watch us both, didn't he. Now you're for it.

WILLY *goes out.*

HOLLARCUT. I'll stay put an' watch you. I'm settled down now.
EVENS. You'll miss something.
HOLLARCUT (*contentedly*). 'S obvious yoo want a get rid a me.
So I'll stay. I can work that out, boy.

EVENS *screws the cap onto the whisky bottle and goes towards the house.*

EVENS. Go and watch the vicar's girls swimming.
HOLLARCUT. Thass right: Mr Hatch say yoo come t' corrupt our
manhood. What yoo get up to in there?
EVENS. I shrink little men and put them into bottles. Then the
Martians stand them over the mantlepiece.

EVENS *goes into the hut and shuts the door behind him.* HOLLARCUT
settles down more comfortably against the side of the house.

HOLLARCUT (*contentedly*). I on't believe that. Thass a tall story,
I *doo* know.

SCENE FOUR

Park House.

*Drawing room. Upper middle-class furniture. Comfortable, hard-
wearing, good. Round table. Bookcase.*

MRS RAFI, MRS TILEHOUSE, MAFANWY PRICE (*thirtyish,
bun*), JILLY (*eighteen, bright cheeks and eyes*), RACHEL (*slightly
plump, and neat and capable*). *The* VICAR (*about forty-three but
looks younger. Wears a grey, summer suit*). ROSE *has just come in.
She is pale and tired. The others are staring at her in surprise.*

MRS RAFI. Go back to your room, Rose. We'll manage without
you.
ROSE. I'll stay.
MAFANWY. Poor thing.

MRS RAFI. You'll bring yourself down.
ROSE. I can see the sea through the windows.

A hushed moan from the LADIES

JILLY. How awful.
MAFANWY. In this town you can't get away from the sea.
MRS RAFI. Pull the curtains.
ROSE. O no.
MRS RAFI. The curtains. The curtains. Shut it out.

LADIES *hurry to close the curtains.*

MRS RAFI. Lights.

Some of the LADIES *change direction and hurry to fetch lights.*

MRS RAFI. Yes, stay with us. We understand. We've all known
    pain in our time. Bereavements, lost hopes. All our lives
    pass through the shadows. Jessica, hand out the books. I
    hope we've all got up our lines.
LADIES. Yes. Oh dear.
MRS RAFI. We shall see.
MRS TILEHOUSE (*to* ROSE). How brave of you to challenge your
    despair. You are right. We dare not fall back under the
    blows.
MRS RAFI. Jessica, stop trying to sound like a woman with an
    interesting past. Nothing has ever happened to you. That
    is a tragedy. But it hardly qualifies you to give advice. Hand
    out the books. Act one, scene three. Enter Orpheus.

A flurry of nervous anticipation.

I have lost my Eurydice. You all have the place? Over-
whelmed with misery I set out on the journey down the
steep rocky path to hell. On either side rise terrible bottom-
less pits blazing with smoky darkness. The rocky cavern
arches over my head. Maddened bats fly through its black-

ened vaults. I reach the river that lies before hell. Wearily I sit down on a rock and survey the dismal scene. I take out my lute and sing 'There's no place like home'.

MRS TILEHOUSE. Louise, dear. Is that the right song?

MRS RAFI. The right song? I always sing 'There's no place like home'. The town expects it of me.

MRS TILEHOUSE. Yes.

MRS RAFI. Then am I to disappoint them? I will not break the stage's unwritten law and comment on my fellow artistes' performance, but I will say, with confidence that comes from many tributes, that my performance of 'There's no place like home' will be one of the highlights of the evening.

RACHEL. We always enjoy it.

MRS TILEHOUSE. Well we'd better get on.

MRS RAFI. Get on, she says – as if we were drawing a glass of water from a tap. I do not know on what level you would find your inspiration – had you been entrusted with a part – but I cannot jump in and out of my part like a lady athlete. (*Silence. She sings.*) 'Bait havver sah hoobull hahs noo-hoo place lake hoo ... (*She cuts quickly to the end of the song.*) dum-di-dum-di – *Ya*-ho-hoo place lake hoo.' Moved by the atmosphere I have created, I cry – together with a large part of the audience, if things go as usual. The sound of my torment attracts Cerberus, the watch dog of hell. He comes swimming over the dark water towards me.

MAFANWY. Louise, couldn't I already be on your side of the river?

MRS RAFI. Would you sit quietly by while I sang? Not at all. You would want to join in the chorus.

MAFANWY. It's so difficult to pretend I'm swimming when I am in fact walking.

MRS RAFI. Act, Miss Price. Remember your audience will do most of the work for you. They have already been set up by the poetry that has gone before.

MAFANWY (*sudden temper*). I can't I can't!

MRS RAFI. Every year the same. One sympathizes with god when he struggled to breathe life into the intractable clay. Do you not wish to support the coastguard fund? Has it no meaning for you?

MAFANWY. How cruel, Louise.

MRS RAFI. Then act. Give yourself to the part and it will carry you through.

MAFANWY. Why must I be a dog? Last year I was the monkey. If we did a pantomime you'd make me be the cat. I want to be one of the floral maids-of-honour who greet Orpheus with rose petals and song when he comes out of hell.

MRS RAFI. You'll be a dog. You collect for your Save the Animals Fund every year and you never go away till we've given twice as much as we can afford. Now you have the chance to earn some more gratitude from your little friends. (*Sighs.*) I know you need all the help you can get. I have foreseen it. Therefore two auxiliary ladies will hold a sheet across the stage. It will be decorated with dolphins, starfish and other sea emblems, and the ladies will be clad in bathing attire. You swim on behind the sheet. Only your head, arms and chest will show.

The LADIES *exclaim happy approval.*

MAFANWY. Oh thank you, thank you, Louise. You have such an inspiration.

MRS RAFI. At the same time – Mrs Tilehouse will crawl along in the dark under the stage and splash water round in a basin.

MRS TILEHOUSE. I can't. There isn't room.

MRS RAFI. Then create room. Don't you aspire to be an artist? Think of the miners who spend their lives crawling through darkness so that you may have light. That also, in its way, is the task of art.

The LADIES *murmur fervent agreement,* MRS RAFI *picks up a loose cover decorated with flowers, stems and leaves.* JILLY *and* RACHEL *hold it shoulder high across the stage.* MAFANWY *swims along behind it, as if the top of her body were coming out of the waves.*

MAFANWY. I come along, spitting water out of my mouth . . .
MRS RAFI. Not the dog paddle, I think. It's too obvious. Eurydice, are you for ever lost?

Normally MAFANWY *manages an acceptable middle-class accent, but the effort to act makes the dog very Welsh.*

MAFANWY. Who calls? What terrible shouts sound through these halls of death? Is that all right?
MRS RAFI. Don't be afraid to attack your part. I start up crazily at the sound of your voice. I cry: Eurydice, is it you?
MAFANWY. I step from the water and shake myself.
MRS RAFI. Shake yourself?
MAFANWY. All dogs shake themselves when they leave the water. I've been studying our Roger very carefully for the part.

MAFANWY *shakes herself.*

JILLY. It's so real, Fanny. I can feel the water. I want to dry myself, Mrs Rafi. I want to put on my overshoes and open my umbrella.
MRS RAFI. Yes, dear. Describe your reactions later over tea. They sound so interesting and fresh.
MAFANWY. From whence this voice of terror? It is the voice of a living man. The dead are spared such sufferings. Oh mortal, do not disturb these shades of darkness.

A knock on the door.

MRS RAFI. Never more shall I be silent. Lo, I tamed the wild beasts, but I cannot tame the torments of my breast —

DAVIS, *the maid, puts her head round the door.*

What is it, Davis?

DAVIS. Begpardonmam. Mr Carson. You said to show him in anytime.

MRS RAFI (*nods to* DAVIS). Ladies, you don't mind?

DAVIS *goes.*

For a few moments they stand and fidget nervously. Then WILLY *comes in. He looks round at the darkness.*

MRS RAFI. Come in, Mr Carson. We're rehearsing a performance.

WILLY. Ah, I'm sorry. Let me come back at —

MRS RAFI. No, no. Do come in. Here is my niece. Rose.

WILLY. Miss Jones. Howdyoudo. I wish our meeting was different. I can only tell you —

MRS RAFI. Hush, hush. Not now, children.

ROSE *shakes* WILLY's *hand. Then she goes back to her place.*

MRS RAFI. Sit down, Mr Carson. Your presence might shame our ladies into some efforts at creativity. I'm about to cross the Styx by ferry. The Styx is made from the tears of the penitent and suffering, which is interesting. Do sit down. There – you'll see everything there.

MAFANWY. Do not disturb these shades of darkness. I use the special tone, Mr Carson, because I am portraying a dog.

MRS RAFI. Eurydice, let me clasp your marble bosom to my panting breast and warm it with my heart.

JILLY *starts to cry.*

JILLY. Oh dear. So sorry. It's so moving. So sad.

MRS RAFI. Let it flow, dear. Be moved. It's to be expected.

JILLY. How awful!

JILLY *runs crying from the room.*

MRS RAFI. I hope you'll all act like that on the night.

RACHEL. I'll go after her.

MRS RAFI. Leave her. Never show any interest in the passions of the young, it makes them grow up selfish. Davis will pat her and give her some tea and a slice of cake. Eurydice, oh speak. (*She embraces* MAFANWY.)

MAFANWY. Away, distracted man. I am a dog.

MRS TILEHOUSE. Shouldn't she get down on all fours?

MRS RAFI. Jessica, I am directing this production. Your job is to sell programmes and assist the stage carpenter. Eurydice, oh speak.

MAFANWY. Alas, you have awakened old Pluto, the god of this place. Now I shall be well thrashed.

Slight pause.

MRS RAFI (*loudly*). Pluto comes. (*Nothing happens. Louder.*) The god of hell. (*Calls.*) Vicar.

VICAR. Oh, dear, I thought I was being summoned by Gabriel. Pardon me, fellow Thespians. I was admiring your bibliographic splendours, Mrs Rafi. A true delight.

MRS RAFI. Never mind books now, Vicar. We're struggling with life.

VICAR. Quite so. I await direction.

MRS RAFI. You come on on the far side of Styx.

VICAR. Like so? Good. Now where are these excellent lines? What is this dreadful wailing? By-the-by, Mrs Rafi. In the interest of light relief might I at this juncture add a reference – a sly reference, ladies – to a certain church choir of my acquaintance?

MRS RAFI. No.

VICAR. I feared not. I do lend myself to these ribald interjections, Mrs Rafi. However. Bad dog, come to your master.

MRS RAFI. Try: bad dog, come to your master.

VICAR. Dear me, if I were Cerberus I would run straight back to hell. However. Down, sir.

MRS RAFI. On your knees, dog.

VICAR. Ah yes. On your knees, dog. Oh excellent, Miss Price. Our Ajax lies just so before the hearth when he comes home from his walk on winter evenings.

MAFANWY. Thank you, Vicar. I've been noting the mannerisms of our Roger in a little book.

MRS RAFI. Ah! Eurydice.

VICAR. The excellent Roger. Yes. I'm sorry to tell you, Miss Price, that Roger has been chasing Ajax. I should explain, ladies, that I've always wanted an Ajax and I had bestowed that name on my dog before I noticed that she was of an altogether inappropriate gender. However, Roger noticed. Yes. I wonder, Miss Price, if I might ask you to —

MRS RAFI. Vicar.

VICAR. Indeed the subject is somewhat delicate. (*To* MAFANWY.) A few whispered words after choir practice will suffice.

MRS RAFI. Ah! Eurydice.

VICAR. Who calls my wife.

MRS RAFI. Ah horror.

VICAR. Yes, she is mine. Oh man, in this cold place of hell I lost my heart to her.

MRS RAFI. Ah horror. Ah horror.

MRS TILEHOUSE. That's only written down once. I hope I shan't be told I can't read – or count.

MRS RAFI. You can say what you like as long as you can carry it off. Ah horror. Ah horror. You shall not come out of hell to fetch that which is not thine or all women shall live in fear of Pluto's lust.

VICAR. He sounds like Roger. I cannot let her go.

MRS RAFI. Then defiance and resistance are my lot.

VICAR. Rise, my sleeping furies. Mrs Rafi, might I here make reference to a certain local congregation toward the end of sermon time?

MRS RAFI. No, Vicar.

VICAR. Furies, up!

LADIES *surround the* VICAR *gesturing and grimacing.*

VICAR. Be warned, oh vain and foolish man. That way lies madness and despair. Oh man, a god pleads with you. You may not put your hand into the iron sea to pluck out the glittering thing. Behold, my ferryman. Think well before you step into my ferryboat.

RACHEL *picks up a punting pole and a straw boater.* LADIES *lay the loose cover flat on the floor.*

RACHEL. I'm sure Mr Carson will think I row like a chump. Here goes.

RACHEL *steps onto the cover. She speaks her part very timidly and can't remember the lines.* MRS TILEHOUSE *whispers prompts to her all the time she speaks.*

RACHEL. I am . . . the ferryman of hell. I . . . come to . . . take you over the black . . . water.

MRS RAFI *is about to step into the boat. She stops and peers down into the water.*

MRS RAFI. I see a white thing shining down in the darkness.

RACHEL. That is the . . . reflection . . . of . . . Narcissus. It is condemned to haunt these . . . waters for ever —

MRS RAFI. Ah horror. *Ah horror.*

RACHEL. – and . . . stare . . . up at the tormented and harrowed . . . faces of those who . . . pass to death. Look, and turn . . . back.

MRS RAFI. I cannot.

MRS RAFI *steps onto the cover.* RACHEL *starts to punt rhythmically.*
MRS RAFI *poses on an imaginary prow and stares at the distant far shore of Styx. The rest of the cast softly hum the* 'Eton Boating

Song'. ROSE *slowly comes into the space on the shore and stands by Pluto.*

MRS RAFI (*ecstatic*). Eurydice. Beloved. I see you.

ROSE. I am queen of this dark place. My heart burns with a new cold fire. Your love, your fear, your hope – what are they to me now? Dust scattered over the sea.

MRS RAFI (*stretching both arms towards Eurydice*). Eurydice I cannot hear you. The wind blows your words over this cold river, I only see you calling me.

ROSE. Go back.

MRS RAFI (*ecstatic*). Beloved, I come.

ROSE. Go back.

MRS RAFI. Yes, I come.

The rumble of very distant guns. The people in the room are silent for a moment. Then they make a low moan of annoyance and regret.

MRS TILEHOUSE. The battery.

RACHEL. Such a sad sound.

MRS RAFI. They practice all day and night! Someone should write to the War Office.

MAFANWY. They have their job.

MRS TILEHOUSE. I gladly embrace the inconvenience. The soldiers are our defenders.

VICAR. Just so, ladies. One reads the newspapers. The continental balance of power is threatened. Then there's the naval question . . .

MRS RAFI. I hope I'm a patriot. But an army belongs in the battlefield or the barracks. Not at the bottom of one's garden rattling the windows. Open the curtains. (*The* LADIES *sigh with relief.*) The mood of art has been pounded away. If I were doing Lear I could rise to it. But one can't play lutes to the sound of gunfire.

VICAR. What a pity. I do enjoy our clash on the bleak strand. Two mighty Titans locked in mortal battle.

RACHEL. I've laid out the designs on the table.

They go up to the round table to look at the designs. ROSE *crosses to* WILLY. *He sits alone on a chair. While they talk the others are admiring and giggling at the designs.*

ROSE. What is the matter, Mr Carson. You're white.

WILLY. It's nothing.

ROSE. Surely you're ill.

WILLY. The guns.

WILLY. They fired when our boat turned over.

ROSE. Can I get you something?

WILLY. No, no. That's very kind. I'm all right.

ROSE. It's an ordeal for you.

WILLY. We'd been friends so long.

ROSE. Yes.

WILLY. I can't say how sorry I am. There's nothing I can do.

ROSE (*nods*). No. There's nothing.

VICAR (*looking at a design; frightened*). Oh Mrs Rafi, do I approve? Is it proper to wear tights in front of one's parishioners? I must have a vestry ruling.

MRS RAFI (*at the round table*). They can't object. I designed them.

WILLY. They say his body will be washed up.

VICAR (*as before*). And the trident?

MRS RAFI. Pitchfork.

WILLY. I know he's dead, but when there's no body there's still a chance he might be . . .

ROSE. Mr Carson, you must go home.

WILLY. No. I sat in that hotel all yesterday. No. And what has been happening here this afternoon, I noticed nothing till the guns . . .? There were people on the beach when the boat turned over.

ROSE. Who?

WILLY. One was drunk and the other stood and shouted at me.

ROSE. Shouted?

WILLY. The man who runs the draper's on the front.

ROSE. Surely you're mistaken.

WILLY. No, no. He swore at me.

ROSE. Swore?

WILLY. Waved his arms. I thought he was mad. Or I was.

The VICAR *has come down to them.*

VICAR. We've shocked you, Mr Carson.

WILLY. How?

VICAR. Rehearsing a play when an inquest is about to take place in our town. You see, it's for our yearly evening in aid of the coastguard fund. Under the circumstances ...

WILLY. Of course.

VICAR. Yet I feel some guilt. (*To* ROSE *as she is about to speak.*) Yes, my dear, pardon me, but I do. I'd be happier on my knees praying for our dead friend. And I would pray for guidance and understanding. He was so very young. God asks much of us. I christened him. I was hardly more than a boy myself, you know. Quite new here. And now he's gone. If the body is found I shall read the burial service. That is always – well, particularly moving, you find, when you bury someone you baptised. (*He starts to mumble some tears.*) Now you must forgive me ... One comes to live the life of the parish. The births and deaths are in part one's own.

The VICAR *goes away.*

WILLY. We were so near the shore. If only I'd been able to get to him. It was so dark. I went back in the water. I think I went in four times. More.

ROSE (*frightened*). Please go home, Mr Carson.

JILLY *comes into the room.*

JILLY. I'm sorry. Aren't I a silly? But I'm better now. I helped
   them to set tea. It's all ready in the conservatory.
MRS RAFI. Shall we go through?

WILLY *stands. Everyone moves towards the door.*

SCENE FIVE

Draper's Shop.

HOLLARCUT, THOMPSON, CARTER *and* HATCH.

HATCH. Read the papers between the lines. It says preparations
   against continental powers. Now what does that mean? Space
   travellers. But London can't say that.
THOMPSON. Count a they'd start up a rare ol' panic?
HATCH. Right. Imagine it, Wad, the enemy from another world!
   People would lose hope. They wouldn't even try to fight.
CARTER. Some on us would.
HATCH. *You* would. But would they at Forebeach?
CARTER. Wouldn't bet on that, true. But how'd yoo know he
   come from space?
HATCH. The guns. You can't get round that. They opened
   up the moment he came. Oh the army knows what's going
   on. That new range's not for practice. They mean business.
THOMPSON. Oh lor'. 'S plain as a baptist's funeral.
CARTER. Well why'd he drown young Bentham?
HATCH. That's obvious. Mr Bentham was about to marry. We
   may hope, he and his lady being nice, clean, well-brought
   up members of the gentry, they'd provide offspring.
THOMPSON (*knowingly*). Oh ah.
HATCH. And that's just what *they* don't want. The fewer we are
   the easier we're overcome.

THOMPSON. What? You mean everytime a chap's thinkin' a gooin' t' church he's liable to be done in?

HATCH. 'Fraid so, Mr Thompson.

THOMPSON. An' every time yoo tak' a gal back of a hedge they're watchin' an' . . . my life.

HATCH. If you only knew the half of it. There's no end to their cunning.

HOLLARCUT. Bet even yoo don't know, Mr Hatch – meanin' no disrespect.

HATCH. I know you don't, Billy. Still, I do know they've got more than one friend in this town.

THOMPSON. ⎱ (together). Who?
CARTER. ⎰ Not just Evens, then?

HATCH. Oh no. You soon spot them behind this counter. You get a fair indication from the way they pay their bill. That shows if they respect our way of life, or if they're just out to make trouble by running people into debt. Oh, some of them don't even know themselves. Their brains are taken out at night, bit by bit, and replaced by artificial material brought here in airships. Course, that's a slow method, it can take years —

HOLLARCUT. Oh you hadn't ought 'a say that, Mr Hatch. That worries a man. I hope there on't no particle a me I warn't born with.

HATCH. Not you, Billy. They wouldn't try it on you. You've led a clean life and now you see your reward. They tried to bribe me, you know.

THOMPSON. Goo on.

HATCH. Oh yes. Leave notes. I found one in the jam. Took the lid off and there it was.

THOMPSON. The devils!

HATCH. Write on a steamy window. That's another of their tricks. By the time you've brought someone to see it it's gone.

CARTER. How much did they offer yer?

HATCH. I didn't read the exact sum. I was too disgusted.

The doorbell clangs. MRS RAFI *and* MRS TILEHOUSE *come in.*

HATCH. Thank you for coming lads. I'll gladly help raise money for new instruments for the town band. That's a worthy cause. Ah, Mrs Rafi, ma'am. I was hoping you'd call. Good day, Mrs Tilehouse. Right lads, out through the back.

MRS RAFI. Thompson, what are you doing here?

THOMPSON. Mornin', missus. I juss come down t' get some seedlin' off the market —

MRS RAFI. Get back to the house. I pay you to work in my garden, not come here and idle and gossip. See me in the morning.

THOMPSON. Missus.

MRS RAFI. Mr Hatch, will you explain why you're holding a mass meeting in secret at eleven o'clock in the morning on a working day? Has the whole town gone on strike?

HATCH. Now, Mrs Rafi, your curtainings have come. Mr Hollarcut was just running up to the house with a message. (*To the men.*) Off you go, there's good lads.

The three men go out behind the counter. HATCH *goes to two large rolls of velvet on the counter and pats them.*

HATCH. Not many houses in these parts can afford to hang this quality at the window, Mrs Rafi. I congratulate you on an excellent choice. That's very like the sample, I think you'll agree. Identical.

MRS RAFI. Mr Hatch, I've been speaking to Mr Carson.

HATCH. Ah yes, and I hope the young gentleman's as well as circumstances allow.

MRS RAFI. Mr Carson tells me that on the night of the drowning he met you on the beach. That he called on you for help. And that you refused – in a language not merely abusive but callous.

HATCH. Ah.

MRS RAFI (*taps the material*). Send it back.

HATCH. What?

MRS RAFI. Mr Hatch, you cannot expect me to patronize a
tradesman who ignores his duty as a coastguard —

HATCH. But you must take it!

MRS RAFI. – for which he is paid ten shillings, and who allows
his fellow man —

MRS TILEHOUSE. And your duty as a Christian!

HATCH. Did you see the storm? What could I do – Christian or
not! – calm the waters, Mrs Rafi?

MRS TILEHOUSE. Oh.

MRS RAFI. Hatch, it's all of a piece. I'd expect you to blaspheme.
Mr Carson tells me you raved and swore at him.

HATCH. He's a liar!

MRS RAFI. A liar?

HATCH. And a scoundrel!

MRS TILEHOUSE. Oh dear.

MRS RAFI (*taps material*). Send it back.

HATCH. Not a liar. No. But he was half drowned. He couldn't
understand me. How could you expect it? The gentleman
was hallucinated. Shocked. I shouted instructions to him. I
tried to help.

MRS RAFI. You let an innocent man drown.

HATCH. I've sent back so many things for you, Mrs Rafi. The
calico. The Irish muslin. The set of renaissance chair
covers, with those wonderful embroidered hunting scenes.
The manufacturers won't deal with me any more.

MRS RAFI. Nor will I.

HATCH. I'm in a *small* way of business, Mrs Rafi. I'm on the
black list. I had to pay for all this before they sent it. And
I made such a fuss about delivery. All my capital has gone
into it.

MRS RAFI. You should have thought of that before. I won't have
it in the house. I'd be afraid to have the curtains drawn.
They'd remind me of the tragedy.

HATCH. I tried to help. I've never seen such a storm. You didn't see it. You were safely tucked up in bed. My name, my goodwill, my whole life's work is at stake. I'm on the edge of a terrible disaster.

MRS RAFI. It goes back. (*Prepares to go.*)

HATCH. I see. You're acting on his instructions already then? What's he said to you? Has he told you to break me? You're his first victim, you've been corrupted.

MRS RAFI (*turning to go*). Good day.

HATCH (*standing between her and the door, some way from her*). I must speak out, Mrs Rafi. Mr Carson is a spy. He murdered Mr Bentham. He's here on a mission. He's sowing the wind of discord. He'll reap the whirlwind.

MRS TILEHOUSE. Mrs Rafi corrupted? Oh! What else did he say? A spy? Murder? Oh dear, I must go home immediately. (*She sits.*)

MRS RAFI. Of course I shall not take your allegations seriously. You always were over-imaginative for a draper. No doubt you should have taken up something more artistic. Certainly you haven't found your proper place in our community. It would be better if you were to close your shop and leave.

HATCH. Yes, yes, I am more in the creative line. They always said that at school. I was head scholar in bible class. You will take the material, Mrs Rafi? This whole shop's tied up in it. The little I've put by – not much, there's no big buyers here. I couldn't set up in the larger towns. No capital. But I've worked hard, much of it against the grain – my inclinations being elsewhere, as you so rightly pointed out. D'you want me to crawl, Mrs Rafi? Feel the stuff, ma'am. Really, an educated person of your taste can't resist a product as beautiful as – (*Crying.*) but oh the pity of it is you don't see the whole community's threatened by that swine, yes swine, bastard, the welfare and livelihood of this whole town! He's tricked you. Only I spotted him. Well I've warned the coastguards. We don't let anyone land here now. They'll drown. I'll kick them under with my boot.

THOMPSON, CARTER *and* HOLLARCUT *come out from the back of the shop.*

MRS RAFI. Thompson, are you still here?

THOMPSON. Missus, missus —

CARTER. Can't you keep your snout clean, Hatch? Now there'll be the devil to pay.

THOMPSON. Don't mind Mr Hatch, missus. He likes t' spout a lot a ol' rot. We coastguards well's we can. We on't put town money in our pocket till we earn en —

HOLLARCUT. Doo watch that stuff, Mr Hatch. Yoo dutty en with yoor cryin'.

MRS RAFI *takes hold of* THOMPSON'*s ear.*

MRS RAFI. Just as you earn money in my garden! Now get back to work.

THOMPSON. Ouch, missus. Yoo'll hev my hid off.

MRS RAFI. I've had enough of this tomfoolery.

MRS TILEHOUSE. Careful, Louise. He's too heavy for you.

MRS RAFI *leads* THOMPSON *out by the ear. The doorbell clangs.* CARTER, HOLLARCUT *and* MRS TILEHOUSE *go out after her.* HATCH *is left alone.*

HATCH. I took an order and there's a copy in the order book. (*He picks up his draper's shears.*) So she'll take delivery and pay. And she can collect – I'm damned if I'll deliver to the door. Pieces of three yards. (*He starts cutting three-yard lengths from the rolls.*) This is the moment that tests and proves. Events are moving and I must act. Three yards. I'll disclose it all at the inquest. Yes, that's my public pulpit. Oh god, what can I do? They'll never believe me. The fools. The swine. (*Cutting.*) Careful. Three yards. Don't let your hand shake. Stop that! No trembling. No complaints. Three yards. I'll take my shears to that little swine. I'll snip him. I'll improve his outline. Send me to the workhouse! Begging like a skivvy-worker. Picking rags. Cleaning drains. 'Here's a crust, my man, here's a mug. Draw yourself some water from the pump.' No! Three yards: one, two, three.

HOLLARCUT *appears in the doorway. He is looking down the street. The doorbell clangs all the while he talks.*

HOLLARCUT. She's leadin' him along the front by the ear. They're comin' out a shops t' gawk. Ol' Mrs Tilehouse's tannin' his arse with her brolly. The ol' tarter. He'll be blacker'n a nigger on a dark night. Hev you ever seen the like? Ho up, lads. Here she come!

HOLLARCUT *runs into the shop. The doorbell stops clanging.*
HOLLARCUT *stops when he sees* HATCH. HATCH *is still cutting the material – slashing and tearing at it when the shears stick. The material unrolls over the floor.*

HOLLARCUT. Whatever yoo up to, Mr Hatch?
HATCH (*points to the pieces he has cut*). Roll them up, Billy. Nice and neat. You can't drop high-class goods in the bottom of a cart like a sack of sprouts. That's the makings of the good draper: finesse, industry, and an understanding of the feminine temperament. They stamp on you but they wipe their little boots first.
HOLLARCUT. I on't touchin' nothin', Mr Hatch. Folks've got their dander up. You must fend for yoorself now.
HATCH. I'll start on the other roll. Bit off each. Three yards. The moment for action, Billy. Time draws near. An army can't watch the grass grow round it. It's out in the open now. People will rally round the truth. You'll see many signs and wonders in the days to come.

HATCH *goes on cutting.* MRS RAFI *comes in. The doorbell clangs.*
HOLLARCUT *goes behind the counter and watches.*

MRS RAFI. Hatch, I'll report this morning's outrage to the constable and the town doctor. I shall certainly see that no one under my influence ever uses *any* shop of yours again.

MRS TILEHOUSE *appears in the doorway behind* MRS RAFI. *Until she comes into the shop later on, the doorbell makes isolated, spasmodic clangs.*

HATCH. Come in, Mrs Rafi. Your order is being attended to.

MRS TILEHOUSE. Louise, don't go in.

MRS RAFI *comes further into the shop.*

MRS RAFI. Hatch, pull yourself together.

HATCH (*still cutting*). The cutting's nearly done. You see I cut it all myself. You have to know cloth. There's an art to this. That's why I don't hire an assistant. They'll never stop long enough to learn the trade. Oh it's not that I can't afford one. Look at that edge. I could have ten assistants. Open departments. Haberdasheries. Riding habits. Liveries. A sporting counter. I could attract the towns to *me*. But no one stays long enough to learn the trade. It takes a life time, Mrs Rafi. Three yards. Always move. Why? Don't they take to me? Am I so hard to ... They must be off. What do they ever see, what are they looking for, what do they ever find? The trade is a respectable vocation. Sons of the gentry haven't been above it. (*In tears.*) I walked my life away on this floor. Up and down ... Three yards ... Why isn't the floor worn through ... Thirty years ... I'm worn through ... (*He goes on cutting, tearing, ripping and slashing.*)

MRS RAFI. Mr Hatch. You're hacking it to pieces. No one can take the material now.

MRS TILEHOUSE. Hollarcut, take his collar.

HOLLARCUT. I on't touch him.

HOLLARCUT *ducks down out of sight behind the counter.*

HATCH (*smiles and cuts*). These shears are part of my hand. Watch how the cloth leads them. That's the gesture of my soul, Mrs Rafi, there's a whole way of life in that ...

MRS RAFI. Mr Hatch, listen to your friends. You make it hard for me to help you.

HATCH. There, Mrs Rafi. Some lengths to be getting on with. Will you take them with you now?

MRS RAFI. No.

MRS TILEHOUSE. Don't beard him, Louise.

HATCH (*cunningly*). Ah, but it must be taken. You see, it's cut. According to the customer's requirement. It's in pieces.

MRS RAFI. No.

MRS TILEHOUSE. What foolishness to bait the unchained lion.

MRS RAFI *turns to go.* HATCH *stops her by cutting off her path.*

HATCH. Are you paying now? Pay the bill and tidy it away. Of course! Don't let these things hang over you.

MRS RAFI. Hollarcut.

HOLLARCUT *looks over the top of the counter.*

HOLLARCUT. Don't antagonize him, missus.

HOLLARCUT *goes down out of sight.* HATCH *holds one end of* MRS RAFI'*s bag and she holds the other.*

HATCH. You've brought the money. Are you too shy to take it out? The company of men? I understand all that. Don't look away, m'am. Each one has his failings. I never put a lady to shame. Let me. I do it all in a nice, clean way. A lady can't be soiled with money.

MRS RAFI. Take it. (*She gives him her bag and turns away. Weakly.*) My legs . . .

MRS TILEHOUSE *hurries into the room. The doorbell clangs and stops.*

MRS TILEHOUSE. Louise, your bag.

MRS RAFI. Nonsense, Mrs Tilehouse. Farthings. Shout in the street. Mr Hatch has made me a prisoner.

MRS TILEHOUSE *collapses in a chair.* HATCH *is struggling with*

MRS RAFI. HOLLARCUT *looks up from behind the counter, yells and runs out. The doorbell clangs.*

HATCH. Farthings! Farthings! All that money under your bed and you won't pay your debts!

MRS RAFI. Mr Hatch, remember who we are.

HATCH. Mr Carson keeps your money now! You're all liars, swindlers, frauds, bankrupts —

HATCH *hits* MRS RAFI *with the shears. She is cut. They stand in silence for half a second.*

MRS RAFI. Hatch, you're a fool.

CARTER *comes in. The doorbell clangs.* HATCH *goes behind the counter.*

MRS RAFI. See to Mr Hatch. He's very poorly. I have only a slight cut.

HATCH. Well, well. How did that happen? She tried to grab my shears, Jack. She must be a lady burglar. She interfered with work on the premises. You know they come in here and whisper, ask for intimate garments. Could I try this on, Hatch. Then they're off to the fitting room before you can stop them and leave the curtain open. All the intimate things. Wriggling into this and that. Is it too tight, Mr Hatch? Is this gusset in order?

CARTER. Thass enough a that, Hatch. You howd yoor noise an' come with me like a good man.

CARTER *goes cautiously towards* HATCH. HATCH *dodges round him and goes out of the shop. The doorbell clangs. As he goes he points to* MRS TILEHOUSE. *She is sitting unconscious in a chair.*

HATCH (*going*). There's the worst. Leaves the curtain open and turns the mirror – brazen! – so you see the darkness underneath.

MRS RAFI *takes a piece of material from the display dummy on the counter and wraps it round her wrist while she talks. She is frightened and angry.*

MRS RAFI. I don't know what you've been up to amongst yourselves. Have you no respect for public opinion —

CARTER. Yes, m'am.

MRS RAFI. Will your wives and children hold their heads up for
years? And your superiors, they'll certainly be pained by
these excesses?

CARTER. Yes, m'am. Please don't goo on, m'am.

MRS RAFI. Put your finger on this knot. (CARTER *holds the knot
while she fastens the material on her wrist.*) You've plunged
the town into scandal. What will they say in Forebeach?

CARTER. Yes, m'am.

MRS RAFI. Thank you. I shall go and alert the town constable.
As it's only midday I suppose he's still in bed. That is, if
he's as conscientious as the rest of the town. I hardly know
if I dare approach a representative of the law. In this state
of anarchy one might find oneself inside. See to my companion – another sentry asleep at her post.

MRS RAFI *goes out. The doorbell clangs.* CARTER *goes quietly to*
MRS TILEHOUSE.

CARTER. Mrs Tilehouse, m'am.

MRS TILEHOUSE (*jumping to her feet*). Help! I am about to be
attacked by a large man.

CARTER. Mrs Rafi tol' me t' say —

MRS TILEHOUSE. Louise is dead! What were her last words?
She apologised to me for it all! I forgive her! I hold no
grudge, however justified —

CARTER. No, no. She's gone for the officer.

MRS TILEHOUSE. Thank god. The town is relieved! We're
saved!

CARTER. She said I'm to see yoo home.

MRS TILEHOUSE. Ah, thank you, Carter. I don't think I could

walk there unassisted, I shall require your arm – in the less public places. (*She sees the shears on the counter.*) Ah! The murderer's shears.

CARTER. Look the other way, ma'am.

MRS TILEHOUSE. Yes. After this I shall regard Gomorrah as a spa resort.

CARTER *leads* MRS TILEHOUSE *out. The doorbell clangs. Immediately* HOLLARCUT *comes on through the back of the shop. He calls softly.*

HOLLARCUT. Mr Hatch . . . Where yoo hidin', Mr Hatch? . . . I'll put some bread an' cheese on the window ledge out the back for yoo, an' a bottle a sweet tea . . . Don't you run out without yoor coat . . .

SCENE SIX

Beach.
The stage is empty except for a body upstage. It is covered with trousers, socks, vest and jersey – all dark. There are no shoes. The jersey is pulled up over the head and the arms, which are lifted up and bent at the elbows in the act of removing the jersey – so the jersey forms a hood covering the head, neck, shoulders, arms and hands. The dark vest covers the trunk. The top half of the body is on the beach and the rest in the water.

ROSE *comes on. She is looking ahead at someone who has gone on in front of her.*

ROSE (*calling ahead*). I must sit down. (*She sits.*)

WILLY *comes on from the direction in which she shouted.*

WILLY. Are you all right?

ROSE. Yes.

WILLY. Shall I leave you alone?

ROSE. Yes.

WILLY (*nods. Slight pause*). I don't like to. You haven't been out here since he drowned.

ROSE (*remotely*). I'll see you back at the house.

WILLY. All right.

Pause. WILLY *doesn't move.*

ROSE. This stupid inquest.

WILLY. Why?

Pause.

ROSE. The coroner will say he's sorry and decide why he died. Why? You might as well have an inquest on birth. They're afraid of me. I'm touched by death. Perhaps you are. I see it when they call to say they're sorry. They look at me as if I'm a dangerous animal they have to pat . . .

WILLY. You're supposed to forget what they look like very soon. It comes as a shock. But it's hard to forget the voice. You suddenly hear that twenty years later.

ROSE. Really they come to be calmed and assured. I have to find some of my pain to share with them. A taste. Then they know that if I can bear it so can they when it comes.

WILLY. He knew more about sailing than I do. But we both knew it was wrong to be out. He wanted to get here quickly. To see you. Perhaps he wanted to show something. I mean: prove. (*Shrugs.*) I said let's go back. I kept asking, 'How close is the land?' He didn't answer. He went on working. Pulling ropes. And he baled water in a bucket. He knew we'd made a mistake. It was dangerous to be there.

ROSE. What did he say?

WILLY. Nothing. Then the boat turned over. I saw the bottom

coming up out of the water. It looked very ugly. It was wet
and suddenly smooth in all that chaos. I yelled but I couldn't
hear him. He was gone.

Pause.

WILLY. Did you love him . . . a great deal?

ROSE. What?

WILLY. I thought perhaps he wasn't sure. I mean about what
you felt. It was clear what he felt.

ROSE. Why are you saying this?

WILLY. Somehow, he was afraid. That was so unnatural for him.
He was sure and firm about everything else. It seems terrible
that he could be afraid . . . I think that would have destroyed
him. A hero's fear.

ROSE. Fear?

WILLY. You were brought up together. Your aunt wanted you to
marry. Everyone knew you would. It was too easy. He was
afraid one day you'd meet another man – perhaps even a
weaker man – and he'd lose you. A hero must be afraid of
weaker men.

ROSE. Why?

WILLY. He never talked of you. No photographs. I didn't know
what you looked like. Sometimes he said he'd written or
you'd been somewhere. Of course I'd formed my own
picture of you.

ROSE. How long did you know him?

WILLY. Seven years. I'm twenty-one. We were the same age.

Silence.

ROSE. If I'd seen him die it would be easier to forget him. I
can see him working and not saying anything. Wet to the
skin. And the noisy sea. But I can't see him when he dies.
(*Pause.*) He was very beautiful. He had dark eyes. I think
of him as a fire.

WILLY. Why?

ROSE. A fire that doesn't die out. I've seen it burn in the sea.

WILLY. What d'you mean?

ROSE. When we were young we lit fires on the beach. At night. The fire shone on his face. I saw it reflected in the sea. It danced because both the flames and the water moved.

WILLY. D'you feel anything wrong?

ROSE. You mean guilty?

WILLY. Yes. When someone dies people sometimes —

ROSE. No. I was always happy with him. There was nothing mean and selfish in it. It seemed perfect. Now I have nothing to live for. There's nothing to look forward to. I don't know what I shall do. I can't think of anything to make one day pass. Yet I have most of my life to live. I don't know how I shall get through it. He was the only person who could understand me now.

WILLY. I understand you a little.

ROSE. Yes, but what does that matter to me?

WILLY. All people matter to each other.

ROSE. That isn't true, of course.

WILLY. No.

Silence.

ROSE. I can't bear to lose him. I don't think I can live without him.

WILLY (*quiet anger*). I think that love can be a terrible disaster. And hope is sometimes pride and ambition. When I'm lost in darkness I'll shut my eyes and feel my way forward, grope like an animal, not be guided by some distant light.

ROSE. How can you escape from yourself, or what's happened to you, or the future? It's a silly question. It's better out here where he died. At home there's so much to do. People coming and going. Why? What does it matter to them? How can I escape from *that*?

WILLY. If you look at life closely it is unbearable. What people suffer, what they do to each other, how they hate themselves, anything good is cut down and trodden on, the innocent and the victims are like dogs digging rats from a hole, or an owl starving to death in a city. It is all unbearable but that is where you have to find your strength. Where else is there?

ROSE. An owl starving in a city.

WILLY. To death. Yes. Wherever you turn. So you should never turn away. If you do you lose everything. Turn back and look into the fire. Listen to the howl of the flames. The rest is lies.

ROSE. How just. How sane.

WILLY *stands and looks upstage.*

ROSE. What is it?

WILLY. He's on the beach. There.

ROSE *and* WILLY *go up to the body.*

ROSE. Why is he like that?

WILLY. He tried to pull the jumper over his head. So he could swim.

ROSE. He drowned.

WILLY. Yes.

They stare silently for a moment.

ROSE. Is it him?

WILLY. Yes. I know his clothes. Go and fetch Mr Evens. I'll keep watch.

ROSE. Yes.

ROSE *hurries out. After a moment* WILLY *crouches down by the body.*

WILLY (*coldly*). How will they get you into the box? You're a corpse and they'll break your arms. They'll cut your clothes

and fold you up like a dummy. What's on your face now?
Is it quiet, or swollen, or scratched?

A sound in the distance. Not a tune, but a high, inarticulate, sing-song whining, mad, with the note of a hunter in it. WILLY *looks at something offstage. He comes quickly downstage and crouches out of sight. The sound comes closer. He waits.* HATCH *comes on. He carries a knife.* WILLY *crouches lower.*

HATCH. More prints. And still someone with him. Always back
to the beach. He can't keep away. What drags him back time
after time? Obsession. You must get him, Mr Hatch. The
fools in this town think they're safe. No, life's being worn
away. Their bodies are crunched underfoot like sand. This
long beach is a stream trickling through god's hands. Their
bones are ground down and fall through the hour-glass.
Time runs and the enemy is closer. Quiet, Hatch. Hold your
noise. Stop your rant. Follow your victim. (HATCH *takes a
few steps towards the body. He stops and looks round.*) Mr
Carson asleep on the beach. Where's the head? In his hands.
That's it! What confidence. Insolence. Sleeping while he
waits for his friends to come out of the sea. This is the quiet
place where the sea monsters breed and play and lie in the
sun. Mr Hatch, you have him. Careful. (*He creeps towards the
body. He still holds the knife.*) A sound and he's gone ...
(HATCH *reaches the body. He falls on it and knives it in a
frenzy.*) Kill it! Kill it! Kill it! At last! What's this? Water!
Look, water! Water not blood? (*Stabbing.*) Kill it! Kill it!
(*He stops.*) More water? (*Stabs.*) The filthy beast!
WILLY (*to himself*). Hit it. That's an innocent murder.
HATCH. No blood. Only water. How do I know he's dead?
Surely, surely! (*Stabs.*) There, that's hard enough. Hack his
throat. Cut it! Tear it! Rip it! Slash it! (*Stops stabbing.
Rambles on quickly to himself.*) Still no blood! Oh who would
have thought of this? Surely they die? Why come here, why
do anything, if you're not afraid of death? Yes. Their worlds'

dying and they'll die if they stay – they know, they know!
Of course they die! Yes – watch and see if they bury him!
You can't bury something that's still alive. (*Looks offstage.*)
Hide, Mr Hatch. They're after you.

HATCH *hurries out.* WILLY *is sitting downstage with his back to the*
body. ROSE *and* EVENS *hurry on.* EVENS *brings a folded blanket.*

ROSE. We saw the draper.
EVENS. The town's out looking for him.
ROSE. Are you all right?
WILLY. Yes. (*To* EVENS.) The body's up there.

EVENS *stares offstage after* HATCH. *Then he goes upstage to the*
body.

ROSE. He's cut. Look. His clothes. His arms.
WILLY. Hatch. He went for him with a knife.
ROSE. How terrible.
WILLY. He thought it was me.
ROSE. How terrible. How terrible.
WILLY. Why? What does it matter? You can't hurt the dead.
    How can you desecrate dust? (*Shrugs.*) He's just dead bait
    for a mad man.
ROSE. But it seems so violent.

EVENS *covers the body with the old blanket. It is pale green or faded,*
dirty white. He lays it out like a square and doesn't tuck it in. The
body makes a bump in the middle.

EVENS (*to* ROSE). Go into town and fetch a horse and cart. Go
    quietly or they'll come out to gape. There's no need for that.
    We'll watch.
ROSE. Yes.

ROSE *goes out.* EVENS *and* WILLY *stand some way apart. They*
face half upstage and wait in silence. The body lies upstage.

SCENE SEVEN

Clifftop.

Open, windy, sunny morning. An upright piano has been carried up on to the cliffs. When it is played the sound is hollow and spread. A chair stands in front of it. MAFANWY *and* JILLY *are alone. They arrange sheet music on the piano.*

MAFANWY. The wind.

JILLY. When *I'm* dead I'll be brought up here to the cliff tops.

MAFANWY. How can you even think about it!

JILLY (*looking off*). They're coming. Why don't you play?

MAFANWY. Mrs Rafi wants to enter to silence.

JILLY (*looking offstage*). Oh isn't she marvellous? Look how she holds the urn. Oh, isn't it small.

MAFANWY. How disgraceful.

JILLY. Whatever is it, Fanny?

MAFANWY. They've brought Mr Evens.

JILLY. Oh where?

MAFANWY. He's lower than a tramp. Louise only does it to annoy.

JILLY. Oh, is that what he looks like? Oh dear. You must let me stand by you. I feel quite afraid. How silly. Are those stories true?

MAFANWY. I haven't listened to them.

JILLY. The girls say that if you go by his hut at night —

MAFANWY (*sharply*). Sh-sh! What is the matter with you? Your neck's gone quite red.

JILLY. Oh dear.

MAFANWY *and* JILLY *stand with bowed heads. Their hands are crossed in their laps. The procession comes on.* MRS RAFI, MRS TILEHOUSE, ROSE, RACHEL, WILLY, EVENS, VICAR, CARTER, THOMPSON *and other* MEN *and* LADIES. MRS RAFI *carries a small urn. Two of the* MEN *carry the town banner. It is a red strip stretched between two poles. It is heavily embroidered with gold-coloured wire and silk. Everyone goes to their place in silence.*

VICAR (*low and considerate*). You'll be more comfortable over there, Mrs Rafi. A trifle more sheltered from the blast.

MRS RAFI *goes silently to her place. The group settles down.*

VICAR. Dearly beloved, we the friends of this poor departed soul in god remember today, as we cast his ashes about this favourite walk, the faithful townsman who has gone before us on the great journey that leads to that home where there is always peace. Let us pray, each in the silence of his heart (*They bow their heads and clasp their hands. A short silence.*) Amen.

ALL. Amen.

VICAR. I heard a voice from heaven saying unto me, write. From henceforth happy are the dead, for they rest from their labours. The first hymn, Miss Price, thank you. Page 432.

Some of the people use hymn books, others know the words. As they sing a rivalry for the most elaborate descant develops between MRS RAFI *and* MRS TILEHOUSE. MRS TILEHOUSE *becomes operatic.* MAFANWY *stamps out the proper rhythm at the piano.*

> Eternal father, strong to save
> Whose arm doth bind the restless wave
> Who bidst the mighty ocean deep
> Its own appointed limits keep
> O hear us when we cry to thee
> For those in peril on the sea
>
> O Saviour, whose almighty word
> The winds and waves submissive heard
> Who walkedst on the foaming deep

>And calm amid its rage didst sleep
>O hear us when we cry to thee
>For those in peril on the sea

ALL	Amen.
MRS TILEHOUSE	(sing) A-a-a-a-a-a-a-a-meeeeeeeen.
MRS RAFI	A-a-a-a-

MRS RAFI (sung). -men.

VICAR. Colin's goodness speaks for him. I will not tarnish that sound with my foolish words. One incident I cannot forbear to relate. Yesterday I went to the battery commander at Forebeach and asked if, during the brief moments of our ceremony here today, his guns might be silent. Without prompting he lifted up his martial voice and said 'Yes. Mr Bentham was a good man, Padre. He goes before the Almighty with a clean record. He is destined for high rank among the heavenly hosts. Would that I had numbered him amongst my own officers.' Saying which this soldier, so reminiscent of some fine hero of the ancient world, raised his sherry glass and sang the opening lines of the Regimental —

In the distance the battery starts to fire. There is an embarrassed silence.

VICAR. Miss Price, perhaps we might go on to the next hymn.

They sing the 'Old One hundredth'. MRS TILEHOUSE *again delays the tune with her descant.* MRS RAFI *glares at her angrily and unconsciously beats time against the urn.*

>All people that on earth do dwell
>Sing to the lord with hopeful voice
>Him serve with fear, his praise forth tell
>Come ye before him and rejoice
>
>O enter then his gates with praise
>Approach with joy his courts unto
>Praise laud and bless his name always
>For it is seemly so to do.

MRS TILEHOUSE *begins to sing* 'amen', MAFANWY *doesn't accompany her.* MRS TILEHOUSE *stops. During the singing the* VICAR *has gone upstage to the edge of the cliff. The guns have stopped.*

VICAR. We commit this body to the air over the deep waters; to be turned to corruption; and we look to the resurrection of the body when the sea shall give up her dead. Amen.

ALL. Amen.

VICAR. I believe you have prepared a few words, Mrs Rafi.

MRS RAFI *goes towards the edge of the cliff. She still carries the urn.*

VICAR. Not too near the edge, dear lady.

MRS RAFI. Be not afraid, Vicar.

MRS RAFI *turns to the congregation and recites. While she does so she mimes to her words. The effect suggests* 'Under the spreading chestnut tree'.

At the same time MRS TILEHOUSE *starts to search in her large handbag. She can't find what she is searching for. She speaks to herself in a sweet, patient, chiding voice, lower than* MRS RAFI's, *but loud enough to be heard, especially in* MRS RAFI's *dramatic pauses. She hands things from her handbag to those next to her to hold.*

MRS TILEHOUSE. Smelling salts. Smelling salts. Dear me, where are you? Did I leave you in my trinkets box? Under this distress I may perchance have left the top off. What misfortune! – the mixture is so volatile . . .

MRS RAFI. Like dust and ash all men become
Broken and old when they reach home

(*She reacts to a sudden idea.*)

I'll throw his ash into the heartless sea
The waves will calm, like water under lee
And in that water that is always night

(*She dramatically gropes a few steps towards the edge. The spectators gasp.*)

His ashes fall, sparkling as light!
There they will drift through ages yet to come
Lighting the deep with dreams of home!

(*She unscrews the top of the urn.* MRS TILEHOUSE *has stood her handbag on the ground and is rummaging in it.*)

Men who live out their little year

(*She stares dramatically into the urn as if she discovers something in it.*)

Are diamonds polished by their labours here!
Fire has burned! It gives no ashes grey!
Diamonds only from this mortal clay!

She snatches out a handful of ashes and holds them up triumphantly. The spectators gasp.

MRS TILEHOUSE. Or might I indeed have lent them to the cook?

MRS RAFI. Arise ye dust, and take the air on wings!
    Pale spirit rise! For hark! the angel —
    Mrs Tilehouse, perhaps you would like to go down and cut
    the sandwiches for our tea?

MRS TILEHOUSE. I beg your pardon.

MRS RAFI. I only wish to spare you your little upset.

MRS TILEHOUSE (*plaintively*). Louise, how can you? I cannot
    help it if my feelings make the use of salts necessary —

MRS RAFI. Feelings!

VICAR. Ladies, let us pray.

MRS RAFI. Is this an exhibition of feelings?

MRS TILEHOUSE (*angrily*). You would not understand, Louise.
    No one has feelings except you, of course.

MRS RAFI. Most people would say it is an exhibition of hysteria.
    It seems to me to be quite close to insanity!

VICAR. Our father which art —

MRS RAFI. Oh do be quiet, Vicar!

MRS RAFI *crosses to* MRS TILEHOUSE. *She still carries a handful
of ashes. As she passes* JILLY *she gives them to her.*

MRS RAFI. Hold these for a moment.

JILLY. Ah! (*She bursts into tears.*)

MRS RAFI. You've deliberately destroyed this occasion. (*She holds up the urn.*) Now what are my last memories of this poor dead boy? Your absurd singing. Your absurd histrionics. Oh, I know what's behind this, madam. (*Going back to her place.*) It's because she didn't get a part in the play.

EVENS *goes to help* JILLY. *He puts his hand on her shoulder.*

EVENS. Allow me, my dear.

JILLY *turns and sees him. She screams. He tries to take her hand.*

EVENS. But I want to help —
JILLY. You beast! You beast!

JILLY *faints and drops the ashes on the ground.*

MRS TILEHOUSE. Look at this poor girl. Another of your victims.
VICAR. Miss Price, the next hymn.

MAFANWY *starts to play* 'Eternal Father'. *She switches to* 'All people'. *She stops in confusion and starts to cry.* MRS TILEHOUSE *is trying to sweep up the ashes in her handkerchief.*

MRS RAFI. Wallow, Mrs Tilehouse. Look at her. Snatch and grab! That's what she wanted all along. She wants to scatter them. Well let her. I won't!

MRS TILEHOUSE. I'll never forgive you. You've gone too far this day, madam.

HATCH *comes in in a frenzy of excitement and triumph.*

HATCH. He's dead! He's dead! The first one's chalked up!
VICAR. The devil's come.
HATCH. Put him in a hole at the crossroads. (*He dodges about. The others try to catch him.*) Put him in quicklime. There's a place for him in the prison wall. The little green where the hangman grows flowers for Buckingham Palace.

MRS RAFI. Ruffian, have you no respect for the dead?

MRS TILEHOUSE. Anarchist!

HATCH (*dancing*). Witches! Hussies!

MRS RAFI. Silence before your betters.

HATCH *attacks them.* HOLLARCUT *runs on.*

HATCH. Push them over the top, Billy. That's where the swine go!

RACHEL *starts to beat* HOLLARCUT *with the sheet music.* LADIES *surround* HOLLARCUT *and* HATCH *and hit them. The* VICAR *kneels.*

VICAR. Page seventy-eight in your prayer books. A prayer in time of war and tumult. Save and deliver us, confound their devices —

MRS RAFI (*throwing handfuls of ashes at* HATCH). Have you no respect for the dead?

HATCH. Billy, save me!

HOLLARCUT. Mr Hatch, help!

CARTER. I'll larrup yoo, lad. I'll bang yoo. I'll knock 'em into next week, Mrs Rafi.

HATCH (*throwing his arms open.*) Take me to my end. My work is done.

Suddenly HATCH *steps in front of* WILLY. WILLY *is taking the empty urn from* MRS RAFI. *He holds it awkwardly upside down. He stares at* HATCH. *The silence spreads.*

HATCH. Alive? (*He half reaches out to touch* WILLY.) Alive? (*He begins crying.*) No. No. No. No. He's still alive. (*He falls to his hands and knees.*)

WILLY. Touch me. I won't hurt you. No one will hurt you here.

HOLLARCUT. Mr Hatch . . . Don't yoo cry. 'Tis better so. (*He goes to* HATCH *and crouches beside him.*) Stop that . . . (*He looks at the others.*) Why yoo do this to Mr Hatch? He on't done yoo no harm.

MRS RAFI. No harm! D'you know what you're saying?

HOLLARCUT. He only stopped yoor spoutin' for a little while.

Not even so much. Take more'n a few whacks t' shut her up.
How hev the likes a him ever harmed yoo? Look on him
now, if yoo can.

MRS TILEHOUSE. He wounded Mrs Rafi's arm.

HOLLARCUT. She on't die a no scratch. She come nearer dyin'
every time she stick her ol' hat pin in.

VICAR. Hollarcut, I have failed. Week after week I laboured at
your side in the heat of Sunday School. For hours I struggled
with your soul. I fought with your rational mind to instil some
order into it. Did you not understand one word?

HOLLARCUT. No.

VICAR. Oh. Excuse me, I must go down and prepare myself. The
time of the great beast cannot be far off.

The VICAR *goes out.* MRS RAFI *shouts after him.*

MRS RAFI. Remember, Vicar: the Lord moves in a mysterious
way. The poor man's gone. (*To* HOLLARCUT.) You bully!
Surely you know it's your duty to look after him? He's
weaker than you!

MAFANWY *fusses round* MRS RAFI *with a shawl.*

MAFANWY. Oh Mrs Rafi, I'm so sorry. You tried so hard to make
everything nice today.

MRS RAFI. Carter, take Hatch down to the town lock up.

CARTER *and* THOMPSON *are holding* HATCH.

HATCH (*afraid*). I don't know if you're all ghosts or if you still
have time to save yourselves. (*He cries to himself.*) I'm out
of touch. I tried to save you from your foolishness and
selfishness . . . (*Cries.*) Now someone else will come and take
my place and no one will help you . . . no one can help you
now . . .

CARTER *and* THOMPSON *take* HATCH *out.*

MRS RAFI. Mafanwy, stop fussing and put your shawl on.

Whenever you catch a cold you behave as if you'd taken the sins of the world on your shoulders and we should all be grateful. You'll be snivelling round self-righteously for half the year.

MAFANWY (*turns away in tears*). How can you be so hard . . .

MAFANWY *starts to collect the scattered sheet music.*

MRS RAFI (*making an announcement*). Ladies, attention. I think I may say that everything was going very well today until Mr Hatch came on with his lunacy. Our behaviour was as usual an example to the town.

LADIES. Yes.

MRS RAFI. No doubt some of us had been moved by the high emotionalism of the occasion —

MRS TILEHOUSE. Ah yes, how true.

MRS RAFI. – but that is only proper. (*A murmur of agreement.*) Indeed it shows the depths of our feelings. (*A few claps from the* LADIES.) No more will be said about that. By anyone. Of course, it was unfortunate that the wind blew some of our articles about – (*She takes the urn from* WILLY.) – but you expect it in these high, exposed places. (*She gives the urn to* EVENS.) Mr Evens, kindly see that is returned to my study. Perhaps you will help me to choose a niche. Our work is done – (*She dusts a speck from herself.*) – and we may safely say the ashes have been well scattered. Where's Rose?

They look round. She is not there.

MRS TILEHOUSE. Something terrible is going to happen. I know it. A thing brushed past me through the air.

MRS RAFI. Nonsense, Jessica. Rose is a sensible girl. She's gone off for a few moments' peace away from this madhouse. Hollarcut, can I trust you to go quietly down to the town with at least the outward show of decorum?

HOLLARCUT. I on't give yoo n'more chance to pin nothin' on me, if thass what yoo mean.

MRS RAFI. You can come and work *hard* in my garden every
   evening for the next two months. There's a lot of especially
   hard digging you can do. That, or I must take up this matter
   with the local magistrates. Which?
HOLLARCUT (*grumbling*). Diggin', I suppose.
MRS RAFI. I'm glad you've got some wits left. I shall assume
   Hatch led you astray – an easy assumption. Present yourself
   at my back door tomorrow at five-thirty sharp.
HOLLARCUT. Mornin' or evenin'?
MRS RAFI. Both.

HOLLARCUT *goes out grumbling to himself.*

   Ladies, you can go down now.
RACHEL   ⎱ But are you all right —
MRS TILEHOUSE ⎰ Oh no, my dear. I won't leave you out here
   unattended —
MRS RAFI. You'll be safe, Jessica. Carter won't let Hatch slip
   away.

The LADIES *and the others go out.* MRS RAFI *and* WILLY *are left
alone. She is downstage and he is upstage. The empty chair still
stands in front of the piano. It has not moved.*

MRS RAFI. Fetch me the chair. Willy.

WILLY *fetches her the chair. He sets it downstage. She sits on it.
He stands a little way from her.*

MRS RAFI. I'm afraid of getting old. I've always been a forceful
   woman. I was brought up to be. People expect my class to
   shout at them. Bully them. They're disappointed if you
   don't. It gives them something to gossip about in their bars.
   When they turn you into an eccentric, it's their form of
   admiration. Sometimes I think I'm like a lighthouse in their
   world. I give them a sense of order and security. My glares
   mark out a channel to the safe harbour. I'm so tired of them.
   I'm tired of being a side-show in their little world. Nothing

else was open to me. If I were a Catholic – (*She looks round.*)
– it's all right, the vicar's gone – I'd have been an abbess.
I'd have terrified the nuns. They'd have loved it. Like living
next door to the devil. But the grand old faith didn't allow
me even that consolation. Of course I have my theatricals –
(*She looks round as before.*) – yes, the ladies have gone – none
of them can act, you know. Oh no. I'm surrounded by
mediocrities. A flaming torch and no path to shine on ...
I'll grow old and shout at them from a wheel-chair. That's
what they're waiting for. They get their own back for all the
years I bullied them. They wheel you where they like. 'Take
me there.' 'You went there yesterday. We want to go the
other way.' 'Take me down to the beach. I want to see the
sea.' 'You don't want to see the sea. You saw the sea yesterday.
The wind's bad for your head. If you misbehave and catch
a cold we'll shut you up in bed. You'll stay there for good this
time.' Subtle. Jessica would probably stick matchsticks under
my nails. I'll see she's pensioned off. She is one of those ladies
who are meant to die alone in a small room. You give up
shouting. You close your eyes and the tears dribble down your
ugly old face and you can't even wipe it clean – they won't give
you your hanky. 'Don't let her have it. She gets into a tizzy
and tears it to shreds.' There you are: old, ugly, whimpering,
dirty, pushed about on wheels and threatened. I can't love
them. How could I? But that's a terrible state in which to
move towards the end of your life: to have no love. Has
anything been worth while? No. I've thrown my life away.
(*She sees someone offstage.*) Come along. They've gone.

ROSE *comes on. She walks calmly towards them.*

MRS RAFI. Go away, Rose. Don't stay in the town and marry the
solicitor or doctor or parson. You can't breathe here.

ROSE. Where shall I go?

MRS RAFI. Colin would have taken you away. He'd never settle
down in this ditch. Oh no. But they've got him now. He's

up on these cliffs for ever. A ghost haunting the sea. Till
that goes – even the sea must go sometime. Even the ghosts.
Ha, ha. You take her, Willy.

WILLY. Will she come?

MRS RAFI. If she's got any sense.

ROSE (*to* MRS RAFI). You didn't go.

MRS RAFI. No. (*She stands.*) I've arranged a burying tea. These
little things break the monotony of their lives. There'll be
chaos if I don't go and rule the tea room. They'll hack
themselves to pieces on the cake knives and empty the
tea pot over the sandwiches. But I shall be thinking of the
sea and dead Colin, and how the world is full of things
that have always been far away from me. Don't come
down – it'll disgust you. Stay up here and shock them.
They'll have a good gossip and it'll help them to get over
the funeral.

MRS RAFI *goes out.*

WILLY. Are you all right?

ROSE. Yes.

WILLY. Shall we go away?

ROSE (*calmly*). Would you like to?

WILLY. . . . Yes.

ROSE. Oh yes, but then I could go away with anyone.

WILLY. Who?

ROSE. Any sailor from the port. I don't mind having my life
messed up. Or I could go to London and work. Don't feel
sorry for aunt Louise. She's such a coward. Haven't you
noticed? It's safer to stay in the garden and shout over
the wall. Don't feel sorry for her. She's a bully and only the
weak ones like being bullied. The town's full of her cripples.
They're the ones she's nicest to.

WILLY. I know.

ROSE (*shrugs slightly*). When are you going?

WILLY. Soon. Everything's done here.

ROSE. If you'd drowned I'd be married to Colin now.

WILLY. I suppose it was a near thing.

ROSE. You missed drowning. You missed the draper's knife. Does living excite you?

WILLY. Shall I kiss you?

WILLY *kisses her in silence.*

ROSE. In a dead man's shoes.

WILLY. The dead don't matter.

ROSE. I'm not sure.

WILLY. Then you're like your aunt. You talk and have no courage.

ROSE. Look, they've left the cover off the piano. Damp spoils the strings. (ROSE *covers the piano with a green or faded dirty white sheet.*) Aunt will order two strong men with a barrow to bring it back. (*She stands the chair in front of the piano.*)

WILLY *turns to go.*

ROSE. Where are you going?

WILLY. For a swim.

ROSE. Today?

WILLY. Yes.

ROSE. In the sea?

WILLY. Yes.

ROSE. Where's your towel?

WILLY. I don't need one.

ROSE. Will you?

WILLY. Oh yes.

He looks at her for a moment and then turns again to go.

ROSE. Wait. (*He stops.*) I'll come down and hold your clothes . . .

WILLY *nods at her and starts to go.* ROSE *follows him off. The stage is empty except for the covered piano and the empty chair.*

SCENE EIGHT

Beach.

EVENS's *hut. Bright, clear morning with some wind.* EVENS *sits on a box. He has a small whisky flask in his hand but he doesn't drink. After a moment he shouts offstage.*

EVENS. You've been hanging round there all morning!
HOLLARCUT (*off*). Oh ay?
EVENS. What's the big stick for?

After a few moments HOLLARCUT *comes in. He looks tired and unshaved. His collar is open. He is exhausted but has the energy of anger.*

HOLLARCUT (*flatly*). What, scum?
EVENS. Come to batter me to death, have you? Batter me with your big stick?
HOLLARCUT (*flatly*). What if I have?
EVENS. You won't.
HOLLARCUT (*flatly*). Oh ay?
EVENS. You haven't got it in you.
HOLLARCUT (*flatly*). No?
EVENS. Not now Hatch is inside.
HOLLARCUT. Don't you dutty his name with yoor foul ol' snout.
EVENS. You don't believe the stories he told you? D'you believe I ride on a broomstick?
HOLLARCUT (*flatly*). What if I don't?
EVENS. Then why d'you come to batter me with your big stick? (*He takes a drink.*)
HOLLARCUT. Who drove him wrong in the hid? Why'd he take up all they daft notions? I don't know no one doo that if that weren't yoo. (*He hits a box with the stick. It breaks.*)
EVENS. Probably.
HOLLARCUT. He allus treat me right. Who else talked t' me

'cept t' say goo here, fetch that, yoo en't got this in yoo, yoo
can't doo that? He on't ashamed t' talk t' me, or listen. He
on't used me like that ol' bitch an' the rest on yer. He wanted
me with him.

EVENS. Yes, I see.

HOLLARCUT. I count in the end. Yoo may not like it but mostly
I'm like yoo an' I count. He knew that. That on't so mad.
Thass all I'll say for today.

EVENS. All right, Billy. But don't do mad things. Drop your
stick on the ground.

HOLLARCUT. Mr Hollarcut.

EVENS. Drop your stick Mr Hollarcut.

HOLLARCUT. No. I'll howd on to en now I got en. That remind
yoo I'm here.

WILLY *comes in.*

WILLY. Hello. I thought I'd walk out this way.

EVENS (*nods*). They had their inquest this morning.

WILLY. Yes.

EVENS. It's all wrapped up.

WILLY. Death by drowning.

EVENS. Satisfied?

WILLY. And the coroner mentioned careless people who go to
sea in bad weather and put the coastguard at risk.

EVENS. When are you going?

WILLY. Now. Morning, Billy. I see Mrs Rafi's got you digging
in her garden.

HOLLARCUT. Mr Hollarcut.

WILLY. Ah yes.

HOLLARCUT. Thass all right – Carson on't it? I'll tell you
something you ought a know, boy. I dig for her – (*He lays
the side of his index finger against the side of his nose and looks
crafty.*) – but will anything grow? . . . Mornin'.

HOLLARCUT *goes out.* WILLY *sits on a box.*

EVENS. Have you come to kill me?

WILLY. I don't believe so.

EVENS. He had.

WILLY. Oh dear. Should we take it seriously?

EVENS (*shrugs*). God knows.

WILLY. Perhaps you'd better move back into town. For a while anyway.

EVENS. I'd rather be battered to death.

WILLY. Tch tch.

Silence.

WILLY. The draper thought there were more people up there. Other worlds.

EVENS. There are countless millions of suns, so there must be more planets. Millions and millions of living worlds.

WILLY. But would they come all this way to visit us even if they could?

EVENS. No, hardly worth the trip.

WILLY. Perhaps they're all busy killing each other and killing other things. But what if they've killed everything up there? Then they might come here to kill us. I mean, that would make the long trip worth while. A space safari. Perhaps we're just violent little vermin to them. Not to be taken seriously. Just sport.

EVENS. Yes.

WILLY. D'you think they kill each other?

EVENS. Must do. Where there's life it kills, after all.

WILLY. But up there. Out there. When I look up into the sky there are things dying and bleeding and groaning?

EVENS. Oh yes. The music of the spheres.

WILLY. How can you bear to live?

EVENS. I really don't know. I don't know why I'm not mad.

Silence.

WILLY. I'm not sure if I can bear it.

EVENS. You don't have to bear it long. The years go very quickly and you seem to be spared the minutes. Have faith.

WILLY. In what?

EVENS (*shrugs*). Well. (*Looks round.*) Would you like some tea?

WILLY. No.

EVENS. It's no trouble. It's already made. I fill two flasks every morning and that sees me through the day.

WILLY. No thanks.

In silence EVENS *takes two flasks from a box. He unscrews one flask and pours tea. He lets it stand in the cup. He takes the small whisky flask from his pocket and drinks. He puts it away again. He picks up the tea and warms his hands on the cup. The two flasks stand on a box beside him. The silence lasts a moment longer.*

EVENS. I believe in the rat. What's the worst thing you can imagine? The universe is lived in by things that kill and this has gone on for all time. Sometimes the universe is crowded with killing things. Or at any rate there are great pools of them in space. Perhaps that's so now. At other times it falls out that they've killed everything off, including each other of course, and the universe is almost deserted. But not quite. Somewhere on a star a rat will hide under a stone. It will look out on the broken desert and from time to time it will scatter out to feed on the debris. A shambolling, lolloping great rat – like a fat woman with shopping bags running for a bus. Then it scuttles back to its nest and breeds. Because rats build nests. And in time it will change into things that fly and swim and crawl and run. And one day it will change into the rat catcher. I believe in the rat because he has the seeds of the rat catcher in him. I believe in the rat catcher. I believe in sand and stone and water because the wind stirs them into a dirty sea and it gives birth to living things. The universe lives. It teems with life. Men take themselves to be very strong and cunning. But who can kill space or time or dust? They destroy everything but they only make the materials of life. All destruction is finally petty and in the end life laughs at death.

WILLY. Then it goes on and on. But if it fails in the end? If it always goes back to the rat.

EVENS. I also believe in the wise rat catcher. He can bear to live in the minutes as well as the years, and he understands the voice of the thing he is going to kill. Suffering is a universal language and everything that has a voice is human. We sit here and the world changes. When your life's over everything will be changed or have started to change. Our brains won't be big enough. They'll plug into bigger brains. They'll get rid of this body. It's too liable to get ill and break. They'll transplant the essential things into a better container. An unbreakable glass bottle on steel stilts. Men will look at each other's viscera as they pass in the street. There'll be no more grass. Why? What's it for? There'll be no more tragedy. There's no tragedy without grass for you to play it on. Well, without tragedy no one can laugh, there's only discipline and madness. You see why the draper's afraid. Not of things from space, of us. We're becoming the strange visitors to this world.

WILLY. Perhaps a better world.

EVENS. Then why will they fill it with bombs and germs and gas? You'll live in a time when that happens and people will do nothing. They'll sit on the ground and say perhaps a better world.

WILLY. What should I do? Come and live here? Work hard? Make money? Become mayor?

EVENS. No.

WILLY. You sound so sure.

EVENS. I'm a wreck rotting on the beach. Past help. That's why I live here out of people's way. It wouldn't help *them* if they lived here. We all have to end differently. . . . Don't trust the wise fool too much. What he knows matters and you die without it. But he never knows enough. No. Go

away. You won't find any more answers here. Go away and
find them. Don't give up hope. That's always silly. The
truth's waiting for you, it's very patient, and you'll find it.
Remember, I've told you these things so that you won't
despair. But you must still change the world.

ROSE *comes on*.

ROSE. I followed you. We mustn't miss our train. What were you
saying?

WILLY. I came to say goodbye, and I'm glad you —

END

Narrow Road
to the Deep North

A Comedy

Narrow Road to the Deep North was commissioned by Canon Stephen Verney as Chairman of the executive of the Peoples and Cities Conference and first presented at the Belgrade Theatre, Coventry, on June 24th, 1968, with the following cast:

BASHO, old, a priest		Peter Needham
KIRO, twenty	⎫	Paul Howes
ARGI	⎪	Malcolm Ingram
TOLA	⎬ priests	Christopher Matthews
HEIGOO	⎪	John Rowe
BREEBREE	⎭	Gordon Reid
SHOGO, twenty-five		Edward Peel
PRIME MINISTER		Peter Sproule
COMMODORE, forty-seven		Nigel Hawthorne
GEORGINA, thirty-nine		Susan Williamson
		Alison King
		Diana Beriman
Peasants		Alan David
Soldiers		Geoffrey White
Tars	⎬	Vandra Edwards
Tribesmen		Malcolm Ingram
etc.		Christopher Matthews
		John Rowe
		Gordon Reid
		Peter Sproule
Directed by		Jane Howell
Designed by		Hayden Griffin
Lighting by		Barry Griffiths

Japan about the seventeenth, eighteenth or nineteenth centuries. The introduction is based on an incident in Matsuo Basho's *The Records of a Weather-Exposed Skeleton*.

INTRODUCTION

Bare stage.
BASHO *comes on.*

BASHO. My name is Basho. I am, as you know, the great
seventeenth-century Japanese poet, who brought the haiku
verse form to perfection and gave it greater range and depth.
For example:
   Silent old pool
   Frog jumps
   Kdang!
I've just left my home in the village here (*points offstage*) and
I'm going on a journey along the narrow road to the deep
north and when I reach there I shall become a hermit and get
enlightenment. But just now when I was walking along this
river bank I heard crying. There's a little baby lying in some
rags on the edge of the river. It's about two years old. Why
did its parents do that to it?

A PEASANT *and his* WIFE *come in.*

WIFE. I must see it once more. I must kiss it for the last
time.
PEASANT. That won't do any good.
WIFE (*kneeling by the rags*). My baby.
PEASANT. You'll upset it.
WIFE. It's smiling because I'm here. It's been lying there
wondering how long it would have to wait.
BASHO. Why have you left it by the river?
PEASANT. We're poor and there's no food. We have five other
children and if we let this one go perhaps the others will live.
Better lose one than all of them. People do it every day. You

just leave the little thing here and hope someone with money finds it and looks after it. You'll come across plenty of them along the river.

WIFE (*cries*). And most of them are dead.

PEASANT. There you are! I told you not to come back.

WIFE. Please take it, sir.

BASHO. No. I've given it all the food I had. But I'm poor, too. And I'm going away to get enlightenment.

WIFE. No one will take him. He's too thin and little. They only want the healthy ones, so they can work later on. (*Cries.*) He'll die, or crawl in the river and drown!

PEASANT (*hits her perfunctorily*). I told you not to come back! (*To* BASHO.) She does this every time.

WIFE. You're right, dear. Leave well alone and hope for the best. (*Cries.*) Will god forgive me?

PEASANT. Back to work.

The PEASANT *takes her hand and they go out.*

BASHO. It's true. They're hungry, and they must feel – some relief because they've got rid of *one* of their problems. She's untidied its clothes. (*He adjusts the rags.*) Ha! He stares at me as if I was a toy. What funny little eyes! (*Turns away.*) It hasn't done anything to *earn* this suffering – it's caused by something greater and more massive: you could call it the irresistible will of heaven. So it must cry to heaven. And I must go to the north.

BASHO *goes out.*

PART ONE

SCENE ONE

The same place. KIRO *lounges half asleep. After a moment* BASHO *comes on from the direction he left. He walks older.*

BASHO. Thirty years since I was here! (*Looks round and nods.*) Yes – I remember this spot! Someone left a baby out to die. I spoke to them – I can't remember what we said. When I left there was only a village here. Now there's a great city with ten bridges, and parks, a palace, law courts, and crowds of merchants and beggars and priests and soldiers and children . . . The people in the north still live in tribes, but they fed me. I had a bowl, these clothes, a paper raincoat and an umbrella. The climate is inferior. (*Turns to* KIRO.) Why are you lying by the river instead of working?

KIRO. I'm sad.

BASHO. Why?

KIRO. My parents died when I was a child and —

BASHO. Is it a long story?

KIRO. No.

BASHO. Because I'm tired. I've been travelling.

KIRO. Please listen. You look intelligent and perhaps you could tell me what to do. My parents died when I was a child. They were peasants. One year the rice just didn't grow and they starved. A priest came to the house. He was begging. The door was open and he looked in and saw me lying with my dead parents. So he took me with him and brought me up. That's what he said anyway, but I don't remember. He told me that when he died I was to find someone who'd got enlightenment and become his disciple. Well,

he died last year. But I still haven't been able to find anyone
who knows very much.

BASHO. What did he teach you?

KIRO. Nothing.

BASHO. Nothing?

KIRO. He said he'd never learned anything worth passing on.
He was a very simple old man.

BASHO. You've been fooled. He was obviously just lazy. I can
see everything's got worse while I've been away.

KIRO. Where have you been?

BASHO. The deep north. I went there to get enlightenment.

KIRO. Did you get it?

BASHO. Yes.

KIRO. Tell me what it is!

BASHO. For twenty-nine and a half years I sat facing a wall and
staring into space. Then one morning I suddenly saw what I
was looking for – and I got enlightenment.

KIRO. Yes?

BASHO (*smiles*). I saw there was nothing to learn in the deep
north – and I'd already known everything before I went
there. You get enlightenment where you are.

KIRO. Let me be your disciple.

BASHO. I don't need disciples.

KIRO. Let me!

BASHO (*looks closely at* KIRO). How many feet has god?

KIRO (*hesitates*). Two?

BASHO. How many hands has god?

KIRO (*slighter hesitation*). Two.

BASHO. How many eyes has god?

KIRO. Two.

BASHO. How many ears has god?

KIRO. Two.

BASHO. How many lips has god?

KIRO. Two.

BASHO. How many hairs has god?

KIRO. How many hairs . . . ?

BASHO (*losing patience*). How much patience has god?

KIRO. I . . .

BASHO. Kwatz! You don't know anything about god. You've only been looking at men. Your old priest was an ass!

KIRO. I know, but if I was your disciple —

BASHO. You're not ready to be a disciple, you don't know the first things! Isn't there a seminary in this city?

KIRO. The old priest told me not to go there.

BASHO. Why not?

KIRO. I don't know.

BASHO. Well go there!

KIRO. But —

BASHO. Is his advice better than mine?

KIRO. No, no —

BASHO. Had he been to the deep north?

KIRO. No.

BASHO. Then go to the seminary —

KIRO. But I've always done —

BASHO. – if they'll take you!

Some PRISONERS *and* GUARDS *come on. Each* PRISONER *holds a sack in front of him and has an iron collar round his neck and each collar is attached by a chain to a pole held by a* GUARD. *'Shogo is my friend' is painted in red on the sacks.*

PRISONERS (*chant*). Shogo is head of the city
      Shogo is protector and friend
      Shogo is guide and leader
      Shogo is head of the city (etc.).

BASHO. What's this?

KIRO. They're prisoners, criminals. They bring some here every day and throw them in the river. They put them in the sacks and hold them under with their poles.

PRISONERS (*chant*). Shogo is head of the city
      Shogo is protector and friend (etc.).

BASHO. Who is Shogo?

KIRO. Shogo's head of the city. He was an outlaw, and two years ago he came here with a little army and killed the old emperor who owned all the south. Then he built this city.

GUARD. Let's hear you! Make me happy!

PRISONERS (*chant*). Shogo gives and we take
                 Shogo asks and we answer.

KIRO. The old priest who looked after me said he was the devil.

PRISONERS (*chant*). Shogo is law and order
                 Shogo is —

GUARDS (*shout*). Shogo is Shogo is Shogo!

PRISONERS (*chant*). – law and order.

BASHO. The world's changed in thirty years! I wonder if my house is still there, and my orchard.

GUARD. Sing up! You won't get many more chances!

PRISONERS (*chant*). Shogo is head of the city
                 Shogo is the tide on the river.

GUARDS (*shout*). Shogo! Shogo! Shogo!

The GUARDS *and the* PRISONERS *go out.*

BASHO. I'm going to watch. (*Afterthought.*) Perhaps I can say something that will comfort them.

BASHO *goes out.* KIRO *is alone. He looks at the ground. A* SOLDIER *comes on pulling an* OLD MAN *with his chain and pole. The* OLD MAN *is either drunk or ill – he stumbles along clumsily. He tries to chant, but it sounds like drunken muttering.*

GUARD. Hup! Hup! Hup!

OLD PRISONER. Shogo is . . . guide and friend . . . Shogo is guide and . . . Shogo . . .

GUARD. You'll be dead before you get there and I'll have to drag your carcass and throw it in the river! Hup! Hup!

OLD PRISONER. Shogo . . . is . . . Shogo . . . is . . .

The OLD PRISONER *and the* GUARD *go out.* KIRO *is alone again.*

GUARDS (*off*). Shogo!

Silence.

SCENE TWO

BASHO *hoes his garden. A* NUN *sits upstage with a pen and book.*

BASHO. I've been back two years. I left my old hut up there in
the orchard and moved here farther down the river, away
from the city. My old hut was by the place where they throw
people in the river. Their friends and relatives used to come
and stand quietly on the bank, with Shogo expressions on
their faces. But when it was over they ran round looking
for somewhere quiet to cry, and they always ended up
behind my hut, crying on my vegetables and treading on them.
(*He bends down to pull out a weed.*) I think the head of the
city will put me in the sack next. (*He straightens.*) He knows
I've got enlightenment – and he doesn't like people who know
something he doesn't. (*To the* NUN.) Write this down. (*He
hoes while the* NUN *writes in her book.*)

> The old horse stops on the bridge
> The carter unhitches and leads her from the shafts
> Leg broken
> Passers-by help to push her in the river
> Wild struggle but she drowns quickly
> Floats at rest
> Head down, mane in eyes.
> The carter goes off between the shafts

Two SOLDIERS* *have come on while* BASHO *dictated and sat on
their haunches.*

SOLDIER. We'll wait. He's writing.
BASHO (*hoes while the* NUN *writes*). Another poem.

   * It can be one.

The soldier leant his spear on the wall
It fell
Clatter
They took him in for idleness

SOLDIER. That's good.

The SOLDIERS *grin.*

BASHO (*to the* SOLDIERS). Why have two soldiers come to my garden?

SOLDIER. We're taking you away.

BASHO. Where?

SOLDIER. Shogo.

BASHO. Let me finish this row. (*He hoes.*) Write this. (*He hoes, and the* NUN *writes.*)

Two soldiers came
The head of the city wants me
They waited
While I wrote this poem

BASHO *has finished the row. He gives the hoe to the* NUN *and goes out with the* SOLDIERS.

SCENE THREE

Five PRIESTS *come along the road. They are* KIRO, ARGI (*long and thin*), TOLA (*young and mild*), HEIGOO (*tough and energetic*), BREEBREE (*humorous and aesthetic*). TOLA *and* HEIGOO *carry a small ark with a pot on it.* ARGI *walks in front. They all wear yellow robes.*

TOLA. I'm hot. (*He puts his end of the ark down.*) I want a rest.

ARGI. You've just had a rest.

TOLA. It's heavy.

ARGI. That's because it's holy.

TOLA. I've earned a drink.

ARGI. You should be earning merit, not —

HEIGOO. Anyway, I want a drink too.

BREEBREE. And me.

HEIGOO *takes a bottle and a cup from under his robe.*

ARGI. Put that away!

HEIGOO (*opening the bottle*). I'm thirsty.

ARGI (*sniffs at the bottle*). You can't drink that here!

HEIGOO. I can drink it anywhere!

He takes two more bottles and three more cups from his robe and hands them round. They pour and drink.

BREEBREE. Here's to the sacred pot! (*He drinks.*)

HEIGOO (*to* ARGI). What about you?

ARGI. I'll have some. If I don't you'll drink it all, and have the sin of gluttony on your souls. (*He takes his own cup from his robes and* HEIGOO *fills it.*) But only one.

TOLA *and* BREEBREE *have started a subdued version of hopscotch in which each throws the stone for the other.* ARGI *goes over to them.*

ARGI. Watch him, he cheats. (TOLA *throws and* BREEBREE *hops.*) The aim is to make your enemy win. (*Suddenly.*) Out! Out! Out! He jumped the wrong way.

BREEBREE. I didn't!

ARGI. You did! Didn't he? (*He starts to hop.*) You went there (*hops*) – there (*hops*) – there (*hops*)! You should have gone there (*points*) – there (*points*) – there (*points*)! – (*He hops three times*) self-deception!

TOLA. I thought he went —

ARGI. You don't know the rules! Come on, I'll play the pair of you. This stone's no good. It would float on water. (*He throws the stone away and looks for another one.*)

KIRO *sits on one side.* HEIGOO *crosses to him.*

HEIGOO. Give me your cup. (*He takes* KIRO's *cup and pours him a drink.*) You're sad.

KIRO. No.

HEIGOO. A lie.

KIRO (*drinks*). Well, I've been in the seminary two years and I haven't learned anything.

HEIGOO. You passed your exams.

ARGI. God throw for me! (*He throws a stone.*)

TOLA. Out!

ARGI. This stone's no good either!

HEIGOO. Any more?

KIRO. Please. (HEIGOO *and* KIRO *drink.* KIRO *wipes his mouth on the back of his hand.*) It's all nothing.

HEIGOO. You've been praying too much. Or meditating too much.

KIRO. No, I don't overdo it.

HEIGOO. Well, I don't understand anything . . . You should go to someone clever.

BREEBREE (*hopping*). That's my drink.

TOLA. Sorry! (*He picks up another cup.*) This must be mine.

ARGI (*to* BREEBREE). He owes you a drink out of his: he had a drink out of yours.

TOLA (*pulls a face*).

KIRO. But who's clever?

HEIGOO. Lots of people, surely . . .

TOLA (*hopping*). I'm hot! (*He stops and comes across to* KIRO *and* HEIGOO.) You look sad.

HEIGOO ⎱ (*Laughs.*)
KIRO   ⎰ No, no.

TOLA. Yes you do.

BREEBREE (*crossing to them*). What's the matter with Kiro, he —

HEIGOO. He's sad.

ARGI. Come back! We haven't finished.

TOLA. I'm too tired.

ARGI. I'll finish on my own.

ARGI *jumps and the others drink. Pause.*

HEIGOO. Tola has beautiful ears.

There is a subdued, relaxed, amused murmur. Pause.

BREEBREE (*sings*).
When I became a monk
The farmers' daughters cried
They brought me tea and rice
I sent them back for wine

HEIGOO (*sighs*).

ARGI. I've won!

BREEBREE (*sings*).
They came back with the wine
They cried and turned to go
I said stay

BREEBREE *starts to drift about, twirling his robes.*

ARGI. Come on, we must go. (*To* TOLA.) It's still your turn to carry.

TOLA (*gets up, trips slightly*). O.

ARGI. You're drunk!

TOLA. I'm over-worked! Someone ought to carry *me*!

HEIGOO *starts to drift round* BREEBREE. *He has a bottle in his hand.*

ARGI. Stop that! Someone might come!

HEIGOO (*pulls* KIRO *up*). Come on! Be happy!

KIRO. Yes!

KIRO, BREEBREE *and* HEIGOO *dance round.* TOLA *claps.*

ARGI. You're all drunk!

HEIGOO. Unfortunately no!

ARGI. Father Abbot will —

ARGI
TOLA } – hear about this!

HEIGOO *grabs* ARGI *and whirls him round.*

ARGI. Stop it! Put me down!

TOLA (*takes the pot from the ark and sits on the ark*). I want a carry!

ARGI. Stop it! You'll give us a bad name!

HEIGOO. Up! Up!

He pulls TOLA *up and dances round with him. All the* MONKS *are whirling except* ARGI.

ARGI. I'm going. (*He tries to push the ark, like a wheelless barrow. He stops.*) I can't leave the relic with them!

The PRIESTS *start to play leap-frog.*

KIRO. Watch me drink and jump!

He jumps over BREEBREE *and drinks at the same time. The others cheer and laugh.*

ARGI. Mind the pot! (HEIGOO *comes up behind* ARGI, *pushes him down and jumps over him. Shouts triumphantly.*) Ah! You've hurt me! You've injured my back! (*The other priests whirl and jump.*) Mind that pot! (KIRO *picks up the pot and runs round with it.*) Put it down! O god! (KIRO *goes to throw it to* HEIGOO. HEIGOO *crouches ready.*)

BREEBREE. No! Don't!

A sudden silence. They stare at KIRO. *He isn't sure what to do. Then he turns the pot upside down and puts his head in it.*

TOLA *and* HEIGOO. Father Abbot will hear about this!

ARGI. It's scandalous!

KIRO *starts to jump and whirl about.* BREEBREE, HEIGOO *and* TOLA *dance with him.* KIRO *tilts his head back and tries to pour drink down the neck of the pot. He splutters and chokes. The drink falls down his robes in a vivid red stain.*

TOLA (*spinning* KIRO). One, two, three! Catch Argi!

ARGI *shouts and ducks about.* KIRO *gropes for him. The others block* ARGI *and* KIRO *catches him and moves his head awkwardly from side to side.*

HEIGOO. He's trying to kiss Argi! (*The others roar with laughter.*)

BREEBREE. Trying to kiss Argi!

TOLA. Trying to kiss Argi!

ARGI. Why not? Why d'you try to make a fool of me? (*He cries in annoyance. He sits down by the ark.*)

The others quieten down. They sit or squat.

HEIGOO. You've got beautiful ears too, Argi.

ARGI *cries for a few seconds in annoyance. Then there is a contented, amused silence.* KIRO *makes a funny noise inside the pot.* HEIGOO *laughs shortly.* ARGI *gives one sniff. Silence.*

HEIGOO (*looks at his empty bottle*). No more.

Silence. KIRO *lifts his hands to take off the pot. It won't come off immediately. He is too exhausted to make any effort, and he puts his hands down again and gets his breath back. The others stare happily into space.* HEIGOO *gives a little chuckle to himself.* KIRO *lifts his hands to take off the pot. Again it won't come off immediately. He stops, but almost immediately tries again – harder still.*

KIRO (*abruptly*). It's stuck.

BREEBREE. I'll do it. (*He stands, goes to* KIRO *and tries to remove the pot. He can't*). It's stuck.

HEIGOO *and* TOLA *come over to* KIRO.

HEIGOO. Hold his shoulders. (BREEBREE *holds* KIRO's *shoulder and* HEIGOO *pulls.*)

KIRO. Ow!

HEIGOO. Brace yourself! (*He pulls.*)

KIRO. OW!

HEIGOO. It won't come.

ARGI. A nice sight if someone comes by.

HEIGOO *suddenly gives the pot another pull.*

KIRO. Ouch!

TOLA. Don't hurt him!

BREEBREE. Lean forward.

TOLA. Lever it.

HEIGOO (*to* TOLA). You do it then!

TOLA (*tries half-heartedly*). It won't come. (BREEBREE *laughs.*)

HEIGOO (*to* KIRO). What d'you want us to do? (KIRO *shrugs.*)

ARGI (*comes over to them*). I knew this would happen.

TOLA. If you can't help shut up!

ARGI. I saw it coming. I think I must have had a vision. (*To* TOLA.) Ha! It's easy to be rude to me. (*Shouts loudly against the pot.*) Have you prayed?

KIRO. No.

ARGI. What a fool! (*He walks a bit away and stops.*) O god, take the pot off his head, amen. (*He goes back to* KIRO, *smartly grasps the pot, and pulls it up.* KIRO *is jerked up with it.*)

KIRO. Whow!

TOLA. You'll break his neck!

ARGI. It's his own fault! He didn't pray hard enough!

BREEBREE. Stop it! Stop it! I'm frightened!

Suddenly KIRO *starts to struggle frantically.*

ARGI. Be careful!

BREEBREE ⎫ Mind the pot! It's holy!
ARGI   ⎭ Yes.

KIRO *runs to the centre of the stage, still tugging at the pot. He crouches and struggles.* BASHO *comes on with the two soldiers. He stops by* KIRO *and watches him. The others are still and intent.* KIRO *struggles and groans.* BASHO *gently touches* KIRO. *Silence.*

BASHO. What's the matter?

ARGI. It's stuck.

BASHO. How did that happen?

ARGI. He put it on his head.

BREEBREE. It's a holy relic. It's a thousand years old.

ARGI. The emperor Kolo hid in it from his brother's army.

BASHO. I recognized it. (*To* KIRO.) Show me your hands.
  (BASHO *glances at* KIRO's *hands.*) I thought so, you're the
  monk who stopped me two years ago and wanted to become
  my disciple. I said no, with foresight.

TOLA. Can you take it off?

BASHO (*to* KIRO). Have you studied meditation? (*Pause.* ARGI
  prods KIRO.)

KIRO. Yes.

BASHO. Good. Think small. (*He waits a second.*) Are you
  thinking?

KIRO. Yes.

BASHO (*tries to remove the pot. He can't*). I can't help you, you
  still haven't learned anything. You live in darkness. (KIRO
  sobs.) You would have to make the pot think big, and that's
  definitely beyond your powers.

TOLA. What will happen?

BREEBREE. He won't be able to eat.

HEIGOO. His neck's swelling.

TOLA. He won't be able to breathe! (KIRO *groans.*)

ARGI. And he's got a hang-over.

TOLA. We'll take him to a doctor.

BASHO. Can a doctor do what I can't?

TOLA. No.

HEIGOO. Shall we try a witch?

BASHO (*looks at* HEIGOO). Anything can be put to good use.
  Bring him with me. There's something *he* can do for us. (*To*
  ARGI.) You won't get it off till he's dead.

ARGI. O!

BASHO *nods to the* SOLDIERS *and they start to leave.*

ARGI. Bring the ark. (HEIGOO *and* BREEBREE *pick up the ark.*

TOLA *guides* KIRO.) We'll cover him with a sheet. Otherwise there'll be a scandal.

They all go out.

SCENE FOUR

SHOGO's *court. A banner or hanging, and a small table with a hammer and sack on it. No one is on stage. There is a shout and a* MAN *comes in with a spear through him. He struggles frantically.*

MAN. It's stuck! . . .

He looks bewildered, dies, and then falls down. SHOGO *comes in talking.*

SHOGO. It missed me and went through the Chief Police Inspector. (*Calls.*) He's in the throne-room! (*He looks at the body.*) He's dead. It's his own fault for not doing his job properly. (*Calls.*) Prime Minister!

The PRIME MINISTER *comes in immediately.*

SHOGO. Have you caught him?
PRIME MINISTER. Not yet, sir.
SHOGO. Have you taken hostages?
PRIME MINISTER. We're taking them, sir.
SHOGO. Well, go and catch him!

The PRIME MINISTER *goes out.*

SHOGO. How do they always get away? When I go out no one is allowed to look at me. They crouch with their faces on the ground. I look at all those bundles of clothes, and every so often one of them suddenly looks up – and I'm looking straight into his face. It's always a different face, but the eyes are the same. He throws a spear, and when we get to our feet again he's gone. I never catch them. They just go . . . (*He walks behind the body and stands with his back to the audience.*) I wanted to say something, but it's gone out of my head . . . The circle that never stops getting smaller. That's an old

saying. (*Suddenly annoyed.*) They won't get him! (*Calls.*)
Prime Minister!

The PRIME MINISTER *comes in immediately.*

PRIME MINISTER (*shaking his head*). Not yet.
SHOGO. Has he got away?
PRIME MINISTER. We've got the hostages.
SHOGO. Go and get *him*!

The PRIME MINISTER *goes out.*

SHOGO (*looks at the body*). . . . I can't be on both sides of a door
    at once. . . .

BASHO *comes in with a* SOLDIER.

SHOGO (*excited*). Yes!
SOLDIER. No, this is Basho the poet.
SHOGO (*calls*). Prime Minister!

The PRIME MINISTER *comes in immediately.*

SHOGO. Fetch it.

The PRIME MINISTER *goes out.*

SHOGO. My police say you've been to the deep north.
BASHO. Yes.
SHOGO. People shouldn't travel. It's bad for the mind.
BASHO. You were only a child when I left.
SHOGO. The police also say you've got enlightenment.
BASHO. Yes. I learned that —
SHOGO. I don't want to know. (*He goes to the body and removes
    the spear and throws it to the soldier.*) Save that. It will come
    in useful.
BASHO (*looks after the* PRIME MINISTER). Is he fetching my
    sack? (SHOGO *smiles.*) You can kill me, of course. It will have
    no importance. But —
SHOGO (*interrupting*). But?
BASHO. I'm going to die. (*He nods in signal to one side.*) No one

can open and shut a door at the same time.

SHOGO (*startled*). What?

TOLA *leads* KIRO *on.* KIRO *is covered with a sheet.*

SHOGO. What's that?

BASHO. You built the biggest city in the world. You can't get a pot off a priest's head. (TOLA *takes the sheet off* KIRO.)

SHOGO. How did that happen?

BASHO. I've tried to get it off, and on our way here we asked several doctors and witches to try: none of us could do it. So I brought him to you. The pot is sacred and very old.

SHOGO (*points to the corpse*). Bury that! (*The* SOLDIER *takes the corpse out. To* BASHO.) I didn't bring you here to kill you. (*Calls.*) Prime Minister!

The PRIME MINISTER *comes in immediately. He carries a* BABY. SHOGO *takes it.*

SHOGO. Have you caught him yet?

PRIME MINISTER. Not yet.

The PRIME MINISTER *goes out.* SHOGO *takes* BASHO *to one side and talks to him privately.*

SHOGO. Two years ago, when I killed the old Emperor, his wife was pregnant. Luckily she died in childbirth. This was the son. I kept him in the palace, but now he's beginning to notice things and I can't keep him here any more. It's too risky. People mustn't know there's someone else who could claim my city. That would start trouble. Take him away and bring him up with some other children – you can get them from the slums, orphans best – and let him think he's an orphan and his parents were peasants. You must never tell him he's an Emperor's son.

BASHO. I can't look after children. I haven't got a wife.

SHOGO. I'm sorry for him. He's done no harm. I've taken everything he was going to have. But you've got enlightenment, so perhaps you can give him something.

BASHO. But I don't know —

SHOGO. Take him. It's better than the sack. (*He puts the* BABY *in* BASHO'S *arms.*) Swear you'll never tell anyone he's the Emperor. *Never.*

BASHO (*nods*). Yes.

SHOGO. Good. (*Turns immediately to* TOLA.) Try a potter.

BASHO. We have.

SHOGO. Well take him away!

TOLA (*desperately*). His neck's swollen. He can't breathe.

SHOGO. Take him away!

A SOLDIER *and the* PRIME MINISTER *come on. The* PRIME MINISTER *pushes a* PEASANT *in front of him. The* PEASANT *is stripped to the waist. He has been hit. The* PRIME MINISTER *forces him down in front of* SHOGO.

SHOGO. Is that him?

PRIME MINISTER. No, but he was standing next to him.

SHOGO. Well done. He's an important witness. (*To the* PEASANT.) Did you see the man who tried to kill me? (*Pause. The* PEASANT *can't answer.*) Did you see him?

PRIME MINISTER. Shall I —

SHOGO (*to the* PEASANT). Which way did he go? (*No answer*). D'you understand my questions?

PRIME MINISTER. It's impertinence.

BASHO. No, you must be patient, he's —

SHOGO. – afraid, and the only thing to do is frighten it out of him. (*He goes to the table, picks up the sack, and lays it down in front of the* PEASANT.) Stand on that. (*The* PEASANT *doesn't move. The* PRIME MINISTER *pushes him forward. The* PEASANT *stands in the sack with the side rucked round his ankles.*) Did you see the man who tried to kill me? Where did he come from? Which way did he go? (*A second's silence.* SHOGO *lifts the sides of the sack till they reach the* PEASANT'S *waist and leaves them there.*) If you go in that sack you'll never come out. (*The* SOLDIER *laughs.*)

PEASANT (*forcing himself to answer the first question*). I – saw –
   him.

SHOGO (*shows him the spear*). Didn't you see he had this?
   Aren't all weapons banned?

The PEASANT *tries to speak. He can't.* SHOGO *lifts the sack to
his shoulders.* KIRO *starts to groan inside the pot. The* PEASANT
tries to speak. Wait.

TOLA (*he puts his head close to the pot*). I can't hear what he's
   saying. I think he's dying.

BASHO (*to* TOLA). Make him stop. He'll crack the pot.

TOLA (*arms round* KIRO). Kiro, Kiro. (SHOGO *turns to watch.*)

SHOGO. What can I do? I can only do what you can do! My
   hands are only like yours. There isn't some political skill or
   trick called taking pots off priests' heads!

KIRO *jerks.* TOLA *sobs. The* PEASANT *tries to speak.*

PEASANT. I – saw – him.

SHOGO *goes to the table, picks up the hammer, goes to* KIRO, *and
breaks the pot.* KIRO *slumps down. His face is blue.* SHOGO *goes to
the peasant, pushes him into the sack and closes it.*

SHOGO (*to the* SOLDIER). Take him off! He didn't see anything, anyway.

BASHO. Then you should let him go.

SHOGO. No, he should have seen something!

The PEASANT *cries in the sack. The* SOLDIER *hauls him out.*

SHOGO *comes towards* KIRO. *He still holds the hammer.*

SHOGO. Is he all right?

KIRO. You broke the pot!

SHOGO. Wouldn't anyone?

KIRO *puts his arms round* SHOGO's *legs. The* PRIME MINISTER
pushes him away.

SHOGO. Poets and priests! I must work. (*He starts to go upstage.*)

KIRO (*lurching after* SHOGO). Let me talk to you!

SHOGO. What?

KIRO *follows him upstage and says something.* SHOGO *laughs and walks on a bit more.* KIRO *talks.* SHOGO *stops and listens.*

BASHO (*to* TOLA). Collect those pieces. (TOLA *collects the bits of pot and offers them to* BASHO. BASHO *turns away.*) Take them to your Father Abbot.

TOLA *goes to one side and kneels.*

PRIME MINISTER (*stares at* BASHO). What's the matter?

BASHO. This city has no future.

PRIME MINISTER. What?

BASHO (*angrily*). He's imprisoned innocent women, orphaned children, made the men soldiers, and killed them. His city is hell, ruled by atrocity. I could put up with that if I could still hope. But how can I hope if he destroys religion? He knew the pot was sacred. Of course, that's only a symbol, but we need symbols to protect us from ourselves. If he destroys them, there's no future. A fool destroys men but a fanatic destroys their hope – and he's a fanatic. (SHOGO *laughs. He is walking and talking upstage with* KIRO.) You needn't tell him what I've said, I'll tell him.

PRIME MINISTER (*to* TOLA). What are you doing?

TOLA. Thanking god for delivering our brother from —

PPIME MINISTER. Go away!

TOLA *goes out.*

PRIME MINISTER. The Chief Inspector was killed today. Last week it was the Chief Fire Officer, the Chief Civil Servant and the Under-Chief Civil Servant. When he goes out he makes all the government officers stand round him. If it goes on like this we'll all be killed.

BASHO. Get rid of him.

PRIME MINISTER. How?

BASHO. Bribe the army or promise them promotion. I understand that's how it's done.

PRIME MINISTER. You can't. He's turned them into saluting and stabbing machines. It's uncanny.

BASHO. Poison him.

PRIME MINISTER. No, I have to taste everything before he eats it.

BASHO. He's a flesh man, isn't he?

PRIME MINISTER. A – ? – O, yes, yes!

BASHO. I've heard you can poison the woman's passage.

PRIME MINISTER. No, I've tried that.

BASHO. I don't like meddling in politics, like most people I have more important things to do. But if politicians can't solve this problem, someone must. (*He looks round and then turns back to the* PRIME MINISTER.) When I was in the deep north I met someone who's more ruthless and powerful than Shogo.

PRIME MINISTER. There is no one!

BASHO. Yes. Five times more ruthless, and he understands magic.

PRIME MINISTER (*interested*). O?

BASHO. He asked me if there were any people in the south, and I said no. I knew he'd attack us if I said yes. I told him it's a desert. But even a witch is better than that man. We can't wait for the river to flood and drown him.

PRIME MINISTER. Come with me and we'll talk about it.

BASHO *and the* PRIME MINISTER *go out.* SHOGO *and* KIRO *walk downstage.*

KIRO. But why is your city perfect?

SHOGO. It has the best drains, schools, churches, water, houses, food, laws, hospitals – but most important it has a purpose: perfection. That gives the people something to do. Instead of arguing and rotting away in hovels, they work for the city, they live for it. If the city wasn't there they'd start cutting each other's throats, there'd be chaos, and that's worse than all the ancient plagues and famines.

KIRO. But why d'you put people in prison and kill them?

SHOGO. To prevent suffering. (*He laughs.*) It's true. It stops the chaos. That's why I have a policeman for every two streets. Sit down, you look tired. (*They sit.*)

KIRO. If you didn't have police there wouldn't be any crime. Anyone knows that. Punishment makes crime.

SHOGO (*laughs*). No, life makes people unhappy, not my city. You think I'm evil. I'm not – I'm the lesser of two evils. People are born in a tiger's mouth. I snatch them out and some of them get caught on the teeth – *that's* what you're blaming me for.

KIRO (*puts his hand on* SHOGO's *leg*). D'you love god?

SHOGO. No. – Your face isn't so blue.

KIRO. You've already forgotten the man in the sack.

SHOGO. Nearly. You pity him. But I'm proud of him – he was a hero. He died for the city – to protect the rule of law and order. Were you afraid inside your pot?

KIRO. It hurt.

SHOGO. How would you run the city?

KIRO (*thinks for a moment*). Some problems have no solution, but it's hard to know which problems these are.

SHOGO. Another problem.

KIRO. Our Father Abbot has a puzzle from China. You have to fit eight pieces of wood into a circle. In fact, they're specially made so they can't fit. But for the last forty-eight years he's spent ten hours a day trying to make them fit – because one day they *might*. He's very holy.

SHOGO. D'you like being a priest?

KIRO. My old guardian told me to become a disciple – but I can't find anyone to follow.

SHOGO. Are you well enough to go now?

KIRO. When you talk about the city you mean you.

SHOGO. Of course. My family were peasants, I had nothing, no
one had to do what I told them – but they did. I am the city
because I made it, but I made it in the image of other men.
People wanted to follow me – so I had to lead them. I can't
help shaping history – it's my gift, like your piety. If you
gave me ten men I'd have an army in two months. If I turned
my back on the ten men the army would still spring up out of
the ground. I *am* those people – at least where it really
matters. In a way, *they* push *me*.

KIRO. That's leadership!

SHOGO. No. (*Smiles.*) Like all mobs they think they run the
dictator – but . . .

KIRO. Yes?

SHOGO. The old Emperor I had to kill was religious. When he
heard I was coming he prayed to god to protect him. I shot
an arrow at him and god put out his hand and broke the
arrow into three pieces. But it so happened that when these
pieces fell to the ground they accidentally fell together, and
their velocity carried them on through the Emperor's heart.
So I'm not pushed. – Say something.

KIRO. What d'you want me to say?

SHOGO. Why don't you stay in the palace? I like talking to you.
Politicians are so stupid.

KIRO. You're married?

SHOGO. Five times. I'll show them to you. Have you ever had
a woman?

KIRO. No.

SHOGO. That's evil. (*Pause.*) There's a line round your neck
where the pot went. I suppose that'll stay.

KIRO *touches his neck.*

SCENE FIVE

The deep north. BASHO *and the* PRIME MINISTER *come on in
travelling clothes.* BASHO *still carries the* CHILD.

PRIME MINISTER. I've never travelled so far before.

BASHO. This is the place.

PRIME MINISTER. Will he be long?

BASHO. No. He got my message.

PRIME MINISTER. I'm worried. Are you sure we should do this?

BASHO. No. He's a barbarian – a bragging, mindless savage. But what else can we do? He's so stupid I *think* I can control him.

PRIME MINISTER. Is the child all right?

BASHO. O yes. (*He looks at it.*) I'm making sure it doesn't die. That's important. Baby-baby.

PRIME MINISTER. Ha! Someone's coming.

BASHO. It'll be him.

The COMMODORE *and* GEORGINA *come on. He wears white trousers, a navy blue jacket with brass buttons, and a navy blue Van Gogh hat. She wears a Victorian crinoline and bonnet. She is shaking a tambourine.*

COMMODORE. Good morning. (BASHO *and the* PRIME MINISTER *bow.*) Nice day.

GEORGINA. Get down to business.

COMMODORE. Yes. You have a proposition?

BASHO. The information I gave you about the south was wrong.

GEORGINA. What did I say?

BASHO. While I was away the place became inhabited and a large city was built.

COMMODORE. Ruled by a native?

BASHO. Yes. This is the Prime Minister.

COMMODORE (*to* GEORGINA). He won't be much trouble.

BASHO (*to the* PRIME MINISTER). I've just told him you're Prime Minister.

PRIME MINISTER (*bows*). Yes?

BASHO. . . . He wishes you prosperity and your ancestors joy.

PRIME MINISTER. Oo ...

COMMODORE. This city-thingummy, is it prosperous?

BASHO. Yes, very.

GEORGINA (*her tambourine trembles*). I beg your pardon. Hem.

COMMODORE. Any manufactures?

BASHO (*shrugs*). No.

COMMODORE. Good! (*He taps* GEORGINA'*s tambourine excitedly*). I'll wire Birmingham. – We march tomorrow.

GEORGINA. Do your coat up, brother. Mr Basho, before we agree to lead your city of the plains out of its ignorance, vice, mischief-making and darkness, I require a few undertakings.

BASHO. Yes?

GEORGINA. Hallelujah! (*She bangs her tambourine.*)

PRIME MINISTER. Who is that dervish?

BASHO. His mistress, but he calls her his sister out of courtesy.

GEORGINA. We will give you soldiers and guns to kill your enemies – and in return you must love Jesus, give up bad language, forswear cards, refuse spicey foods, abandon women, forsake drink and – and *stop* singing on Sundays —

COMMODORE. Er —

GEORGINA. – except hymns and the authorized responses.

PRIME MINISTER (*to* BASHO). What?

BASHO. She appears to be in a trance. (*He nods and smiles at her.*)

GEORGINA. *Secondly*, you will leave the education of all children to me. In this suburb of hell they are all orphans of Jesus, and I claim them on His behalf. Hallelujah! (*She bangs her tambourine.*)

BASHO (*nods and smiles at her: to the* PRIME MINISTER). She's possessed. How noble of the Commodore to keep her.

PRIME MINISTER. He's indulging himself. She's obviously over-sexed. (*He smiles at her.*) Perhaps when the Commodore's finished with her – or she's finished with him – he'll pass her on to me.

GEORGINA. Hallelujah! (*She bangs her tambourine.*)

PRIME MINISTER. But perhaps my other wives wouldn't get on with her.

GEORGINA (*points at the baby*). What's that? A baby!

COMMODORE. Haw haw!

GEORGINA. Another soul for Jesus. (*She bangs her tambourine in the baby's face.*)

BASHO (*steps back*). This is the Emperor.

GEORGINA. What emperor?

BASHO. The head of the city killed the old Emperor, and this is his son. He owns the city. (GEORGINA *and the* COMMODORE *go to one side.*) We shall tell the people we are fighting for the new Emperor, and they will support us. Otherwise it would be a long war.

GEORGINA (*to the* COMMODORE). He's very young.

COMMODORE. Yes, we needn't worry about him for fifteen years and with luck I'll have had an idea by then. (*To* BASHO.) Good. (*To the* BABY.) Chk-chk! We'll put a whiff of gun-shot up their rear, won't we, little chickabiddy?

BASHO (*to the* PRIME MINISTER). They talk like that to keep their spirits up.

GEORGINA. Come on, brother. We're wasting time.

They go out.

SCENE SIX

The stage is bare and empty. KIRO *comes on.*

KIRO. The barbarians have knocked down the city walls with their new weapons, and now they're marching on the palace. (*He looks off. In the distance a military band starts to play* 'The British Grenadiers'.) Shogo's turned me out because I won't fight. They'll beat him. That devil's music is enough to frighten his men away. (*Undecided.*) He should be beaten! He's a tyrant and god will destroy him! (*The music is nearer.*) He'll be dead in an hour! I'll go and talk to him, and try to make him escape with me.

KIRO *goes out. Some* TARS *wheel on an enormous cannon. The* COMMODORE, GEORGINA, BASHO, *the* PRIME MINISTER *and a* JAPANESE SOLDIER *come on.* BASHO *still carries the* BABY. *The* TARS *prepare the cannon.*

BASHO. The Emperor will be proclaimed head of the city, and the Commodore can be Vice-regent. I shall be Prime Minister, and the Prime Minister can be – Chief of Police.

The TARS *are loading the cannon with a ramrod.*

COMMODORE (*to* BASHO). Mr Basho, a word in your ear about little chickabiddy.

BASHO. Yes?

COMMODORE. This Go-slow chappie worked out a little scheme for its education, I hear?

BASHO. Yes.

COMMODORE. Georgina thinks we ought to stick with it: bring him up as a peasant. Open air, healthy sort of life.

BASHO. But he's head of the city.

COMMODORE. No use getting the little fellow involved. Wouldn't do it to one of my own.

BASHO. But the people expect —

COMMODORE. Tell them there was an accident. Say you dropped it. Could happen to anyone. Bring the little fella up to the quiet life. If he never knows what he is, he'll never know what he's missed. Is that right? Haw haw. In England we have a saying: ignorance is bliss. That's a favourite of mine. You must come to England some day – for a short visit. They'd love you. You'll learn a lot. The English countryside, calm, peaceful, green, orderly, civilized, the distant cry of ladies riding to hounds and digging out old Tom Badger. Georgina's firing the opening shot.

GUNNER TAR. Weeping willow one o'clock. Hundred yards. Quarter past one. Big palace.

GUNNER TAR'S MATE. Big palace it is, Ron.

COMMODORE. I'll make you – er Minister for – er, orphans, yes? (BASHO *nods*.) By the way, my sister says your old P.M. will have to leave the cabinet. He's got bad breath. Aren't you chaps good at ornamental gardens? I admire a nice piece of rockery.

GEORGINA. Isn't it ready yet?

GUNNER TAR. Got a do it right.

GUNNER TAR'S MATE. As the mathematician said to 'is girl friend.

GUNNER TAR. Don't want it comin' out the wrong way.

GUNNER TAR'S MATE. As the girl friend said to the mathematician.

GEORGINA. Fortunately that's my deaf ear.

GUNNER TAR (*stepping back from the cannon*). That'll put a curl in the end a their pigtail.

COMMODORE. I'm glad that's settled. – Whiff of whats-it up their thingummy, haw?

GEORGINA. Two lines of Abide With Me. (*Sings.*) Abide with me, fast falls the evening light. Three cheers for Jesus! Hip hip! (*Shouts and tambourine :* 'Hoorah!') Hip hip! (*Shouts and tambourine :* 'Hoorah!') Hip hip! (*Shouts and tambourine :* 'Hoorah!' *She drops a light on the cannon. There is a flash and a roar. The men cheer.*) I saw an angel hovering over it with a Union Jack!

They all start to rush out.

COMMODORE (*to the* PRIME MINISTER, *the* GUNNER TAR'S MATE *and a* JAPANESE SOLDIER). You – you – and you – stay here and stop the stragglers.

All the others leave. Shouts and fight sounds are heard, off. A PEASANT *and his* WIFE *come on. He carries a small bundle.*

PRIME MINISTER. Stop. (*The* PEASANT *and his* WIFE *stop.*) Where are you going?

PEASANT. Friends very loyal to Emperor.

SOLDIER. But which one? What's in that bundle?

PEASANT. Our home!

SOLDIER. Turn it out.

The PEASANT *opens his bundle.* KIRO *and* SHOGO *come on downstage.* SHOGO *is disguised as a* PRIEST. *They see the* PRIME MINISTER *and the others and turn to go, but the* SOLDIER *sees them. They stop.*

KIRO. Pretend to beg. I'll talk to them.

SOLDIER (*calling across*). Wait there. I'll be with you in a minute.

SHOGO. Let's fight. We can manage them.

KIRO. Put your sword away.

PRIME MINISTER. You have *three* spoons. Why is that?

PEASANT. The other one's for our son.

PRIME MINISTER. Where is he?

PEASANT'S WIFE. In the palace.

PRIME MINISTER. Ah! Traitors!

PEASANT. No, no! Against his will! Shogo made him a soldier. (*Angrily to his* WIFE.) Leave this to me!

PRIME MINISTER (*poking in the bundle*). What's this?

SOLDIER (*coming down to* KIRO *and* SHOGO). Where are you going? (*The* GUNNER TAR'S MATE *comes down and watches.*)

KIRO. We're begging priests. (*He holds out his bowl.*)

SOLDIER. The barbarian's mistress has banned begging. I'll have to run you in. (SHOGO *makes a movement. Turning to* SHOGO.) Yes?

KIRO. The fighting's made him nervous.

The PRIME MINISTER *makes the* PEASANT *and his* WIFE *squat on the floor with their hands on their heads.*

GUNNER TAR'S MATE (*to the* SOLDIER). Begging? (*The* SOLDIER *nods.*) Of course, if they wasn't to tell us they'd been begging, and taking into account there's nothing in their bowls, we wouldn't know they'd been beggin', an' they could be on their way, in a manner of speakin', an'

mention me in their prayers, which would be very 'andy-like
if the unlikely ever 'appens an' I was t' go t' 'eaven and the
Almighty turns out t' be a Buddhist an' not a Wesleyan after
all.

SOLDIER. The barbarian says you can go.

KIRO. Thank you.

The PRIME MINISTER *comes down.*

PRIME MINISTER. Who are they?

SOLDIER. Priests.

PRIME MINISTER. There's all sorts of people trying to sneak
off. (*He looks at* KIRO. *He turns to* SHOGO.) How many
hands has god?

The PRIME MINISTER, *the* GUNNER TAR'S MATE *and the*
SOLDIER *look at* SHOGO. KIRO *is behind them. He holds up ten
fingers.*

SHOGO. . . . . Ten.

PRIME MINISTER. How many feet has god? (KIRO *holds up
six fingers.*)

SHOGO. Six.

PRIME MINISTER. How many ears has god? (KIRO *holds up
three fingers.*)

SHOGO (*slight surprise*). Three?

PRIME MINISTER. How many eyes has god? (KIRO *holds up
one finger, but* SHOGO *speaks immediately.*)

SHOGO. One.

PRIME MINISTER. How many tongues has god? (KIRO *holds
up seven fingers.*)

SHOGO. Seven.

PRIME MINISTER. How many . . . how many – noses has
god? (KIRO *holds up two fingers.*)

SHOGO. Two.

The COMMODORE *and* BASHO *come on and join them.* KIRO *and*
SHOGO *see them.*

PRIME MINISTER. How many testicles has god?

Silence. KIRO *tries to gesture. The* PRIME MINISTER, *the* SOLDIER *and the* GUNNER TAR'S MATE *look at the* COMMODORE *significantly.*

SHOGO (*desperately*). Eight thousand seven hundred and five –
PRIME MINISTER (*turning back to* SHOGO *in triumph*). Ah!
SHOGO. – not counting the right one.
PRIME MINISTER. Yes. Good. (*To the* COMMODORE.) They're priests.
COMMODORE. Get rid of them before Georgina sees them. Next to a Roman the thing she hates most is a heathen.
PRIME MINISTER (*motions them off*). Quick.

KIRO *and* SHOGO *cross downstage. The* GUNNER TAR *comes on and salutes.*

GUNNER TAR (*to the* COMMODORE). Palace taken present and correct sir!
COMMODORE. Did you get this No-dough fella?
GUNNER TAR. No, sir, but we're rakin' the ashes.

GEORGINA *and the others come on.*

KIRO (*to* SHOGO). We'll go along the narrow road to the deep north. It's safe there.
COMMODORE (*going up to the* PEASANTS). What's this?
PRIME MINISTER. Traitors. They tried to break the firing gun.
COMMODORE. Spike Big Betty?

KIRO *and* SHOGO *go out.*

GEORGINA. The city's taken and now I can begin my mission. Amen.
ALL (*sung*). A-a-a-men.

PART TWO

SCENE ONE

ARGI, HEIGOO, BREEBREE *and* TOLA *sit down left. They wear robes.* GEORGINA, *the* COMMODORE *and* BASHO *are upstage.*

GEORGINA. I've been running the city a week, haven't we, George? I've relaid the sewers, straightened the streets, shut the 'music' houses, put a curfew on for nine-thirty, and recoded the law. That was on Monday. On Tuesday I shut the drinking shops and the theatres, unveiled a statue, gave a garden party, laid twelve foundation stones, and brought the curfew down to eight-thirty. I haven't time to go through the rest of the week, but I would like to mention that we now only allow people out for an hour at luncheon. Next I must deal with the priests. Tomorrow's the Sabbath so it's urgent. (*She gives each* PRIEST *a clerical collar and a tambourine.*)

HEIGOO. Does she want us to play in a band?

GEORGINA. In England they want to abolish the collar and have a tie with crosses on it. I won't let that happen here. I shall preserve a little corner of England in the Pacific.

BASHO. She says you're now Christians.

ARGI. Can I bless people?

BASHO. Yes.

ARGI. And tell them they're born evil?

BASHO. Yes.

ARGI. Good! We've got a lot of people like that here.

GEORGINA. Tell them they're going to help me run the city. Our's is a religion of love, that means we teach sin and —

HEIGOO. Praise Buddha!

GEORGINA. Did I understand him? (BASHO *nods*.) He's possessed by a devil. We must drive it out! (*She bangs her tambourine*.) Out! Out! Hallelujah!

ARGI (*bangs his tambourine*). Out! Out! Hallelujah!

TOLA *and* BREEBREE *hesitate and then half-heartedly bang their tambourines.*

COMMODORE (*trying to intervene*). Georgina!

ARGI (*bangs his tambourine at the* COMMODORE). Out! Out!

HEIGOO. Praise Buddha!

HEIGOO *runs out. The other* PRIESTS *run after him, banging their tambourines.* ARGI *stops and turns back.*

ARGI. Can I do faith healing?

BASHO. Yes.

ARGI. Hallelujah!

ARGI *runs out banging his tambourine.*

COMMODORE. I need a drink. (*Calls*.) Waiter!

Immediately the PRIME MINISTER *comes on. He has a towel over his arm and carries a small round tray with a glass and syphon on it.*

COMMODORE. Ah, whisky and soda. Good man! We'll make something out of you yet!

PRIME MINISTER. Say when. (*He squirts the syphon*.)

COMMODORE. Whenny-when-when!

PRIME MINISTER (*to* BASHO). I'm learning English quickly, but I never understand him.

BASHO. Their military caste use the language of the nursery. It protects their confidence.

PRIME MINISTER. The old hen's looking ragged round the gills. Perhaps the old cock's too old to crow.

COMMODORE (*wipes his mouth on the back of his hand*). That's better.

BASHO. Cocks that crow loudest at morning are quietest at night.

GEORGINA. Is there a Japanese proverb about the hen?

BASHO *stares at* GEORGINA *and the* PRIME MINISTER *drops the tray.*

COMMODORE. Naughty-porty! They don't drop trays at the Army and Navy. Back to form one.

GEORGINA. George, dear, go and inspect the guard.

COMMODORE. Yes. (*He starts to go and then stops.*) Why?

GEORGINA. They like you.

COMMODORE. Ah.

The COMMODORE *goes out. The* PRIME MINISTER *looks at* GEORGINA, *picks up the tray, and hurries out.*

BASHO. You speak Japanese.

GEORGINA. I had a spare hour last Wednesday and I thought it would be useful. I want to be able to talk to intelligent people. My brother has a lot of good qualities – yes he has – but no one could deny he's a bore. That's why they sent him out here. The English send all their bores abroad, and acquired the Empire as a punishment. (*She laughs.*) Those poor priests – shouting 'Hallelujah' and banging their tambourines!

BASHO. D'you mean you weren't . . . sincere?

GEORGINA (*laughs*). Did you think I was?

BASHO. Yes . . . I admired you for it.

GEORGINA. Why?

BASHO. You run the city better than Shogo.

GEORGINA. How?

BASHO. Well, you don't use the sack.

GEORGINA. O, there'll be a few hangings.

BASHO. But the people are happier.

GEORGINA. Of course they're not! You sound like my brother.

BASHO. I don't understand.

GEORGINA. Well, Shogo ruled by atrocity.

BASHO. Yes.

GEORGINA. It didn't work, because it left people free to judge
him. They said: he makes us suffer and that's wrong. He
calls it law and order, but we say it's crime against us – and
that's why they threw spears at him. So instead of atrocity I
use morality. I persuade people – in their hearts – that they
are sin, and that they have evil thoughts, and that they're
greedy and violent and destructive, and – more than anything else – that their bodies must be hidden, and that sex is
nasty and corrupting and must be secret. When they believe
all that they do what they're told. They don't judge you –
they feel guilty themselves and accept that you have the right
to judge them. That's how *I* run the city: the missions
and churches and bishops and magistrates and politicians
and papers will tell people they are sin and must be kept
in order. If the devil didn't exist it would be necessary to
invent him. I learned all this from my Scottish nanny. She
taught our Prime Minister, the Queen, the Leader of the
Opposition, and everyone else who matters. They all
learned politics across her knee. I am enjoying this conversation.

BASHO. You don't believe in god?

GEORGINA. Yes. But we've been talking about the devil. We
must get our priorities right. We need the devil to protect
people from themselves.

BASHO. You Westerners are inscrutable. Let me tell you
another Japanese proverb: people who raise ghosts become
haunted.

GEORGINA. Haunted? I don't understand that. Haunted?

BASHO *goes out.*

SCENE TWO

The deep north. KIRO *stands in a fighting pose with a sword in each hand.*

SHOGO. Come on. I'll teach you.

KIRO. I want to think.

SHOGO. It'll give me something to do. I'm fed up with this place! I don't like the northern climate. Up! (*He prods* KIRO *with a sword.* KIRO *stands. He gives him a sword.*) I won't be rough. (*He assumes a threatening pose and then attacks. They fence for a few moments.* KIRO *makes no effort. Suddenly* SHOGO *gets behind him and gives him a hard whack across the back.*)

KIRO. Ouch! (*He turns round and attacks* SHOGO *more forcefully.*)

SHOGO. That's better, now you've been hurt. (*They fence. It's obvious that* SHOGO *could kill* KIRO *if he wanted to.*) Good – yes! (*He hits* KIRO *across the legs and* KIRO *falls.*)

KIRO. No more.

SHOGO. Come on, up! (*He pulls* KIRO *to his feet, steps back a little way, and then rushes* KIRO.) There could be an accident! You could get killed. (*He lunges.* KIRO *parries him crudely but effectively and* SHOGO *is trapped off guard.* KIRO *grins and* SHOGO *looks at him.*)

SHOGO. We'll stop now.

KIRO. I was just starting to enjoy it. I like to keep fit. (*He bends and touches his toes.*)

SHOGO. Give me that. (*He puts the swords away.*)

KIRO. Perhaps I should have been a soldier. (*He sits and grins.*)

SHOGO. You'll get piles.

KIRO. What?

SHOGO. Always sitting like that. (*Pause. He doesn't know what to do.*) Are you thinking?

KIRO. Yes.

SHOGO (*slight pause*). What about?

KIRO (*giving in*). D'you want to talk? (*No reply*) D'you want to fight?

SHOGO. No.

KIRO (*after a pause*). Where are your parents?

SHOGO. Dead.

KIRO. D'you miss them?

SHOGO. Yes.

KIRO. What were they like?

SHOGO (*irritably*). Simple! Poor! My father joked a lot! I left home as soon as I could.

KIRO. Why?

SHOGO. Food! We only had a little bit of field – we couldn't both work it.

KIRO. Didn't they try to stop you?

SHOGO. No! It was a question of food! (*He changes the subject.*) Why did you become a priest? (*A long silence.*) Well?

KIRO. I'll repeat it. (*Another silence.* SHOGO *makes a movement of annoyance. Calmly amused.*) It's a joke.

SHOGO. I can't stand this place! Nothing, nothing — (*He can't finish.*) – How can you get enlightenment here?

Silence.

Please don't start thinking again!

KIRO. Why d'you go to the village so much?

SHOGO. I've got a girl there.

KIRO. Is that all?

SHOGO. No. (*Pause.*) You're thinking again!

KIRO. I'm watching the fish. (SHOGO *comes to the front of the stage, stands across from* KIRO, *and watches with him.*) The water's clear. The old man who brought me up had yellow teeth. I didn't like him to laugh in public.

SHOGO. That was mean.

KIRO. I know.

Pause. They look into the water and not at each other.

SHOGO. It goes fast.
KIRO. But there are no waves.

Pause. Their voices when they talk as they look in the water are calm and rapt. Individual words are not emphasised.

SHOGO (*still looking in the water*). An odd thing happens to me sometimes. I wake up and think I've done a crime. It's the worst crime that's ever been done.
KIRO (*still looking in the water*). You mean you dream?
SHOGO. No. I'm suddenly wide awake and there's this idea in my head. I *know* I've done it.
KIRO. What?
SHOGO. I don't know. But I *know* I've done it, and I have to hide it.
KIRO. What sort of thing?
SHOGO. I don't know. I just know I've done it. If I said I remember my name, I wouldn't be *sure* I did, I *might* be making a mistake – but this *is* sure. It worried me when I was young, but not now. Why should it? – nothing happens.

Silence. They still look in the water.

KIRO. It could be anything. You're always killing people.
SHOGO. It's not that. I remember all that. But my life goes on and on like a finger reaching out to point . . .

Slight pause. Still neither of them looks up.

KIRO (*tries to think*). . . . The circle gets smaller and smaller.
SHOGO (*still looking at the water*). . . . What?
KIRO. The circle gets smaller and smaller.
SHOGO. Yes . . . and the shadow gets bigger . . .

Pause. They still look at the water.

KIRO. . . . Some problems have no solution . . . (*He looks at*

SHOGO, *shrugs and breaks the mood*.) You're woken up by the sound of your neck snapping. You're going back.

SHOGO (*shrugs slightly*). I'm not sure.

KIRO. Don't.

SHOGO (*turns away*). Stay here and die of damp?

KIRO (*ironically*). Hh.

SHOGO. The barbarians will destroy my city.

KIRO. You can't stop them.

SHOGO. It's my city and —

KIRO. An arrow only falls together once.

SHOGO (*shocked*). . . . . That's trite.

KIRO (*regretting it*). I'm sorry, I —

SHOGO. That's it! That's the noise a priest makes! Did you believe my story about the arrow?

KIRO. No, I . . .

SHOGO (*angrily and hurt*). Yellow teeth! You don't live, you sit and play with yourself and think of god! O god, this place! No one could build a city here!

KIRO. Don't go!

Three TRIBESMEN *come on upstage.*

SHOGO. You're late.

FIRST TRIBESMAN. We're sorry, we tried —

SHOGO. Late! Have you spoken to your tribes?

FIRST TRIBESMAN. Yes —

SHOGO. And they'll attack the city with me and release the child Emperor?

SECOND TRIBESMAN (*hesitantly*). . . . . Yes . . .

SHOGO. Well, will they?

FIRST TRIBESMAN. The barbarians have strange weapons . . .

SHOGO (*goes upstage and comes back with a rifle*). Like this. It's a firing gun. Made by barbarians. (*The* TRIBESMEN *make soft exclamations. The* THIRD TRIBESMAN *touches it.*) I have enough for two-thirds of our men. With these we'll take the city in a day.

THIRD TRIBESMAN. Does it kill?

SHOGO. O yes. (*The* SECOND TRIBESMAN *steps back*.) It's all right. Watch. (*He demonstrates*.) This is a bullet.

THIRD TRIBESMAN (*touches it*). Bullet.

SHOGO. The magic piece. Now, first pull this little stick – and there's a little hole. Push the bullet in – like that – and push your little stick – like that – and now it's up inside. When you're ready, squeeze this little curved thing below, and it goes bang and shoots through the top – and there's your dead man. (*The* TRIBESMEN *exclaim gently and clap politely*.)

THIRD TRIBESMAN. Let me see. (SHOGO *gives him the rifle and the other* TRIBESMEN *crowd round and touch it*.)

SHOGO (*goes back to* KIRO *immediately*). I've got an army of two thousand men. The barbarian's got three hundred.

KIRO. But the whole city will fight for the little Emperor!

SHOGO. The whole city's not worth one of me! Look, I came to this wilderness with nothing and an army fell in on my doorstep! When I wanted guns, an Arab merchant trading guns to China is shipwrecked on my beach! The arrow mends!

KIRO. But you've lost the city!

SHOGO. Yes – I made a mistake. They used the little Emperor against me. That won't happen again. Not again.

SECOND TRIBESMAN. The bullet comes out there.

FIRST TRIBESMAN. He said out here.

THIRD TRIBESMAN (*looks down the barrel*). I can't see it.

SHOGO. I can't leave you here on your own.

KIRO. I can't go through another war.

SHOGO. All right, stay here now, and when it's over I'll send a messenger for you. You'll sit here for ever and learn nothing. Will you come?

KIRO. Yes.

The gun fires. The THIRD TRIBESMAN *falls dead. The other* TRIBESMEN *stare at him.* SHOGO *turns to them.*

SHOGO (*immediately*). There! See how it works! We'll take the
city in a day!

SCENE THREE

The river bank. GEORGINA *hurries on with five* CHILDREN.
*They are dressed in identical suits and look alike. Two of them
carry tambourines.* GEORGINA *is dirty and dishevelled.*

GEORGINA. Kneel, kneel. Quickly, children. Not too near
the river. (*The* CHILDREN *kneel.*) Hands together. Eyes
tight. No fidgeting. O lord Jesus, save us from the soldiers
and keep us in your care. Tojo, eyes shut, please. O Jesus,
not by our deserts but by our needs. (*She looks round
and shouts.*) Basho! – Tojo, hands together. (*The sound of
guns. Some of the children stand.*) It's nothing children.
The men are playing. On your knees. Eyes shut. Hands
together.

A PEASANT MAN *and* WOMAN *come in.*

GEORGINA. Where's Basho?
WIFE. Gone.
GEORGINA. But he must look after his children! Where did he
go?
PEASANT. With Commodore.
GEORGINA. But where?
WIFE. Ran, ran.
GEORGINA. I don't believe it. (*She turns away.*) They wouldn't
desert us!
PEASANT (*looks off*). The soldiers are coming.
WIFE (*looks off other way*). They're coming this way!

The PEASANTS *kneel.* GEORGINA *goes back to the* CHILDREN.

GEORGINA. Pray together. Eyes kept shut. That's a good
Tojo.

SHOGO *comes on with* SOLDIERS.

GEORGINA. Eyes shut, children. Nice and tight. I can see your prayers going up.

SHOGO. These are Basho's children?

GEORGINA. Yes.

SHOGO. Where is Basho?

GEORGINA. I don't know.

SHOGO. Where is Basho? (*She doesn't answer.*) Find him!

A soldier goes off. Silence. SHOGO *walks up and down. He sees the* PEASANTS.

SHOGO. Get them out of the way!

The PEASANTS *are pushed out.*

GEORGINA. Eyes shut, children. Jesus sees us.

SHOGO (*walks up and down in the silence. Suddenly*). Basho!

The SOLDIER *comes on.*

SOLDIER. We're looking for him, sir!

SHOGO. Look faster!

The SOLDIER *goes out.*

SHOGO. Clear this bank! I want everyone off.

Two SOLDIERS *go out.* SHOGO *walks up and down. He goes off one side. He comes back immediately.*

SHOGO. Which is the Emperor's son?

GEORGINA. I don't know.

SHOGO. Tell him to step forward.

GEORGINA. Eyes shut very tight.

SHOGO. You must know. You're in charge.

GEORGINA. I found them by the river. Your guns frightened them. So I told them to stay with me, that's all.

SHOGO *goes off the other side. He comes back immediately.*

SHOGO. You're lying.

GEORGINA. If I knew I would lie, but I don't know.

SHOGO (*calls*). Have you found him yet?

The SOLDIER *comes in.*

SOLDIER. I think he's dead.

SHOGO (*horrified*). He can't be dead!

SOLDIER. Most of the people are dead. There's some in the river. He could be in there. We're trying to fish them out before they float away.

SHOGO (*goes up to the river*). Basho! Basho! Basho! (*To the* SOLDIER.) Go and find him!

The SOLDIER *hurries out. The other two* SOLDIERS *come back.*

He's hiding! (*Goes towards* GEORGINA.) And this bitch lies!

GEORGINA. Pray, children.

SHOGO. Which is the Emperor's son?

GEORGINA. Only Mr Basho knows.

SHOGO. Which of them is best at his lessons?

GEORGINA. I don't know anything.

SHOGO. Which one draws best? Which one sings best? Which one has the best manners?

GEORGINA. They're brought up to be the same.

SHOGO (*goes to the* CHILDREN). Which is the Emperor's son? Which of you's the strongest? Point at him! Which one wins the arguments? Which one's the subtlest? Which one's the leader? Which one d'you hate? Hands out! (*He looks at a* CHILD's *hands.*) He bites his nails! (*He looks at the other* CHILDREN's *hands.*) They all bite their nails!

GEORGINA. Eyes nicely shut.

SHOGO (*to a boy*). Who was your mummy and daddy? (*To another* BOY.) Were you brought up in a palace? D'you remember soldiers and lots of toys? (*To another* BOY.) Have you seen me before? You remember me, don't you? Don't you? (*He shakes the* BOY.) Answer when you're told! –

Which one of you's the Emperor's son? Please! D'you want
to make me do something terrible? (*Shouts*). Basho! Basho!
Help me! Help me! Help me!

A long complete silence.

SHOGO. All right. Let's go on. I don't know who's the
Emperor's son so I kill them all.

GEORGINA. Monster!

SHOGO. Then help me! Tell me —

GEORGINA. I don't know!

SHOGO. Why do they all look alike? (GEORGINA *cries.*) Kill
them!

GEORGINA. He's not there, my brother took him away, they've
gone!

SHOGO. Liar!

GEORGINA. No.

SHOGO. Kill them! Kill them! Kill them!

The SOLDIERS *take the* CHILDREN *out.* GEORGINA *tries to
follow.*

SHOGO. Stay there. (*A* SOLDIER *keeps her back.*)

GEORGINA (*sings*). God be with us in our labour . . .

She stops and listens intently. A brief silence. Then the sound of
CHILDREN's *voices, like gentle, polite surprise at a party. It dies
into silence. A wait. The* SOLDIERS *bring the bodies on and put
them in a heap.*

SOLDIER (*counting the bodies*). Three. Four. Five.

SHOGO. Put barriers on the bridges and the roads. I want the
Commodore brought in. Identify all corpses and kill the
prisoners. Afterwards give the men a day's leave, one quarter
at a time. All officers will report to me in the morning. I'll
level the city and begin again, and this time there won't be
any mistakes. My city will last a thousand years. (*He points
to the bodies.*) Drop them in the river.

The SOLDIERS *pick up the bodies and everyone goes out except*
GEORGINA.

GEORGINA. My chicks, my chicks . . . All dead, all dead. (*She
finds a tambourine*). Who dropped this? (*Plays and sings. Two*
PEASANTS *come on and watch her.*) All things bright and . . .
all creatures great and . . . My little chicks all gone . . . Hands
together, eyes shut tight . . . Who's the Emperor's son?
. . . That one and that one . . .
WIFE. What's the matter with her?
PEASANT. She's haunted.

They hurry out.

GEORGINA. Naughty boys . . . Dirty hands . . . Nasty hands . . .
Keep your hands still! Tight together! . . . Stop playing
with your sins! . . . What comes to naughty boys? . . . (*She
dances, plays the tambourine and sings.*) He gave them snow in
winter . . . and lips that we might tell . . . all things bright
and . . . dead . . . (*She plays and dances a few steps.*) . . . All
dead.

SCENE FOUR

The same place. Empty.

KIRO *comes on. He is tired. His robe is dirty.*

KIRO. Shogo sent his message. He's won the war, and he's
rebuilding the city. This time it will last for ever. No one will
take it from him . . . I've walked all the way from the deep
north. It rained. I'm tired. I'll rest here by the river and go
on into the city tonight.

A procession comes on upstage. BASHO, *the* COMMODORE,
SOLDIERS, OFFICERS *and* SHOGO. SHOGO *is in chains. He has
been beaten. There is dry blood round his mouth.*

COMMODORE. We'll wait till the crowd's settled down. (*The procession stops. To* BASHO.) Georgina's out again. I used to rely on her advice. Now she keeps shouting 'Do your buttons up', and they're not undone. Perhaps it's time she went home to England . . . Mr Basho, I've decided to make you Prime Minister.

BASHO. Thank you.

COMMODORE. While Georgina's ill I need all the responsible advice I can get —

SHOGO *suddenly dashes forward.*

SHOGO. I won't die! The city's mine – they can't kill *me*!

SHOGO *pushes* BASHO *aside.* BASHO *is carrying a folder of loose pages with his poems on them. The pages are thrown in the air.* SOLDIERS *grab* SHOGO.

COMMODORE. Gag him. Tie him tighter. He's got no pride. He'll interrupt the trial.

SOLDIERS *truss and gag* SHOGO. BASHO *picks up some of the sheets.*

COMMODORE. I'm sorry about your poetry, Mr Basho. (*He picks up a sheet.*) We'll soon get them all —

BASHO. It's of no importance, I have copies. (*The* COMMODORE *drops the sheet.*) But we won't leave them here, it looks unsightly. (*He motions two* SOLDIERS *to pick them up. They collect large handfuls while the procession forms up again.*)

COMMODORE (*looking off*). I think they're ready.

GEORGINA *comes in. She has her tambourine. She sees the sheets.*

GEORGINA. Snow. Snow. It's a cold winter that blows nobody any good.

COMMODORE. Georgina, dear —

GEORGINA. Do your buttons up. (*Picking up sheets.*) Let me.

Let me. (*She gives them to one of the* SOLDIERS *who are collecting them.*)

COMMODORE. Come and see the trial. It may give your poor mind some rest.

GEORGINA. I haven't time to rest. All these sheets! Then I've got to sweep the water! (*She shouts at the* SOLDIER.) Sweep the water! No one else remembers! (*She knocks his pile of sheets into the air.*) Pretty, pretty!

COMMODORE. Help her!

SOLDIERS *try to catch her. She darts about and then stops.*

GEORGINA. It's all right. It's finished now. I'm better. (*She picks up a few sheets.*) I'll watch the trial with you. (*She gives the sheets to the other* SOLDIER.)

SOLDIER. Thank you.

GEORGINA *knocks the bundle out of his hands, laughs and dashes out right.*

COMMODORE. Pick them up! Court martial him for carelessness!

The SOLDIER *goes to the back of the procession. Two other* SOLDIERS *start to collect the sheets quickly. The procession walks out.* SHOGO *is struggling to talk. He hasn't seen* KIRO.

KIRO. I've just come from the deep north. I heard Shogo had taken the city.

SOLDIER (*collecting papers*). That was last month. The barbarian had gone to see his people, and he came back up the river with big ships and guns and took the city again.

KIRO. Where are they going?

SOLDIER. To the trial. They've collected all the people on the bank. They say they've found out how Shogo was born!

OTHER SOLDIER. Come on! We'll miss it.

The SOLDIERS *pick up a few more sheets and hurry out. Only a few sheets are left close to* KIRO. *He sits. The voices of the trial are heard down the river. They come through a microphone and sound very loud and hard.*

COMMODORE (*offstage*). Shogo is the murderer of innocent little children in cold blood — Five little throats . . . He ruled this city with iron — the streets were prisons, the houses cells — Mr Basho will now recite.

KIRO (*picks up the sheets*). Poems. (*He looks through them.*)

BASHO (*off*). The river was red with fire and blood. — Dogs howled at him. — If his shadow fell on a tree it died. — Stone flinched. — Coffin breath . . .

KIRO (*reads*). A feather falls from the sky
        There are no birds here
        The nests are broken and
        The migration's over

BASHO (*off*) — After thorough investigation I found evidence that explains all that has happened — Shogo called himself head of the city as if his ancestors — Princes, poets, samurai — But he was a peasant's son . . .

KIRO (*reads another page*).
        The soil was dry
        The flower bent its petal mouth
        To drink from the soil
        The soil was still dry

BASHO (*off*) — Shogo's father was an honest working man who knew his child — He saw the snake arms writhing in the cot and said: My dear, our child's a monster. So they left him on this river, praying he would starve —

CROWD (*off, groans*).

KIRO. I understand now. Shogo was left by the river when he was a child. The upturned boat knocks against the pier.

BASHO (*off*). Now I come to the worst of all — I, Basho, saw
 that child, I saw it in its rags by the river, already lying in its
 own filth. I looked at it and went on. O god forgive me! —
 If I had looked in its eyes I would have seen the devil, and
 I would have put it in the water and held it under with these
 poet's hands . . . (*The* CROWD *groans*.) . . . I am a poet and I
 would have known . . .

KIRO (*he turns a sheet and reads*).
>   I drain the cup
>   At the bottom
>   Flags

CROWD (*off, loudly*). Guilty!

KIRO *puts the sheets down. Silence. The* CROWD *gasps once.
Silence. The* CROWD *shouts on a rising scale once. It ends in
some short metallic sounds. Silence. A longish, sighing exhalation
from the* CROWD *with five diminished pulses in it. Silence. A
band playing out of tune — a Sullivan medley or 'Sussex by the
Sea'. The procession comes on, but it is now disorderly. A huge
white placard is carried in on two poles, with a smooth white
sheet carried in front of it as a mask. People mill round, shout and
make gestures.*

COMMODORE (*shouting through a microphone*). The head of the
 city has paid for his sin. The city is purged. (*The sheet is
 dropped*.) Feed your eyes and rejoice!

SHOGO's *naked body is nailed to the placard. It has been hacked
to pieces and loosely assembled upside down. The limbs have been
nailed in roughly the right position, but the whole body is askew and
the limbs don't meet the trunk. The head hangs down with the
mouth wide open. The genitals are intact.*
    *People mill round shouting and waving. Someone rings a hand-
bell. Some hit tambourines.*

CROWD. Hallelujah! Rejoice! Hip hip!
BASHO (*shouting through a microphone*). This is your Prime-

Minister addressing you! Shogo is dead! The sin is broken! Let the new city live for ever!

The procession goes out, leaving debris behind. KIRO *is still sitting in the same place.* GEORGINA *comes on. She carries her tambourine. She sees* KIRO *and stops.*

GEORGINA. One of those priests! (*She bangs her tambourine at him.*) Out! Out! Out! O god, the devil's everywhere! Ha! Ha! (*She looks in panic over her shoulder. She turns round.*) There! There! (*She bangs her tambourine at space.*) Out! Out! Out! (*She sees* KIRO *again.*) There he is – running round! Out! (*She kneels and prays silently, her mouth working.*) Is he gone? Yes. (*She opens her eyes and looks at him.*) He's there! Still there!

KIRO *unfastens his robe and lets it slip down. He is naked to the waist.*

GEORGINA. Ah! He's going to rape me! I'm going to be raped! (*She shuts her eyes and prays.*) Jesus, help me! Help your little girl! He'll split me up and open me out! He's got his clothes off! I can feel him! (*She tries to move her arms.*) Ha! My arms are chained! (*She tries to move her legs.*) My legs are chained!

She looks at KIRO. *He takes out a knife.*

GEORGINA. He's going to murder me! Murdered before I'm raped! I shan't know what it's like! (*She prays.*) O god, spare me! I'll lead a cleaner life! My mind! Jesus-us-us-us-us! (*She tears open her dress.*) O Jesus, Jesus hears! Yes, yes! Jesus hears! Dead and no shame? Jesus hears!

KIRO *sticks the knife blade in the left side of his stomach, draws it across to the right on a line just below the navel, twists it and gives it a little jerk. His face has been expressionless, but on the final jerk he stretches his neck, bends his head back and a little to the right, flattens his lips and inhales – as if he was trying to stop a sneeze. (If the actor is left-handed the cut can be made from right to left.)*

GEORGINA (*eyes shut in prayer*). He's coming! I can hear him coming! There's something wet!

Two SOLDIERS *come on upstage. One sees* GEORGINA *and points at her. They creep towards her.*

Coming! Coming! (*The* SOLDIERS *grab her.*) At last! Now! Up! (*They jerk her to her feet. She opens her eyes and sees a* SOLDIER. *She screams. She sees the other* SOLDIER *and screams again. She hits them with the tambourine.*) No! No! My shame! My shame!

SOLDIER. The ghosts are in her.

OTHER SOLDIER. Yes, she's haunted!

SOLDIER (*hits her*). Shut up!

OTHER SOLDIER. You'll be quiet when you're locked away!

GEORGINA *struggles and the two* SOLDIERS *take her out. A second's silence.*

A MAN'S VOICE (*Off. Distantly*). Help. (*Pause. Nearer.*) Help! (*Pause.*) Ah!

Silence. A MAN *clambers up at the back of the stage. He is naked except for a loin-cloth. He is soaking wet and spits water.*

MAN. Didn't you hear me shout? (*He shakes water from his hair.*) I shouted help. You must have heard and you didn't come.

He picks up a cloth from the CROWD's *debris, shakes it, and wipes himself on it. He rapidly dries his legs, arms, chest and back. He takes off his loin-cloth and wrings it out. Then he dries the rest of himself with the cloth.*

MAN. I could have drowned.

The MAN *is drying under his arms. In one movement* KIRO *lurches forward on to his back and straightens his legs. His robe is vivid red where the bowels have fallen.*

The MAN *has his back to* KIRO. *He dries himself.*

Black Mass

Black Mass originally formed part of 'Sharpeville Sequence: A Scene, a Story and Three Poems' written for the Sharpeville Massacre Tenth Anniversary Commemoration Evening, held by the Anti-Apartheid Movement at the Lyceum Theatre, London, on 22 March 1970.

A church at Vereeniging. An altar and a large cross. The altar is plain and covered by a white cloth. The cross is made of simple wood. A lifesize Christ is nailed to it. A PRIEST *and a* PRIME MINISTER. *The* PRIME MINISTER *kneels for communion.*

PRIEST. Ye that do truly and earnestly repent you of your sins and are in love and charity with your neighbours and intend to lead a new life make your humble confession to almighty god meekly kneeling upon your knees. (*Pause.*) Meekly kneeling upon your knees . . .

PRIME MINISTER (*after a pause*). You said something, padre?

PRIEST. You have a lot on your mind.

PRIME MINISTER. True.

PRIEST. Something in particular, prime minister? Perhaps I can help.

PRIME MINISTER. You are a help, padre. It's nothing in particular. I wish — I wish I got a little more understanding. Something more in the way of appreciation. Even a bit less abuse. But you know, padre, I tell myself — I only tell myself in secret, of course — that men of vision are bound to be misunderstood in their own time and being misunderstood is part of the privilege of being a man of vision. Well, let's get on. There's a cabinet meeting this afternoon. You were saying?

PRIEST. Meekly kneeling upon your knees.

PRIME MINISTER. Ah, yes. Almighty god judge of all men we acknowledge and bewail our manifold sins and wickednesses which we — and now there's that crowd of Kaffirs down the road — from time to time most grievously have committed by thought word and deed — just stuck there — we do earnestly repent and

are heartily sorry for these our misdoings the remembrance of
them is grievous unto us the burden of them intolerable have
mercy upon us — you'd think they'd have the decency to go,
they get pleasure out of causing trouble and giving me a bad
name abroad — padre, yes, have mercy upon us — and what can
I do, they tie my hands and stand in front of the gun and when
I squeeze the trigger it's my fault because they're aggressive
enough to get hit, I must make a note of that for the cabinet
meeting (*he writes in a little notebook*) — did I say we acknowledge
and bewail our manifold — note how I'm on my knees, I wish
they could see that abroad, I'm not ashamed to pray for
guidance, how else could I be sure I was doing the right thing ? —
But I mustn't stay here talking, padre, enjoyable though that is.
We must put our hand to the plow, amen.

PRIEST. Lift up your hearts.

PRIME MINISTER. We lift them up.

> *An* INSPECTOR *comes in. The* PRIEST *goes to the altar and
> prepares communion.*

INSPECTOR. The Kaffirs are still there, sir.

PRIME MINISTER. You showed them the planes ?

INSPECTOR. Did do, sir.

PRIME MINISTER. And they still stayed ?

INSPECTOR. So we brought in reinforcements. The lads didn't
   like it. They were playing rugger, tennis, cricket, and other
   mind-cleansing and body-building games, but they came when
   they heard the summons.

PRIME MINISTER. What about the Saracens ?

INSPECTOR. As useless as the planes.

PRIME MINISTER. Oh.

INSPECTOR. They're British made so you wouldn't expect them
   to work. You might as well send them out on the milk round.
   Never mind, we've got our own personal weapons, all made in
   the home country — they'll shift them. (*He goes to the altar,
   where the* PRIEST *is making ritual gestures.*) Could I disturb
   you for a moment, padre ? (*He takes rifles from under the*

altar.) Could you say a prayer for the boys while you're at it
padre?

PRIEST. I'm always praying for the boys.

INSPECTOR. Thank you padre. We'll do you a good turn some-
day, man.

The INSPECTOR *leaves. The* PRIEST *turns to the* PRIME
MINISTER *with the bread and wine.*

PRIME MINISTER. Time spent on your knees is never wasted.

PRIEST. I wish more people thought like you, prime minister.

PRIME MINISTER. So do I.

PRIEST (*Offering the bread*). Take and eat this in remembrance
that christ died for thee and feed on him –

Loud rifle fire, off. After twenty seconds the PRIEST *speaks again*

PRIEST. Do you hear a noise, prime minister?

PRIME MINISTER. No.

PRIEST. I think perhaps there *is* a sound. Perhaps we should go
and see if we can –

PRIME MINISTER. I don't know what you hear, but I can't hear
it. *My* mind is entirely concentrated on the appropriate holy
thoughts.

PRIEST. Oh so is mine! But I thought I – well, your hearing is
better than mine.

PRIME MINISTER. Then let's get on. I can't keep the cabinet
waiting.

The rifle fire stops and the INSPECTOR *comes in.*

INSPECTOR. We had to use fire, sir.

PRIME MINISTER. Dear me.

INSPECTOR. They wouldn't go. And the lads were impatient.
They'd been pulled away in the middle of their matches, you
see, sir – naturally they were keen to get back and win! There's
no fun in shooting at people nowadays. Too many rules in the
game. It doesn't really qualify as a sport any more – though
mind you the lads still try to play in the spirit of the old ama-
teurs, even if they've turned professional. But it can't hold a

candle to wildfowling. You've shot one man and you've shot them all. Still, the lads put up a show.

PRIME MINISTER. What was the final score?

INSPECTOR. 69—0. They certainly didn't let the opposition walk over them. The lads really put their backs into the training. There *were* a few they could have brought off if they'd been on the ball. They set them up, but they couldn't follow it through. Still, they showed real style and you can't ask fairer than that. They've gone off to the shower. Might be as well if you had a word with them, sir. After all, they won. They're good lads and I don't doubt for one moment they're their own hardest critics. I watched their faces and you could see how when one of them missed he knew he'd let the team down. The lady folk have prepared some beer and sandwiches and a few party dainties — perhaps you'd care to join us, padre?

PRIEST. Later on, I'd like that.

PRIME MINISTER. We'll just give them a pat on the head now, while they're hosing down. They like to see the board going round straight after the whistle—show them you take an interest.

The PRIME MINISTER, INSPECTOR *and* PRIEST *go.* CHRIST *comes down from the cross. He raises his hands to speak, but drops them. He puts something in the communion wine, and goes back on to the cross. The* PRIME MINISTER *and* PRIEST *return.*

PRIEST. Most of them were shot in the back.

PRIME MINISTER (*kneeling*). It's the nature of the Kaffir to turn his back when confronted with the white man's weapons.

PRIEST. Shall we finish this?

PRIME MINISTER. It's a long day but it has its rewards.

PRIEST (*offers bread*). Take this and remember that Christ died for thee.

PRIME MINISTER (*swallows*). You know, the lads think it's all over now and they can go home and sleep quietly in their beds like little chidren, but I'll be burning the midnight oil — the paperwork a thing like this involves — the paperwork — it never stops! I only wish you could dispose of paper as easily as you dispose of people. Paper's far more difficult to handle.

PRIEST (*offers wine*). Drink this in remembrance that christ's blood was shed for thee and be thankful.

PRIME MINISTER. I don't begrudge them their sleep when they've earned it — but there are times when I would gladly lay down the burdens of the helm. (*Dies.*)

    The INSPECTOR *comes in.*

INSPECTOR. Did I hear a body falling? Too late! I shall examine the scene of the crime for clues and pounce on the accused with professional speed. Note how, as he faced his maker, he showed the whites of his eyes.

PRIEST. I wish it could have happened somewhere else. It looks bad here.

INSPECTOR. That's the mark of the black hand — no respect for the proprieties. This is a typical Kaffir foul — behind the umpire's back. I'm on to something here! A row of little spots. The accused was crying — unless I'm mistaken and he was peeing himself.

PRIEST. In church?

INSPECTOR. Just a little joke, padre. No intention of mocking the cloth. (*He follows the trail of spots to the cross.*) And here we have just what I was looking for: a little puddle. (*To* CHRIST.) Just a moment, sir. (*Takes out a notebook.*) Would you mind telling me your name, permanent address and occupation and explain what you're doing trespassing on these premises?

PRIEST. I think there's a mistake, Inspector.

INSPECTOR. You know this fellow, sir?

PRIEST. Yes.

INSPECTOR (*starts to put his notebook away*). In that case I take it you're prepared to vouch for this gentleman's bona fides.

PRIEST. Well . . . not entirely.

INSPECTOR. I see. Dearie me then. In that case I must ask the gentleman to accompany me to the station.

PRIEST. No. I — let me pray for guidance.

INSPECTOR. In the circumstances I think prayer comes under the Conspiracy Act.

PRIEST. That makes it difficult. I'll have to guess the answer. (*To* CHRIST.) I'm afraid I must ask you to leave.

INSPECTOR. I'm sorry, padre. It's gone further than that.

PRIEST. This is the best way. The whole incident could be blown up out of proportion.

INSPECTOR. You mean the gentleman has friends abroad?

PRIEST. Frankly I'm not sure, but it's not worth the risk.

INSPECTOR. In that case I'll leave the matter in your hands, as there's no one here to represent Interpol.

PRIEST (*to* CHRIST). You've heard, I've been able to spare you some of the public disgrace. But now I must ask you to collect your things and go immediately. I can't risk your contaminating the young people we have here. I'm very disappointed in you. Oh, I'm not thinking of myself and all the wasted effort I've thrown away – but you've let yourself down. It's too late to say it now, but you weren't without promise – and you've thrown all that away. You'll regret it in a few years and you'll look back on this and see we were right. I hope by then you'll have learned something. You'll never make anything of yourself if you go on the way you've started. I shall say no more. (CHRIST *comes down from the cross and starts to leave. He stops when the* PRIEST *talks again.*) God knows what your family will think of this. You've got a good family and they gave you a start in life many others would envy – and you've let them down, too. I shan't go on. Please leave quietly. It's too late for explanations and apologies. It's past amends. There is some conduct that's too underhand to be put right. I've finished now. (CHRIST *leans against the cross in boredom.*) Why didn't you say if something was troubling you? You know you could always turn to me. I'm not a hard man. I'm fairly reasonable and open – I think I can say that. There's nothing more to be said. The whole thing is best left in silence. In fact I'm too upset to speak. (CHRIST *hangs one arm over the horizontal bar of the cross.*) I'd give you

another chance if I thought it would help. But there's no point.
I have to remember the others in my charge. It's not fair on
others to allow someone like you to continue to be in a respectable institution like this. Go, and I hope you find somewhere
where you can fit in. Have I made myself clear? (CHRIST *goes*.)
It leaves a space. I shan't get used to a space up there. It seems
wrong. The congregation expect something.

INSPECTOR. I'll help you out, padre.

> The INSPECTOR *gestures offstage. A young* POLICEMAN
> *comes on. He is dressed in a fascist-style uniform with an*
> *armband.*

Here we are, Kedgie. Here's a nice easy job for you. Stand up
there on that wooden appliance. Up you get, lad.

PRIEST. Won't he find it tiring?

INSPECTOR. No. He's used to controlling traffic. He'll be all right
if he puts his mind to it. You can do anything if you put your
mind to it. Comfortable, Kedgie? Keep staring straight ahead,
lad. Just think how they taught you to keep watch on the
frontier. (*To* PRIEST.) That makes the place look tidier.

PRIEST. True, it's an improvement.

INSPECTOR. Didn't like the look of the other one. You can pick
them out when you've had a few years in my job.

PRIEST. I sometimes had doubts myself. But he had such good
references, so what can you —

INSPECTOR. You're looking fine, Kedgie. You'll be relieved in
two hours, lad. Do you know what to do? We'll just have a little
rehearsal. We don't want any slip ups. Church parade is a
parade like any other parade. The same smartness and superior
turnout and every movement at the double. (*Shouts order.*)
Relief christ, to your post — *march*! (*A replica of* KEDGIE
marches in.) Relief christ — *halt*! (*The* RELIEF CHRIST *halts in
front of the cross.*) Old christ — descend — *cross*! Smartly,
smartly, there! Stop waving your arms about you're not blessing
the multitude now! Watch your step, eyes front, head up, don't
look down or you'll fall through the water! By god, I'll make

martyrs of the pair of you! (KEDGIE *has come down from the cross.*)
Relief christ – wait for it, wait for it, don't anticipate the word of
command – mount – *cross*! I don't want to see you move, I want
to see you there! Get up that cross there! Halt! Put your arms
out, put your arms out, lad! Don't stand there with your arms
dangling, you look as though you're going to start playing with
yourself! Wank in your own time, not the army's! (*Turns to*
PADRE.) There we are, padre, now we're beginning to get
somewhere, we're playing on our home ground.

PRIEST. I feel much safer. There's someone up there watching
over me and I can trust and rely on him. (*Indicates bread and
wine.*) It's a pity to waste all this. Would you like to take
communion?

INSPECTOR. Oh I –

PRIEST. I've changed the wine.

INSPECTOR. In that case – it's a very civil thought of yours padre,
and I'd be glad to oblige. Call on me any time.

> The INSPECTOR *kneels and the* PRIEST *offers him communion.*

(Curtain)

Passion

A play for CND

Passion was first presented in an open-air production at Alexandra Park Racecourse by the Royal Court Theatre as part of the CND Festival of Life on Easter Sunday, 11 April 1971 with the following cast:

NARRATOR	Chris Malcolm
OLD WOMAN	Susan Engel
DEAD SOLDIER	Marc McManus
QUEEN	Penelope Wilton
PRIME MINISTER	Nigel Hawthorne
MAGICIAN	Roddy Maude-Roxby
CHRIST	Norman Beaton
BUDDHA	Bob Hoskins

Directed by Bill Bryden
Designed by Di Seymour
Staged Managed by Peter Allday
Amplification organized by Dick Lock

These scenes can be played indoors or outdoors. Microphones can be used. The Narrator need not be seen. The characters should be played as types or even archetypes, not individuals. Clothes and make-up should be exaggerated. The title of each section should be given by the Narrator, or shown, before it is played.

THE GARDEN

NARRATOR. There was once an old woman. Her only son was made a soldier and sent to war. When he was killed his body was sent back to her. She was sitting in her garden when it was carried in on a stretcher.

The OLD WOMAN *sits daydreaming on a stool. The* DEAD SOLDIER *is carried in on a stretcher. It is covered with a blanket. The* OLD WOMAN *rises and goes to the stretcher. She makes the gestures and movements of mourning while the voice of the* DEAD SOLDIER *speaks for her.*

DEAD SOLDIER. They have killed my son. They took my only child away and dressed him up for a holiday. They put money in his pocket and he got drunk. He sailed away in a boat to see the world. They said people will welcome you everywhere and you will be called their friend. They said you will destroy the people's foes and punish the wicked. Then they had a battle and the two armies destroyed each other. Afterwards the soldier was lost. He wandered about for days in a cold and empty wilderness. He was afraid to sleep because marauders were cutting the wounded men's throats and robbing them. All he'd had to eat for a week was the biscuits and bits of bread he found in the pockets of the dead soldiers' uniforms. One morning he was lying in a ditch half mad. He heard the wind blowing and he thought it was calling his name. He lifted his head and was shot in the face. He was a young, healthy, strong soldier and it was very difficult for him to die. When it was getting dark the crows found him and he felt their claws as they landed on his face and he heard them cawing. Then he felt them picking at strips of his flesh as if they were tugging worms from the earth, and in a little while he died.

NARRATOR. The old woman stopped crying.

OLD WOMAN. Well, I must stop crying and think about money. After all, I have to live. It's very difficult for an old woman on her own. I can't manage and that's a fact. I need my son to keep me. I shall go to the queen and ask for him back. She's clever and lots of clever men work for her – she can give my son his life back. It's a bit impertinent taking up her time, my worries must seem very trivial compared to the important things she has to do. But she won't grudge an old woman. It'll only take her a few minutes, I expect. And after all, I gave her my son when she needed him, so she can give him back now I need him.

NARRATOR. So the old woman left her cat with the neighbours and set out for the court.

> *The* OLD WOMAN *goes out and the* DEAD SOLDIER *on the stretcher is carried out or put upstage.*

THE COURT

NARRATOR. The queen was busy in the palace having great thoughts on behalf of her people.

> *The* QUEEN *comes on singing 'The Camptown Races' and playing with a yo-yo.*

The Prime Minister was granted an audience as he was anxious to compare his great thoughts with hers.

> *The* PM *comes on singing 'A Life on the Ocean Waves' and playing with a yo-yo.*

QUEEN. Good day.

PM. Good day, mam.

QUEEN. Ideal weather for bowling/swimming/running/jumping/
giving a garden party/getting crowned/getting married/making
your will/taking in lodgers/lifting up your heart/counting your
blessings/or departing this life. Select the word or phrase of
your choice and delete the others as appropriate.

PM. Yes, mam.

QUEEN. And how is your wife/mistress/mother/boy friend/dog/
aunt/son/pet alligator/lady love/fancy man/little bit on the side/
the old other/your Saturday night grunt and grind? Take
appropriate action as already indicated.

PM. Woof-woof is fine, mam.

QUEEN. And would you like a drink/tea/coffee/health beverage/
cocoa/cigarette/smoke/twist/roll/wad/fix/or burn?

PM. I'll have whatever your majesty's having, mam.

QUEEN. Yes. (*Slight pause.*) I see. (*Slight pause.*) Well in that case,
I'm having something/nothing/a little/a lot/just a drop/I'm
fasting this week/help yourself/never touch the stuff/after you.

PM. That's just what I fancied.

QUEEN. Well, I'm delighted/shattered/crestfallen/woebegone/
elated/filled with foreboding/bowled out/seriously perturbed/
hysterical/and totally indifferent to everything you say.

NARRATOR. The conversation meandered on in this pleasant and
well-bred way for three days and then the Prime Minister
mentioned why he'd come.

PM. I have a problem.

QUEEN. O dear/tut tut/dearie me/whatever next/lawksa muckey/
always safe in your hands/thank God I bank abroad/my duty is
to serve/not a glimmer showed on her marble brow.

PM. No, mam, your majesty doesn't understand.

QUEEN. Nonsense! I understand everything except dirty jokes.

PM. I meant I hadn't made myself clear, mam.

QUEEN. That obviously would be a formidable task.

PM. An old woman's come to court. Her son was a soldier –

QUEEN. Hup hup/salute/salt of the earth/last bastion/noble mind
in a noble body/fire on the count of three.

PM. – who was killed –

QUEEN. Dearly beloved/half a minute's silence/honoured dust/
gave his all/heard the summons/history is written in blood.

PM. And now she wants him back.

QUEEN. I see. Her faith in the monarchy is certainly touching.
Well as it happens I've done all the resurrections I intend to do
this week, so instead I shall offer her something. Would she like
a drink/tea/coffee/health beverage/cocoa/cigarette –

PM. I think I know someone who could help us. He's a very
clever man. Knows everything. Comes from Oxford – or
Cambridge – or Sussex – or somewhere. Anyway, he's been
taught to play with two yo-yos!

QUEEN. Two! Let him in.

PM. I shall set him a test for your majesty to see. I've written our
problem on this card.

The PM *takes out a card, beckons off stage, the* MAGICIAN
hurries on, and the PM *hands him the card.*

PM. Read this and give your answer in sixty seconds.

MAGICIAN (*looks at the card. Immediately*). Eureka! The old
woman can't have her son back because you still need him. He's
being turned into bronze and will stand in the main square to
remind us of all the young men our enemy's killed. Would your
majesty care to unveil him?

QUEEN. What a clever/wonderful/stupid/boring/dazzling/wet/
happy/disgraceful/infantile/sublime/uninteresting idea.

PM. Thank you, mam.

QUEEN. Have you any more ideas? You wouldn't know what's
going to win the four o'clock?

MAGICIAN. No. But I've invented a bomb with a bang twice as
loud as anyone else's. I propose to drop it on our enemy.

QUEEN. How nice/charming/amusing/crude/fascinating/silly/vul-
gar/narrowminded/mean spirited/and dull. Well, it's a pity
about the four o'clock but I can see you're still a great asset to

any government and I needn't waste words on that! Tell me
about yourself? Have you a family?

MAGICIAN. I did have but they left me. I don't know why. All
except my son – he was one and a half and too little to walk.
But he's gone too now. I had to go out one day to give a lecture
to my students. I left him playing happily on the mat in front
of the fire and I gave him a box of matches, a loaded machine
gun, several large plastic bags and an open razor to amuse himself with. When I came back from the lecture – which was called
Science and the Responsible Citizen and which by the way
was a great success – I found the little chap had had an accident.
Robin or William or Charles, or whatever it was I'd christened
him, was dead. But one feels that being so clumsy he would not
have grown up to be a scientist anyway –

QUEEN. O dear/tut tut/dearie me/lackaday and woe alas.

MAGICIAN. – so I'm resigned to my loss.

QUEEN. What a noble sentiment! Nobility of mind always makes
me so pleased/moved/stirred/frigid/relaxed –

PM (*interrupting*). Shall we unveil the monument and drop the
bomb now?

QUEEN. – elevated/bored/reduced to tears/yawn/scream/over-
flow/faint/drop off/ button up/lose myself in flower arranging –

They all go out, the QUEEN *still talking.*

THE MONUMENT ON A LAUNCHING PAD

*The Monument stands behind the players throughout the play. Till
it's unveiled, in this scene, it's covered with a large white sheet. The*
OLD WOMAN *comes on and looks at the monument. There is also a
small stand with two buttons on it.*

OLD WOMAN. What a great day in our lives! Who would have

thought that my son, born in a very simple home, would one day be so honoured?

The QUEEN, PM *and* MAGICIAN *come on from the direction opposite to the way they left. The* QUEEN *wears a large hat and carries a large handbag. She is still talking.*

QUEEN. – shout hallelujah/retire to Elba/sign the pledge/take up crochet work/or emigrate to Australia.

A LITTLE GIRL (*or* SKINNY, ANGULAR SCHOOL MISTRESS) *steps forward with a bunch of flowers. She hesitates in confusion and then decides – she goes to the* PM, *bobs, and hands him the flowers. He hits her once or twice with the flowers, shoves them back in her hand and pushes her across to the* QUEEN. *The* LITTLE GIRL *bobs again and holds out the flowers. The* QUEEN *smiles and takes them.*

QUEEN. What lovely blooms! Aren't they pretty/bright/colourful/exotic/well arranged/red/blue/my favourites/nice/nasty/bad for hay-fever/good for asthma/cheering.

While the QUEEN *speaks the* LITTLE GIRL *mimes grotesque shyness. Now she stands on one leg, bobs, almost falls over, starts to cry and runs out. The* PM *takes the* QUEEN *to the small stand.*

PM. This is the monument, mam, and here we have two buttons. That one drops the bomb and that one unveils the monument. I suggest we drop the bomb first and then that will be out of the way.

QUEEN. I see. Now which button is which again? I don't want to get it wrong.

PM (*points*). That's for the bomb.

QUEEN. Yes, well there are two of them and that's very confusing. However, I will make an effort and do what I can. Now I'll just say a few words. (*She hands the flowers to the* PM, *takes a sheet of paper from her handbag, and reads from it very exactly.*) Yakety-yakety-yak-yak, yo-ho-ho and yoo-hoo-hoo.

PM. Hear, hear.

QUEEN. Furthermore. Bla-bla-bla, hands, knees and boo-see-daisy, hickery-dickery-dock.

PM. Amen.

QUEEN. Thank you. Not only that but also bla-bla-bla, one small step for mankind, hey-diddle-diddle, I wonder what we're having for dinner, ba-ba, moo-moo, cheep-cheep, and quack-quack!

PM. Well put.

QUEEN. It now gives me great pleasure to press this button and may God bless all who sail in her. (*Slight pause.*) Prime Minister, did you tell me which button was which? I don't want to press the wrong button.

PM. Press *that* one, mam.

QUEEN. That one. Well, it *is* very confusing but I think I can remember that for five seconds if I empty my mind and stop wondering what won the five-thirty. So let's have another try. And may God bless all who sail in her. (*She presses the button. A moment's pause. She looks round.*) Shouldn't something have happened? Oh, I see what it is: I forgot to lift my finger off the button. Prime Minister, why didn't you remind me that would be necessary? O dear. Now it's stuck. (*Loudly to the audience.*) There'll be a slight – (*She pulls her finger.*) – but it's all right. (*To* PM.) The hole's a shade too small for my – (*Loudly to audience.*) Don't panic, it's all under control. My finger is stuck. In the hole. We won't keep you a moment. (*Still trying to pull her finger out.*) Talk amongst yourselves – or hum a little tune. (*Furiously to* PM.) Do something! Don't stand there twitching! I'll change the government. (*Loudly to audience.*) Are you having a nice time? I'll be with you soon. It's my finger. I depressed the button and because my finger is stuck the button is now unable to return to its correct position and consequently – (*To* PM.) Do something! My arm's going dead! (*Loudly to audience.*) Perhaps someone would like to tell us an amusing story?

PM (*hitting* MAGICIAN *with the flowers*). Do something! Do something! I know who put you up to this! The bounder! It's a socialistic plot!

QUEEN. I'm going to faint.

MAGICIAN (*pulling her arm*). There's nothing wrong with the hole! You press too hard.

QUEEN (*hitting him with her handbag*). I spend my life pressing buttons! I know when a button's pressed and when it isn't! (*Yells.*) Ow! You're pulling my arm off!

PM (*cries and hits the* MAGICIAN *with the flowers*). You'll get me sacked! I'll lose my lovely job!

MAGICIAN (*still pulling*). Her finger's too big!

QUEEN. There's nothing wrong with my finger; it's your hole!

The finger suddenly comes out. There is the sound of a great rushing wind as the bomb is sent off. The three wave after it.

MAGICIAN. It works! My bomb works!

PM. Hip hip hooray! Hip hip hooray! Hip hip hooray!

QUEEN. Bon voyage/send us a postcard/don't drink water from the tap/be kind to the froggies, remember they haven't had our advantages. (*Sighs.*) Well, that's that. (*The* PM *and* MAGICIAN *shake hands and laugh.*) Now, let's finish our other little chore. I hope there's nothing wrong with this button –

MAGICIAN. There was nothing wrong with the other one –

The QUEEN *hits him with her handbag and the* PM *hits him with the flowers.*

QUEEN. Shut up! – because if there is I'll suspend your grant and you'll spend the rest of your academic life working on a cure for the common cold. Well, you've been warned. Now, where's my speech? (*She searches in her handbag, takes out a sheet of paper and reads.*) Dear Bootykins, I was on sentry go last night and as, by a lucky mischance, my sentry box is under your window, when you was switching on the electric light I saw – No, that's from a friend of mine, a dear, comical, whimsical fellow, though I can never get him to wipe his feet when he calls. (*Takes another paper from her bag.*) One sliced loaf, one jar of Oxford marmalade – No. (*Takes another paper from her bag.*) List of suspects to be followed by my dear husband in plain clothes. No. It's here somewhere. (*Searching in bag.*) Green Shield stamps. No. Little Black Book. No. Big Black Book. No. Here it is! (*She takes out a paper and reads.*) The Monument, a poem by our Poet Laureate.

> This monument is very nice
> It stands so still in wind and ice
> And never frowns or makes a cry
> Just stares ahead into the sky
> It does what all good people should
> That's why I think it's very good.

Well, I don't know that that was worth looking for, though the sentiment is, of course, admirable. Still, I must have a word with someone about him. Now, I have great pleasure in declaring this monument open.

The wind has died down to a low, sinister howl. The QUEEN *presses the button and the white sheet falls. There is a full-size cross and on it is nailed and bound a crucified pig. A soldier's helmet is nailed over its head. (The pig is to be obtained from a slaughter house and not killed for the performance. It may seem unnecessary to state this because it is hard to imagine actors leaving rehearsal to kill a pig. But directors are a different matter – experience shows it's a mistake to take chances with them.) The* QUEEN, PM *and* MAGICIAN *salute. The National Anthem is played in the Elgar version..*

OLD WOMAN. That doesn't look very like my son. But then I haven't seen him naked since he was a child. I don't recognize his hands, but of course they've made him into a soldier and taught him to hold a rifle so his hands are bound to be changed. And now I look I do see my son's face – and his mouth – and his eyes. He was a quiet, kind, inward boy. He seemed to

suffer such a lot and I could never really help him. Yes, I
know him now. That's him. I can see the old suffering in his
face. My poor child! I'm glad I live in the country and not in
this city. I couldn't walk by him and look at his face every day.
It's opened my heart and my eyes are full of tears. Dear, dear.
I must go away. I must go away.

The wind has faded almost into silence.

NARRATOR. Unfortunately the enemy king had a magician who
was cleverer than the Queen's magician and he could play with
three yo-yos. When the enemy saw the queen's bomb coming
towards them they fired their own bomb, and that was even
bigger.

*An explosion. Light. Noise. Smoke. Movement. The people
onstage run round in panic.*

PM. Help!

QUEEN. I'm lost! Where's my palace? Where's my robe? I've
lost my crown! Has anyone seen my crown? Who's taken my
throne? It's all lost!

PM. I'm lost! Where are my files? My reports? I can't find any
documents! What's burning? Are my despatches burning? I'm
lost!

MAGICIAN. Caramba! What a bomb! How did he do that? I must
find out! Where are my books? My microscope? My electro-
scope? My telescope? Where's my laboratory? Can anyone see
my test tubes? Don't tread on my test tubes! Where are my
animals? Where are my cages?

OLD WOMAN. O dear! Where is the city? What's become of it?
It was here and now it's gone! Just like that! Where are all the
people? They've all gone! I'm lost!

NARRATOR. There was nothing left. Everything was burned or
broken and blown away. There was only a storm of dust and
a howling wind. They could hear dogs yelping in the ruins but
they could never catch one to eat. They wandered about for

days, round and round and on and on, and they got hungrier
and more tired and unhappy. They were lost.

THE WILDERNESS

While the Narrator has been speaking the QUEEN, OLD WOMAN
PM *amd* MAGICIAN *have been wandering round the stage. Now the*
QUEEN *sits.*

QUEEN. I've come to the end. Prime Minister, this is a crisis. Do
something.

PM. The matter is receiving my urgent attention/being completely
ignored/is under review/has got out of hand/is being left over/
awaiting developments/totally beyond my very limited capaci-
ties.

QUEEN. What a ridiculous way to speak. He's gone mad. (*To the*
MAGICIAN.) You do something!

MAGICIAN. I'm examining the dust. I'm taking specimens of
dust from everything. I have the dust of trees. This is the dust
of rocks. The dust of earth. This must be the dust of clothes.
The dust of men. The dust of birds. I've even got the dust of
sand. I'll soon be on to something. The answer lies in dust. Dust
will save us. I'm wrestling with it and soon it will yield up its
secrets to my relentless, probing mind.

NARRATOR. Just then a bird began to sing joyfully. It was the
first happy sound they'd heard since the bomb fell on them.
They looked up and saw Christ and Buddha coming towards
them over the ruined fields.

CHRIST *comes in supported by* BUDDHA. CHRIST *wears a robe
and* BUDDHA *a loin cloth.*

QUEEN. Haven't we met somewhere? I don't know that strange,
swarthy fellow – though I may have bumped into him when I
was running around the colonies, only they all look alike –
but I know you ... Now I know! We're from the same family,
almost. Howdyoudo. (*She shakes his hand.*) I suppose the
Almighty sent you. Why couldn't he come himself? Well, you're

here now – not before time. You know I've lost my crown and
my palace – everything. I suppose you've come to get them
back for me.

CHRIST. I'm sorry, I can't stop now.

QUEEN. What? Don't you realize how urgent this is?

CHRIST. This is Easter and I'm going to be crucified.

BUDDHA. It's a long way to go. He's tired and I'm helping him
so that he has enough strength to die properly when he gets
there.

CHRIST. Yes, my friend, thank you for your compassion. We've
come a long way and there will be only suffering and bitterness
at the end. But you help me. When I feel your arm holding me
I don't mind the stones and dust so much, and when I die I
shall look at your smile and be at peace. But we must go on
quickly. Everywhere children are crying, mothers and fathers
are groaning, and old men and women are shrieking as if they
were mad. All the animals are broken and bleeding. I must die
soon so that the world can be healed. When I have dived to the
bottom of the sea all this suffering will end.

BUDDHA. Look, my brother, isn't this your cross? Surely we're
here.

   CHRIST *goes to the foot of the cross and looks up at the crucified*
   pig.

CHRIST. I am too late. I can't be crucified for men because they've
already crucified themselves, wasted their lives in misery,
destroyed their homes and run mad over the fields stamping
on the animals and plants and everything that lived. They've
lost their hope, destroyed their happiness, forgotten mercy and
kindness and turned love into suspicion and hate. Their
cleverness has become cunning, their skill has become jugglery,
their risks have become reckless gambles, they are mad. What
are my sufferings compared to theirs? How can one innocent
die for the guilty when so many innocents are corrupted and
killed? This is a hell worse than anything my father imagined.

BUDDHA. Cry and I'll wipe your tears and lead you somewhere else. Lean on me. We'll find another world where they'll accept our priceless gift of peace.

CHRIST. But where? This is our place. There was to be love and kindness and good sense here. There was to be peace.

MAGICIAN. I have it! I have it! I'm sure my figures are right! Yes! I can make a bomb out of dust! We're saved!

QUEEN. Is this true? Has God answered my prayers? Hurrah! I'll give you a medal! All my medals!

PM. I knew we'd bounce back. We land on our feet. You can't sink the island race. I'll scout round and muster up a few soldiers, there must be a few men or women and children left – we all serve when the hour sounds.

BUDDHA. You see they are mad. They have no pity. They can't pity each other, so how could they ever listen to us?

QUEEN. My strength's returning! I shall make a speech. (*She clears her throat.*) People advance! Forward/onward/backward/ ladies and infants to the side/over the hills·into the blue/the horizon beyond the dust/sound of the trumpet/up and down and on . . .

CHRIST *and* BUDDHA *have gone out quickly while the* QUEEN *talks. Now the* QUEEN, PM *and* MAGICIAN *go out quickly.*

PM (*going*). Hear hear!

MAGICIAN (*going*). Caramba!

NARRATOR. It was at this moment that the old woman found the body of her son. It had been blown out of its grave. She lifted him up by the shoulders and rested him against her and as she did so he seemed to speak. It was only gas escaping from his decaying belly and passing out through his teeth, but he seemed to say this –

The OLD WOMAN *has sat the* DEAD SOLDIER *up. We hear him speak.*

A DEAD SOLDIER'S THOUGHTS

My tanks set fire to corn
My bullets stripped trees
I made where I was a grave
And walked and laughed in it
Once in a little quiet
I watched a singing bird
Build a nest
In the cardboard boxes we used to put bodies in

My flares blind stars
My guns shatter thunder
I ravaged more than plagues and famine
My bayonet was sharp
Whetted on blood and cries of unpitied men
I crippled to make men happy
Built prisons to set them free
The simpleton drooling in a bath-chair inherited under my will
I am the father of millions of orphans

I am dead
The bird sang
When blood ran out of my arms
It sings still
I lie in my grave and it has the sky
If I could rise now on wings and fly
I would sing
I would sing

Madmen, peace!
You who bend iron but are afraid of grass
Peace!

The dust on my wings shines in the sun
I have learned to sing in winter and dance in my shroud
I have learned that a pig is a form of lamb
And power is impotence
Madmen, you are the fallen!

Methuen World Classics

Aeschylus (two volumes)
Jean Anouilh
John Arden
Arden & D'Arcy
Aristophanes (two volumes)
Aristophanes & Menander
Peter Barnes
Brendan Behan
Aphra Behn
Edward Bond (four volumes)
Bertolt Brecht
  (three volumes)
Howard Brenton
  (two volumes)
Büchner
Bulgakov
Calderón
Anton Chekhov
Caryl Churchill
  (two volumes)
Noël Coward (five volumes)
Sarah Daniels
Eduardo De Filippo
David Edgar
  (three volumes)
Euripides (three volumes)
Michael Frayn
  (two volumes)
Max Frisch
Gorky
Harley Granville Barker
  (two volumes)

Henrik Ibsen (six volumes)
Lorca (three volumes)
David Mamet
Marivaux
Mustapha Matura
David Mercer
  (two volumes)
Arthur Miller
  (four volumes)
Anthony Minghella
Molière
Tom Murphy (three volumes)
Peter Nichols
  (two volumes)
Clifford Odets
Joe Orton
Louise Page
A. W. Pinero
Luigi Pirandello
Stephen Poliakoff
Terence Rattigan
  (two volumes)
Ntozake Shange
Sophocles (two volumes)
Wole Soyinka
David Storey
August Strindberg
  (three volumes)
J. M. Synge
Ramón del Valle-Inclán
Frank Wedekind
Oscar Wilde